T0330582

Managing Competences

Managing Competences

Research, Practice, and Contemporary Issues

Edited by
Benoît Grasser,
Sabrina Loufrani-Fedida, and
Ewan Oiry

CRC Press
Taylor & Francis Group
Boca Raton London New York

CRC Press is an imprint of the
Taylor & Francis Group, an **informa** business

First edition published 2020
by CRC Press
6000 Broken Sound Parkway NW, Suite 300, Boca Raton, FL 33487-2742

and by CRC Press
2 Park Square, Milton Park, Abingdon, Oxon, OX14 4RN

© 2021 Taylor & Francis Group, LLC

CRC Press is an imprint of Taylor & Francis Group, LLC

ISBN: 978-0-367-48892-5 (hbk)
ISBN: 978-1-003-04335-5 (ebk)

Typeset in Garamond
by Deanta Global Publishing Services, Chennai, India

Contents

Editors

Benoît Grasser is a professor of human resource management (HRM) at the University of Lorraine, France. He's a member of the CEREFIGE (European Research Centre for Financial Economics and Business Management). His current research topics are competence management, organizational routines, and the dynamics of management tools. He has also published numerous articles or book chapters on the links between work, competences, and organizational dynamics. In addition, he has also published handbooks on human resource management or organizational theory.

Sabrina Loufrani-Fedida is a professor of HRM and project organizing at the Université Côte d'Azur, France. At the IAE Nice Graduate School of Management, she is the head of management and corporate communications programs. She is also associate dean for the Group of Research in Management. Her teaching and research interests are competence and talent management, human resources communication, and development of project teams. Her work has appeared in international research journals such as *Long Range Planning*, *International Journal of Project Management*, *International Business Review*, and in famous French reviews such as *Revue de Gestion des Ressources Humaines*.

Ewan Oiry is a professor of HRM at École des Sciences de Gestion – Université du Québec à Montréal (ESG-UQAM), Canada. His current research topics are competence management, HRM practices, and policies and their link with firm strategies. He has published numerous articles or book chapters on these topics. For several years, he has managed a think-tank on competences' management with Sabrina Loufrani-Fedida and Benoît Grasser. This think-tank brings together researchers in management, HRM, and strategy, as well as consultants and HR directors.

Contributors

Christoph Barmeyer is a professor of intercultural communication at the University of Passau, Germany and co-director of the master international cultural and business studies. His areas of research and teaching are constructive intercultural management, intercultural competences development, international transfer of management practices, and French–German management. He has published books, such as *Intercultural Management: A Case-Based Approach to Achieving Complementarity and Synergy* (Palgrave, 2016) and articles in journals like *International Business Review, International Studies of Management and Organization, International Journal of Intercultural Relations*, and *International Journal of Cross-Cultural Management*.

Dominique Bouteiller is a professor at HEC Montréal, and a graduate of the Institut des Hautes Études de l'Information et de la Communication de l'Université de la Sorbonne à Paris (CELSA), France. He holds a master's and doctorate in industrial relations from the Université de Montréal, Canada. He is especially interested in the implementation of new competency-based human resources management tools, as well as learning and transfer dynamics within organizations. He is also an associate researcher at the Centre Interdisciplinaire de Recherche/Développement sur l'éducation permanente (CIRDEP), Canada.

Brigitte Charles-Pauvers is an associate professor of HRM at the IAE (Business Administration Institute), University of Nantes, France, and a member of the LEMNA (Laboratory of Economy and Management Nantes Atlantique). Her research interests are focused on the organizational behavior (work commitment) in connection with the evolution of the politics of HRM, arisen from the transformations of employment (social solidarity economy, cooperative enterprises, and cultural and creative industries) as well as on the intercultural management.

Frédérique Chédotel is a professor of HRM at IAE Angers, France, and a member of the GRANEM research laboratory (Groupe de recherche angevin en économie et management, University of Angers, France). Her research explores the relationship between team competence and social innovation. She has published and presented articles in international refereed management journals and conferences. Her current projects cover telework in dispersed teams, collective intelligence and transformation, and creativity and improvisation in teams.

Pénélope Codello is a professor at HEC Montréal, Canada. Her research and teaching interests focus on soft skills and professional growth. She has developed several courses on these topics. Her research joins educational and managerial perspectives and is based on these experiences. She is also particularly interested in the role of relations between people in the development of leadership. She develops coaching based on the Gestalt approach. Finally, she has major administrative responsibilities in her institution.

Thierry Colin is an associate professor in HRM at the IAE Nancy School of Management, (University of Lorraine) France, and researcher at CEREFIGE (European Research Centre for Financial Economics and Business Management, University of Lorraine). He is co-director of a master's degree in HRM. His research focuses on the impact of the institutional context of HRM, organizational learning, skills and employment management, and labor relations.

Sophie D'Armagnac is an assistant professor at TBS Business School in Toulouse, France. Her research interests include talent management, competence management, and organizational learning. She is in charge of the MSc in aerospace management in TBS.

Michel Ferrary is a professor of management at the University of Geneva, Switzerland – Graduate School of Economy and Management – and an affiliated scholar at Skema Business School. He received a PhD in Management from HEC Paris, France (1997) and an HDR from the University of Toulouse, France (2004). His research interests are related to social networks, complex network theory, stakeholder theory, and management of innovation. He has published several papers in prominent academic journals on these different topics. He is frequently a visiting scholar at Stanford University to analyze the Silicon Valley ecosystem of innovation.

Patrick Gilbert is a professor emeritus at Sorbonne Business School (IAE Paris, France) and Research Director at the Mutations Anticipations Innovations Chair. He has a PhD in Management and a graduate in Organizational Psychology. He is (or was) also member of the board of several scientific societies such as Association francophone de Gestion des Ressources Humaines (AGRH) and Association Internationale de Psychologie du Travail de Langue Française (AIPTLF). His recent books: *Management Tools: A Social Sciences Perspective*, Cambridge University Press (2019), *Technological Change*, ISTE/John Wiley & Sons.

Nathalie Jeannerod-Dumouchel is a human resource teacher and researcher in Université Gustave Eiffel (IRG Laboratory), France. She has a strong professional practice in HRM and general management as she worked in large French companies for more than 20 years, mainly in France Télécom/Orange. Her main areas of research are competences, role tensions, recognition, and generations at work.

Alain Klarsfeld is a senior professor at TBS Business School in Toulouse, France. His research interests include talent management, competence management, diversity management, and comparative human resource management. He has taken part in multiple international research projects as well as edited special issues and books in international human resource management. He routinely publishes in French-language journals as well as international journals such as *International Human Resource Management Journal*, *European Management Journal*, *European Management Review*, and others.

Cathy Krohmer is an associate professor of management and organization in the faculty of Economics and Management of Aix-Marseille University, France, and a member of the LEST (Laboratoire d'Economie et de Sociologie du Travail, CNRS). Her research concerns the dynamics of change in individual and collective competence and how to manage them. She is currently working on competence in high-tech organizations.

Sihem Mammar El Hadj is an associate professor of HRM at Université Catholique de l'Ouest, France. Her research explores team competence and collective work. She published an article in a refereed French management journal and international conferences.

Ulrike Mayrhofer is a professor of international business at IAE Nice, Université Côte d'Azur France, where she is program director of the Executive MBA (Master of Business Administration) and a member of the GRM-lab (Groupe de Recherche en Management). Her teaching and research interests concern intercultural and international management, corporate strategy, and marketing. Her research is published in books (e.g., *Management of Multinational Companies: A French Perspective*, Palgrave Macmillan, 2013) and in journals such as, *European Management Journal*, *European Management Review*, *International Business Review*, *International Studies of Management and Organization*, and *Journal of International Marketing*.

Ingrid Mazzilli is a associate professor at Aix-Marseille University, France and LEST (Laboratoire d'Economie et de Sociologie du Travail), with a PhD in Management Science. Her current work focuses on cooperation and cross-sector partnerships in the field of work, employment, competence, and human resources development.

Fabien Meier is a human resources director in a French high-tech company. He is doctor in management. His PhD work at CEREFIGE (University of Lorraine), conducted in parallel with a professional activity, focused on the processes of competence transmission in an aeronautical factory.

Nathalie Raulet-Croset is a professor in Management and Organizational Theory at Sorbonne Business School (IAE Paris, University Paris 1). Her research focuses on the role of space and territories in organizations, on cooperation in and between organizations, and on new and alternative forms of management and organization. She also develops research in the field of nonprofit organizations and on the role of management in societal issues, particularly in terms of collaboration between private, public, and nonprofit organizations around environmental and societal problematics.

Eve Saint-Germes is a former student of the Ecole Normale Supérieure in economics and management and is an associate professor in management sciences, specializing in HRM at the Université Côte d'Azur, France. She mainly teaches at the Economics and Management Graduate School and runs a master's degree course in HRM (Organization and Social Responsibility Consulting). A member of the GREDEG (a joint research unit of the university and the CNRS), her research focuses on the management and evaluation of employability, employability-competences links and articulation, talent management, social support for change and restructuring, and territorial approaches to employment and HRM.

Nathalie Schieb-Bienfait is associate professor of Small Enterprise Management and Entrepreneurship at the IAE (Business Administration Institute), University of Nantes, and Director of research. She was co-founder and responsible for the Centre for Entrepreneurship – Creactiv –, Université of Nantes, France, for 8 years. Her research interests are focused on the process of new business, entrepreneurial strategies, entrepreneurial support, and entrepreneurship education.

Régine Teulier is an engineer and a doctor in economics. She is a researcher at the CNRS and associate researcher at the CRG-I3 Interdisciplinary Institute of Innovation, UMR 9217 CNRS Ecole Polytechnique. She has been working on the conditions and processes of cooperation at work, focusing on individual and collective practices. She is currently working on cooperation and competences in building information modeling and participates in the MINND project.

Delphine Theurelle-Stein is an assistant professor at Strasbourg University, France. Her research and teaching interests focus on competences, soft skills, and professional growth. She has developed for EM Strasbourg Business School a digital tool to enhance students' soft skills. This platform has been awarded by the IdEx

(French national prize on educational innovation). Prior to her academic career, she worked 18 years as a global manager in the fashion industry.

Caroline Urbain is an associate professor of Marketing and Innovation at the IAE (Business Administration Institute), University of Nantes, France. Her research interests are focused on the attitude and behaviors toward money, free, and prices particularly in the cultural sectors and on the cultural consumption access and social innovation. As researcher, she is a member of the LEMNA (University Nantes) and the Association Française de Marketing.

Introduction to the Handbook

Benoît Grasser, Sabrina Loufrani-Fedida, and Ewan Oiry

Human capital, skills, abilities, knowledge, know-how, competencies, competences, etc., these different terms are used to talk about what people know and know about how to do their work. Yet, their meanings vary significantly according to theoretical, academic concerns, as well as to cultural, geographical, or institutional approaches. If we refer to the individual level and professional contexts, these different terms have the common goal of designating the cognitive, affective, emotional, social, or psychomotor capacities held by employees, which can be mobilized in specific or more generic activities, depending on the approaches in question. To stabilize the vocabulary used and for reasons that will be discussed in more detail in Chapter 1, we have chosen to use the term "competence" for this research Handbook.

Competences have always been an issue for organizations and management. This can be illustrated historically by the example of the royal factories created in France under Louis XIV, which aimed to consolidate competences considered strategic for the state and to control their reproduction and use within an organized framework. In a much more modern way, Taylor's scientific organization of work can be viewed as a desire to control the workers' competences and ensure their adequacy with an organization's needs and their reproducibility over time. Several variants for considering competences in management emerged throughout the 20th century, giving greater or lesser importance to labor markets and institutions such as labor legislation, education systems, or industrial relations systems, thus making it possible to support the growth of economies and societal changes. In France, this historical movement can be analyzed, on the one hand, as a continuous shift from a quantitative approach to labor toward a qualitative approach considering competences. On the other hand, it may be viewed as a process that is increasingly institutionalized (Gilbert, 2006).

The 1990s saw the first paradigm shift with the questioning of work standardization and prescription. Today, however, we are witnessing a renewal of thinking on the very nature of competence management, under the combined effects of various extremely profound trends that are affecting work. The Organisation for Economic Co-operation and Development (OECD) has identified several major transformations that are significantly changing the content and place of work, for individuals as well as for companies (OECD, 2017a). The development of technology makes it possible to automate an increasing number of tasks traditionally performed by humans, including non-routine tasks given the progress of artificial intelligence. In addition, companies need to organize themselves to innovate continuously and experiment with more organic forms of organization, with a higher potential for creativity and adaptation, while using more autonomous and transversal forms of work. From a demographic point of view, the share of the working-age population is decreasing rapidly in some countries and increasing significantly in others. This raises questions of shortages, redistribution, and the transmission of competences. Globalization has had a significant impact on the distribution of the value chain and the specialization of activities at the international level, while the reduction in transport and communication costs is accelerating technological dissemination. At the same time, people's tastes and values are changing, both in terms of consumption and in terms of finding new ways to balance private and professional life. The result is the search for new flexibilities in working hours and places of work and in relations between employers and employees. These multiple developments have an impact on the way work is organized and carried out and, consequently, on the competences used in production activities. These trends raise concerns about the risk of further polarization of labor, which would challenge traditionally accepted national and sectoral borders (OECD, 2017b). The risk of polarization thus concerns all countries and all sectors of activity as the global value chain is repositioned, forcing researchers, companies, and institutions to better identify competences, how they emerge and are transmitted, and how they integrate organizational dynamics.

The challenge is therefore for companies, for individuals, but also for national education systems to enable the continuous emergence of the competences necessary for economic performance and the maintenance of employability. Human capital is probably today more of an element of corporate competitiveness than it has ever been before, and it is becoming essential to design competence-based human resources management which takes into account the importance of employee competences (Sienkiewicz, 2014; Brockmann et al., 2008). This type of management seeks not only to improve the acquisition process on the labor market, but also, and above all, to develop and combine the competences of employees to achieve better performance in terms of productivity, innovation, flexibility, quality, and the ability to create and seize business opportunities. For individuals, the challenge in this changing and complex context is to maintain their employability throughout their working lives. In addition to having the competences required for a job, this implies developing specific competences such as learning to learn, communicating, working in a team, and problem solving (Brewer, 2013). While the competences necessary for employability enable individuals to secure their jobs or their passage through the labor market, they may also be an aim for companies, because they guarantee better control of technological or organizational changes, and can moreover contribute to improving the social climate and working conditions.

Economic and scientific globalization, as well as new and much more complex issues, are now confronting researchers and practitioners in competence management with common problems. Yet managerial thinking about competences has developed historically in a much contextualized way, due in particular to local specificities in capitalism, labor institutions, or the traditions shaping industrial relations. The aim of this book is therefore to facilitate dialogue between the different approaches to competences, by offering a significant overview of the French approach and its characteristics, within an international framework.

The book is the result of work held by the Thematic Working Group "Competence Management – Didier Retour*" (TWG), affiliated to the Association francophone de gestion des ressources humaines (AGRH), a French-speaking academic society that brings together researchers specialized in human resources (HR) management. Created at the beginning of the 1990s, the TWG's objective has been to clarify the concepts, challenges, and tools of competence management based on research conducted mainly in the French context. Three collective books have been written under the auspices of the TWG, and its members have published their work on numerous occasions in national and international journals. We are not seeking in this book to set out French specificities as such. On the contrary, our objective is to show that these specificities have led to the development of analyses and approaches that can be generalized in order to enrich the international scientific debate on competence management at a time when it is facing new challenges.

The dimensions we wish to highlight start from a definition that is agreed within the TWG: individual competences are defined as a combination of resources that make a person at work capable of carrying out an activity in a specific context. Four characteristics flow from this definition. The first characteristic is that potentially everyone can be competent, and everyone can be competent in their own way. Indeed, both the resources available (knowledge, know-how, behavioral and

---

* The dynamic of this TWG owes a lot to Didier Retour, who was Professor in Human Resources Management at Grenoble Alpes University in France. By his great qualities of being a researcher, his legendary good humor, and his constant dynamism, he greatly contributed to federate this TWG, to encourage us to deepen our reflection and to push the limits of science. By his desire to deepen the concepts, his wish to dialogue internationally (with Brazil, China, or Peru, for example), and his attention to making research also useful for organizations, he is fully present in the thematic of this book. A stroke brutally separated us from him in 2010 but his legacy remains very much alive: the dynamics of the TWG, which today adopted his name and this book, are living proofs of this liveliness.

relational abilities, etc.) and the ways of combining them to deal with a professional situation are specific and personal. This approach is therefore inclusive in nature.

The second characteristic is the importance given to context. The individual is not universally competent, but is in an identified professional situation. One of the profound implications of this characteristic is that individual factors are as important as organizational factors in analyzing the successes or failures of an activity. Moreover, we believe that the relationship to the working context is dynamic; the development of individual competences can be encouraged, hindered, or guided by organizational choices, while the organization can draw on individual competences by integrating them into its operational, structural, or strategic decisions. We believe that the analysis of competences should not be limited to the question of adjusting individual competences to organizational needs identified *ex ante*. Instead, the analysis should be open to a more dynamic vision in which individual and organizational competences transform each other through the continuous exercise of an activity. It is therefore essential to identify clearly the different levels, from the most micro to the most macro, through which competences flow and are transformed within an organization, as well as the transformation mechanisms themselves. For example, the organizational learning mechanisms theorized by Argyris and Schön (1978) can explain how organizational learning and individual learning can feed into each other.

The third characteristic is to make individual competence an object of management by companies. Determining the place of individual competences in a company's business model is the first step, especially if it is a question of building competitive advantages based on the individual competences of the members of the organization. From an operational point of view, management tools specifically dedicated to the identification, assessment, and development of competences are the means by which management can encourage and guide the development of individual competences toward the objectives set by the organization. The extensive work carried out on these management tools has highlighted their essential role as well as their non-functional nature. Indeed, far from leading to desired results mechanically, these management tools only produce their effects through their use in real contexts, thus paving the way for cognitive and/or political learning and appropriation processes. The instrumentation of competence management corresponds to a set of tools, concerning the evaluation of competences and the multiple HR levers that have an impact on their development (training, mobility, tutoring, learning organization, etc.). But this instrumentation also concerns the processes from the design of the tools to their actual use and understanding by the different sets of actors involved.

Finally, the fourth characteristic is to consider competence as a subject of negotiation. First of all, competence is an element that enhances the value of work, just like performance, positions, diplomas, or experience. As a result, it is naturally intended to be part of negotiations between employers and employees, particularly when pay is concerned. Secondly, by definition, it is not possible to control the mobilization of competences. The less it is possible to prescribe work, the more individuals must take personal initiatives to cope with professional situations, their accidents, and irregularities. As a result, it becomes necessary to design and negotiate compensatory measures that encourage employees to really apply their competences. In addition, developing competences requires costly efforts in terms of time and money, both for the employer and the employees. Therefore, an agreement among an organization's stakeholders on the distribution of the gains and efforts related to the implementation of competence management is a prerequisite for its success.

The objective of this book is therefore to bring this approach to the attention of an international and, in particular, a North American readership, in order to stimulate debate and exchanges and to address the global issues we have identified here in a more collective way. Reflecting the work of the TWG team, the book contains 14 chapters, set out in three parts.

Part I focuses on the history and concepts of competence management. Chapter 1 (Grasser, Loufrani-Fedida, and Oiry) metaphorically evokes the transatlantic travels of the concept of competence. It aims to show how different conceptions of competence have been gradually developed, and at the same time, how fruitful it is to differentiate them and make them interact. Taking this historical perspective further, Chapter 2 (Bouteiller and Gilbert) focuses on the evolution and permanence of competence management tools over time. The next three chapters move away from the historical perspective and seek to enrich the concept of competence, by putting it in perspective with related concepts, including talents in Chapter 3 (D'Armagnac and Klarsfeld), soft skills in Chapter 4 (Codello and Theurelle-Stein), and employability in Chapter 5 (Saint-Germes).

Part II aims to link competences at non-individual levels. Chapter 6 (Chédotel and Krohmer) thus seeks to understand how competences exercised collectively exceed the mere addition of individual competences. Chapter 7 (Mammar El Hadj) moves on to show that it is also possible to think in terms of a collective competence, when employees belonging to several distinct organizations are working on a common project. Then Chapter 8 (Mazzilli) explores the possibilities for analyzing competences at the level of a territory, considered as a structuring framework for the activities of organizations of different natures. Finally, Chapter 9 (Ferrary) concludes the second part of the book, by placing competence management at the interface between organizations and markets. It shows that the competitiveness of companies in product markets may depend on their competitiveness in the labor market, i.e., their ability to attract the competences needed to strengthen their competitive advantage.

Lastly, Part III looks at the importance of taking into account real contexts in the analysis and management of competences. Chapter 10 (Colin and Meier) thus shows the importance of activity in the process of transmitting competences, based on research conducted in the aeronautic sector. Chapter 11 (Dumouchel) uses ergonomic approaches to reveal the richness provided by detailed analysis of work, and Chapter 12 (Raulet-Croset and Teulier) uses an interpretative approach to show that new competences (in this case in sales activities) emerge at the micro-level of activity, through interactions between salespeople and customers. Chapter 13 (Charles-Pauvers and Schieb-Bienfait) shows that the specific context of the social and the solidarity economy can lead to the emergence of particular entrepreneurial competence. Finally, Chapter 14 (Barmeyer and Mayrhofer) presents research perspectives for taking intercultural contexts into account in the process of competences' emergence.

References

Argyris, C., & Schön, D.-A. (1978). *Organizational Learning: A Theory of Action Perspective.* Reading, MA: Addison Wesley Longman Publishing Co.

Brewer, L. (2013). *Enhancing Youth Employability: What? Why? And How? Guide to Core Work Skills.* Geneva, Switzerland: International Labor Organization (ILO).

Brockmann, M., Clarke, L., & Winch, C. (2008). Knowledge, skills, competence: European divergences in vocational education and training (VET) – the English, German and Dutch cases. *Oxford Review of Education, 34*(5), 547–567.

Gilbert, P. (2006). *La gestion prévisionnelle des ressources humaines.* Paris, France: Editions La Découverte.

OECD. (2017a). Future of work and skills. In Paper Presented at the 2nd Meeting of the G20 Employment Working Group, 15–17 February.

OECD. (2017b). *Investing in Innovation and Skills: Thriving in Global Value Chain.* OECD Science, Technology and Innovation, Policy Papers, n 44.

Sienkiewicz, L. (Ed.). (2014). *Competency-based Human Resources Management: The Lifelong Learning Perspective.* Institut Badan Edukacyinych, Warszawa, publication co-financed by the European Social Fund of the European Union.

Chapter 1

The Conceptual Travel of Competence: Building a Bridge between North American and European Approaches

Benoît Grasser, Sabrina Loufrani-Fedida, and Ewan Oiry

Contents

1.1 Introduction

Due to its cross-cutting nature, the concept of competence has been studied extensively in management sciences since the mid-1990s (Sanchez et al., 1996; Nordhaug, 1998; Drejer, 2001; Delamare Le Deist and Winterton, 2005; Capaldo et al., 2006; Håland and Tjora, 2006; Sandberg and Pinnington, 2009; Lindberg and Rantatalo, 2015). Many contributions were produced both in terms of competence management and in terms of the design of human resource (HR) tools and the management of organizations, as well as more societal contributions about the recognition of work or even about the limits of this kind of management. More recently, however, research in competence management has entered an era more open to doubt, reflecting on a series of questions: Is there actually a solid theoretical foundation that supports the concept of competence? What is the contribution of research on employee's competences to human resource management (HRM) specifically and, more generally, to management? Is there not a risk of diluting the concept of competence by considering it at the individual, collective, organizational, and strategic levels? Can we and should we still talk about competence when the notions of talent and human capital are more and more present in the literature? Is it still possible today to manage competences in a world where the boundaries of organizations are more and more porous? Should we even continue to manage competences when the progression of knowledge and innovations quickly make obsolete any attempt at formalization? These questions, and many others, probably explain why, in a field which seemed well identified and well structured yesterday, analyses of competences today are very diffused, both for researchers and for practitioners.

These observations, however, suggest a kind of paradox, as the questions surrounding competences are experiencing a sharp rise in attention, as evidenced by the growing dissatisfaction of companies with the traditional tools of competence management or the many questions raised by international institutions concerning labor competences for the future (OECD, 2017; WTO & ILO, 2017), in relation to employability (Loufrani-Fedida et al., 2015; France Stratégie, 2017) and innovation (Toner, 2011).

Concerning specifically the concept of competence, it has often been criticized for being fuzzy and catchall (Chen and Chang, 2010; Delamare Le Deist and Winterton, 2005). In particular, for Delamare Le Deist and Winterton (2005), there is considerable confusion surrounding the term "competence," including a confusion of concept with neighboring but distinct concepts and incoherent uses. Some authors use the singular ("competence" and "competency") and the plural ("competences" and "competencies"). Elkin (1990) associates the term "competences" with the micro level of competence (job competences and individual competences, which are centered on the individual) and the term "competencies" at a macro level (managerial/management competencies for the future). Others use "competency" when they refer to professional competence, while others still treat the terms as all being synonymous. Burgoyne (1988), for example, distinguished "being competent" (meeting the job demands) from "having competencies" (having the attributes necessary to produce a performance with competence). In this Handbook, we have chosen to use the terms of competence in the singular and competences in the plural, to be coherent with our analysis of the travels of competence as a concept from the United States to Europe and back again to the United States ("competence" being the term most used in the United States).

In our opinion, two main reasons explain this diversity in the concept of competence. Firstly, the concept is multidisciplinary. Indeed, it is increasingly successful in fields as diverse as linguistics, work psychology, ergonomics, education, and training sciences, as well as sociology (all disciplines that have integrated competence as an essential dimension of humans at work). But it is also used in the fields of economics (mainly through the evolutionary theory of the firm or, more recently, the territorial economy) and management (in which competence finds a particular resonance in the field of research in strategy). Secondly, competence may be seen at different levels of analysis: individual, collective, organizational, and inter-organizational. Indeed, the concept of competence has found its place "naturally" within the company context, first by positioning itself in three levels of analysis: the individual (with individual competences), the organization (with organizational competences, some of which are considered as strategic), and then the team (with collective competences). But with the opening of organizational boundaries and strategies of vertical disintegration (or outsourcing of activities), a fourth level has emerged, namely that of inter-organizational competence (some of which is territorial). Accordingly, the researcher in management sciences is often asked whether he/she should opt for an observation at the individual or collective level, or whether he/she would prefer another unit of analysis such as the organization as a whole, inside or outside its borders.

This chapter is organized into two parts. Part I identifies how American scientific research has produced two different streams of literature in management sciences. Following the seminal work of McClelland (1973), the first perspective considers competence as a personality trait that explains the high performance of certain employees. The second perspective is based on a conceptual framework that comes from strategic management, with the resource-based view (RBV) (Wernerfelt, 1984; Barney, 1991) which has deeply influenced the research in the field of strategic HRM (Lengnick-Hall et al., 2009). Part II shows how in Europe different literatures from Great Britain, Scandinavia, Austria/Germany, and France (often independent of each other) have developed a perspective on competence that is quite different and which pays much more attention to the context in which competence is built. We believe that this perspective has allowed us to enrich the American literature on competence and to propose new concepts such as collective competence and inter-organizational competence.

1.2 The Focus on Individual and Strategic Levels of Competence in the United States

1.2.1 Competence at the Individual Level

In American scientific research, McClelland's article (1973) is rightly considered to be a founding contribution in understanding the concept of competence in human resource management (HRM). However, he was not the first to address the issue. White's (1963) work on the "meaning of competence" contains many of the elements that McClelland (1976, 1998) later mobilized. McClelland's article (1973) has an unusual form in scientific journals, and has been particularly controversial. It is written in the form of a sharp criticism of the intelligence tests that he proposes to replace with competence assessments. It ends with lengthy proposals for managers, HR managers, and even executives on what they should do to go beyond the limits of intelligence testing in their recruitment practices, by adopting competences assessment tools. In this article, McClelland has a dual, scientific and social, agenda. At the scientific level, the article intends to found the concept of competence theoretically. At the social level, it intends to fight against racial discrimination. In his article, McClelland (1973) points out that the so-called intelligence tests actually measure mainly the knowledge that is acquired at school. Since access to schooling is very strongly influenced by social origins and, particularly in the United States, racial origins, he proposes replacing the tests of intelligence/knowledge acquired at school by tests of competence, competence being for him innate and therefore not socially determined. This article immediately positioned competence as a subject of debate, involving researchers, practitioners, and social actors, which has been the case ever since (Boyatzis, 1982; Spencer and Spencer, 1993).

Despite its unusual form, McClelland's article founded a whole stream of research on competence. This involved considering competence only at the individual level, and the field of research on individual competences has been the subject of much debate. For example, McClelland positioned competence as the characteristic that distinguishes the best performers from other employees. Others criticized this position by considering that all employees can be competent, even if these skills can be of very different kinds. This debate is also reflected in the literature on the concept of talent: Gallardo-Gallardo et al. (2013) discuss whether talent characterizes best performers (exclusive vision) or whether all employees of an organization can be considered as the repository of a form of talent (inclusive vision).

Another debate on the innate or learned origin of competence has also strongly structured this current of research. On this point too, McClelland adopted a clear position. Competence is similar to personality traits, and so it is pretty innate. On the other hand, other authors rather supported the idea that competences are built and acquired: through training and on-the-job training, or by the observation of other employees. For example, Bandura (1986) talks about vicarious learning, i.e., learning that takes place by observing co-workers. Spencer and Spencer's (1993) proposal to distinguish the "hard and soft" dimensions of competence has helped to build a certain consensus in this debate: the "soft" dimensions of competence are similar to personality traits and are therefore rather innate, while the "hard" dimensions of competence are more constructed and can therefore be the subject of learning. The image of the iceberg is now widely used to reflect the diversity and heterogeneity of resources that, when combined, make up competence. In this metaphor, the hidden part of the iceberg corresponds to soft skills (motives, traits, self-image, and social role) while the emerged part corresponds to hard skills (skills and knowledge).

This line of research, which positions competence only at the individual level, has produced particularly convincing results. Even if the debates mentioned above continue, the acronym KSOA (knowledge, skills, and other abilities) produced to designate the different components of competence is now unanimously considered in HRM as a satisfactory representation of resources that, when combined, constitute competence (Ployhart and Moliterno, 2011).

1.2.2 Competence at the Strategic Level

Strategic competence is part of another academic field (strategy), which undoubtedly explains why it has developed as a separate line of research since the 1980s, in a way that is relatively disconnected from the various studies we have just mentioned. Like McClelland (1973), some strategy researchers (Wernerfelt, 1984; Prahalad and Hamel, 1990; Barney, 1991; Grant, 1991) have grasped the concept of competence with their own social and scientific agenda. At the scientific level, these strategy researchers are clearly part of an attempt to surpass the work of the Harvard School, whose standard-bearer was Porter (1985). This school of strategic positioning makes the analysis of the external environment the key to a company's strategy. It is by studying the different forces that exist in a given sector of activity (an "industry" in Porter's terms) that researchers and managers can identify the markets in which it is profitable to develop and those which it is advisable not to try to enter. In a context of market saturation, some authors (Wernerfelt, 1984; Barney, 1991) quickly perceived the limits of this positioning logic. If most markets are saturated, the tools of the positioning school are no longer really useful. The only solution is to invent a new market. Such a "blue ocean" strategy differs from a "red ocean" strategy, in which competition is cutthroat and the water is bloody. It thus appears to be the way to salvation in an economy where most of the major known markets are saturated (Kim, 2005). Apple and Steve Jobs, with their ability to innovate by inventing the iPod, iPhone, or iPad market, appear as the archetypal players in this new strategic perspective.

Drawing on the work of economists such as Penrose (1959), researchers like Wernerfelt (1984) and especially Barney (1991) highlighted the concept of an organization's strategic competence and gradually structured a resource-based view (RBV) approach which, without rejecting the relevance of external context analysis, emphasizes that an organization's strategy is based on its ability to identify its internal resources and combine them in an original way in order to build one or more key competences. These key competences will enable the organization to invent an innovative product that customers will accept to buy, often at relatively high prices. The VRIN/VRIO model is nowadays considered as a satisfactory synthesis of the characteristics of a strategic competence. Such competences are *v*aluable (allowing new products or services to be invented that can be sold on a market), *r*are, difficult to *i*mitate, and *n*on-substitutable. Barney's work (1991) proposed an initial identification of the mechanisms by which these key competences can be built. He thus refers to the learning processes by which the resources necessary to build a key competence are developed. He defines resources as: "all assets, capabilities, organizational processes, firm attributes, information, knowledge, etc. controlled by a firm that enable the firm to conceive of and implement strategies that improve its efficiency and effectiveness" (Barney, 1991, p. 101) and includes "human capital resources" which cover "the training, experience, judgment, intelligence, relationships, and insight of *individual** managers and workers in a firm" (ibid., p. 101).

This RBV approach has really contributed to renewing strategic thinking. A great deal of research has been done in this regard (Foss, 2007). Even on the more specific issue of key competences, much work has been done to advance analysis. For example, the work of Spender (1996) and Grant (1996) has focused on a particular type of resource (knowledge) and thus founded the knowledge-based view (KBV) approach, which clearly enriches Barney's (1991) approach. By definition, knowledge is rather intangible, difficult to communicate and disseminate. They are therefore archetypes of resources as conceived by the RBV approach.

Similarly, the "dynamic capabilities" approach is another particularly interesting addition to Barney's (1991) original definition. As early as 1997, Teece et al. highlighted that companies must not only create a competitive advantage by combining their resources; they must also maintain this competitive advantage for it to become sustainable. In a changing economic environment, this objective is particularly difficult to achieve (Eisenhardt and Martin, 2000). Since the initial contribution of Teece et al. (1997), there have been major advances in the field of dynamic capabilities. In particular, over the past two decades, significant theoretical

---

* Barney's own emphasis.

progress has been made to clarify the concept. Several key definitions have been developed (Eisenhardt and Martin, 2000; Teece, 2007; Helfat and Winter, 2011). All of them position dynamic capacity as the company's ability to build and renew its competences, to adapt and act on its environment, and to maintain its competitive advantage. They also emphasize the central idea of change (i.e., the dynamics of competence development) and underline the intentionality of the actors in the development of a firm's resources and competences.

However, the RBV approach was highly criticized in stimulating and challenging ways. Several authors have highlighted its tautological and *ex post* dimension (Porter, 1991; Priem and Butler, 2001). It has also been highly criticized for its lack of operationalization (Priem and Butler, 2001). As we have seen, from the outset, Barney (1991) focused on individuals who, through their intelligence, judgment, or experience, contribute to building an organization's resources. Yet he has never been able to develop a clear conceptualization of the role of the micro level in building strategic competences. The RBV has therefore been the subject of recurrent criticism about its operationalization: How do resources actually combine? What are the roles of HRM, tools, and policies in this dynamic? The RBV has always had the greatest difficulty in providing clear answers to these types of questions (Nordhaug and Gronhaug, 1994; Priem and Butler, 2001). However, several attempts have been made. For example, the work of Prahalad and Hamel (1990) is particularly interesting because, by adopting questions closer to HR, they examine in detail the mechanisms that make it possible to build this strategic competence. For example, they highlight the role of the leader who becomes, from their point of view, a "competence architect" and mention the role of HR policies in training and developing the resources needed to build strategic competence. Nevertheless, the RBV approach has the greatest difficulty in identifying the mechanisms by which individual resources or competences combine to build key competences at the strategic level of the organization.

1.3 From the United States to Europe: A Contextualized Perspective on the Individual and Strategic Levels of Competence and the Emergence of Collective and Inter-Organizational Competences

The European scientific literature also offers original perspectives on competence. Some of them have been in contact with the US literature. Others are clearly parallel to it, in particular because, as in the United States, each research field responds to different social agendas. We will therefore first see that the European literature has developed a rather contextualized vision of individual competences (in Great Britain, Italy, France, and Sweden) but also a contextualized vision of strategic competences (in Austria and Germany). Next, we will see that this literature has also developed concepts that have not strictly speaking existed in the US literature: collective competences and inter-organizational competences. However, we would like to point out that roots of thinking similar to these concepts do indeed exist in the United States and that the hybridization of this literature will undoubtedly be relatively easy.

1.3.1 A Contextualized Perspective on Individual and Strategic Competences

1.3.1.1 A Contextualized Perspective on Individual Competence

Faced with the same saturation of mass markets and the same need to develop industries that offer quality, innovative, and personalized goods, various European countries are engaged in an examination of "flexible" organizations that make it possible to preserve economies of scale while offering varied products (Lorenz and Valeyre, 2005). This thinking on new organizational models was immediately accompanied by an analysis of the new competences that workers must develop to be effective in such a new type of work organization. Taylorism was based on the principle of workers' obedience to prescribed tasks, to ensure optimal mass production, economies of scale, and their associated profits. The need to ensure flexible production in which products are varied and adapted to customer demands implies thinking about the competence of workers. The new bases for companies' profitability in this case include: workers' competences, in particular, their ability to identify and correct defects as soon as they occur, to deal with continuous and significant variations in products and processes, to cope more frequently with unexpected situations, and to formulate proposals for improvement. Such thinking can be found in Great Britain (Tether et al., 2005), France (Zarifian, 2001), Italy (with the Professionalità, Rouvery and Tripier, 1973), and Sweden (Charron and Freyssenet, 1994).

Like McClelland's article (1973), these reflections are part of a particularly strong social agenda. Realizing that profits are now more clearly linked to the ability of workers to intervene adequately in the production process, these new analyses call for what can be considered as a "just" retrocession of the value thus created, given a context of strikes and industrial conflict. The strikes at Fiat in Turin, which gave rise to the "Professionalità" movement of reflection and action, were particularly emblematic of this social agenda of thinking about competence (Zarifian, 2001). In France, it has rather been the employers and management that have promoted competence, thus trying to bypass collective agreements and company agreements negotiated with trade unions that they have perceived as too limiting of freedom to undertake change (Dumont, 2000; Zarifian, 2001).

While also seeking to respond to market developments (see in particular the work on the organizational models renewed at Volvo and in particular at its

Uddevalla plant), the Swedish and Scandinavian literature in general has paid strong attention to context. In particular, Sandberg's (2000) work also focuses on individual competence, but is at odds with McClelland's approach, which the latter radically refuses to take into account the context of the competence. By contrast, Sandberg (2000) makes it a major element of his definition of competence. First, he considers competence as "lived," a "life experience" that takes place in a unique professional and personal context. This context has a direct impact on how competence is perceived, implemented, and developed. This concern for context is also reflected in some of the work in Great Britain (Stokes and Oiry, 2012).

On the basis of this work, in France and partly in Europe (but also in Brazil; Ruas et al., 2011), the literature agrees in defining individual competence as "a combination of resources that makes a person at work capable of carrying out tasks in a professional situation, *in a precise context*" (Defélix et al., 2006, p. 2). This definition therefore expresses McClelland's perspective: competence is indeed a set of resources ("knowledge, skills, and other abilities"), but it is directly related to the work that a particular individual actually does (Singleton, 1978). Since the late 1970s, the work of Singleton (1978), but also that of French ergonomists De Montmollin (1984) and Leplat (1990), has shown that it is not possible to treat the capacities of individuals separately from their productive context, only because the physical dimensions, and in particular the sensory dimensions that intimately link the individual to his/her context, are essential to exercising know-how. The same is true for the time dimension: the characteristics of time, intensity, and rhythm are specific to a given context and constitute a constraint on activity, and it is precisely control at work that leads to a regular and fluid unfolding of the activity, despite variations and hazards. Under these conditions, the exercise of individual and collective competences results in the emergence of organizational routines, embedded in an organization. These routines inextricably combine competences and organizational contexts, both from a static point of view (reciprocal adequacy) and from a dynamic point of view (transformative dialectics between competences and organizational contexts). Exceptionally, some research in the US literature reflects this contextualized approach to individual competence: see, for example, Capaldo et al. (2006).

1.3.1.2 A Contextualized Perspective on Strategic Competence

As we have just seen, there is an original literature on individual competence in Europe that offers a much more contextualized perspective. The same type of literature is available for strategic competences. In particular, the Austrian and German literature, within the field of "competency-based management," has structured this perspective (Sanchez et al., 1996; Sanchez and Heene, 1997; Freiling et al., 2008). This approach proposes to integrate into a common conceptual framework the work that had been scattered across a growing number of trends in strategic management. These authors reaffirm that RBV has constituted a profound renewal of the analysis of corporate strategies, but consider that the multiplication of research and trends has gradually made it less effective as an explanation. While deepening the analysis, the knowledge-based view (KBV) approaches (Grant, 1996; Spender, 1996; Wright et al., 1994), "core competence" (Prahalad and Hamel, 1990), and "dynamic capabilities" (Teece et al., 1997; Eisenhardt and Martin, 2000) have helped to spread research into areas that sometimes struggle to dialogue with each other. Competency-based management proposes to re-found the RBV line of research conceptually, epistemologically, and methodologically (Freiling et al., 2008) and does so by placing competences and organization (and therefore context) at the heart of its thinking.

Competency-based management integrates the various works resulting from the RBV, by positioning them in relation to the concept of competence. Researchers who belong to this theoretical field define competence as "an ability to sustain coordinated deployments of resources in ways that help an organization to achieve its goal" (Sanchez and Heene, 1997, p. 306). This trend therefore immediately goes beyond the individual definition of McClelland's competence to position it in a context of organization and competence management. Competence cannot be defined in a purely individual way. It can only be understood in an organizational context. The "ability to sustain coordinated deployments of resources" does not exist in itself. It only makes sense in connection with an organization and in its ability to help it achieve its goals. Given this attention paid to context, Sanchez and Heene (1997) analyze in detail how competences can be developed and built. For example, they consider that *"competence leveraging* occurs when a firm sustains coordinated deployments of resources in ways that do not require qualitative changes in the resources the firm uses or in the modes of coordination used by the firm" and that *"competence building* occurs whenever a firm acquires and uses qualitatively different resources or modes of coordination" (Sanchez and Heene, 1997, p. 306). These authors then point out that the so-called "modular" work organization is the one that best ensures the development of employees' competences (Sanchez and Heene, 1997, p. 82).

1.3.2 Emergence of Collective and Inter-Organizational Levels of Competence

1.3.2.1 The New Concept of Collective Competence

Beyond a contextualized vision of individual and strategic competences, the European literature on competence also proposes new concepts. In particular, recent work has focused on collective competence, especially in France, noting first of all that collective competence still remains the poor relative, or weak link, in the literature on HRM (Retour and Krohmer, 2006).

In the United States, however, two schools of research quickly brought them to the forefront. First, Lawler's (1994) founding work rapidly moved beyond the individual and purely HR characteristics of competence to make it a strategic, organizational, and managerial issue. The author was thus not only interested in individual competence but rather in the organizations and collectives that enable individuals to build and develop their competences. Similarly, the work of Prahalad and Hamel (1990) quickly identified the importance of the collective level in the construction of key competences. They write that the key competence is "the collective learning in the organization, especially how to coordinate diverse production competences and integrate multiple streams of technologies" (ibid., p. 82). However, this line of research has never reached a satisfactory conceptualization of the collective dimension in the analysis of competence.

Conversely, the collective level has long been the subject of a very abundant literature (Forsyth, 2014), including the notions of teams, groups, and communities of practice for instance. Several scientific journals are even dedicated to them (see for example *Group Dynamics, Theory, Research and Practice*, or *Group and Organization Management*). Work on the collective level is also very interested in the appropriate leadership to manage these groups (Morgeson et al., 2010; Krasikova et al., 2013). But the collective competence of these groups has been relatively little studied in comparison to the work on the individual and strategic levels of competence.

However, research is beginning to develop in HRM and team management, both to define collective competence and to understand its generating mechanisms in different team contexts: here, collective competences result from the combination of individual competences in a team (Arnaud and Mills, 2012). More precisely, the notion of a collective competence can be defined as "a group's ability to perform together towards a common goal, which results in the creation of a collective outcome, an outcome that could not be accomplished by one member due to its complexity" (Ruuska and Teigland, 2009, p. 324). Such competence is said to take place at the group level, and as such, it is a collective competence that integrates both practical and interpersonal competence. Practical competence refers to the team members' ability to integrate their individual competences and solve problems together. It includes a combination of learned competences, working routines, and processes, as well as thinking chains and reasoning. Interpersonal competence refers to the ability of team members to interact and collaborate with other members, while accomplishing the team's tasks (Ruuska and Teigland, 2009). However, it is not enough to bring people together to become collectively competent or, in other words, it is not enough to create a team for its members to cooperate and a collective competence to emerge (Chédotel, 2004). Thus, the most recent work on collective competence (Salas et al., 2009; Melkonian and Picq, 2010; Arnaud and Mills, 2012) seeks to detect the mechanisms underlying the emergence of collective competence and so attempts to identify and propose management tools that can channel it. The aim is then to analyze how collective competences are built in team contexts, in order firstly to define one or more mechanisms (i.e., explanatory ingredients) of the emergence of collective competence from the individual competences. Secondly, prior studies aim to understand how these mechanisms operate, and thirdly, how the team is constructed from the individuals. Thus, many studies focus on the emergence of collective competence in the functioning of teams, in diversified contexts: emergency hospital service (Colin and Grasser, 2009), innovative projects (Loufrani-Fedida and Missonier, 2015), public-private partnership projects (Ruuska and Teigland, 2009), consultancy teams (Klarner et al., 2013), or teams in extreme situations (Melkonian and Picq, 2010).

1.3.2.2 The New Concept of Competence at the Inter-Organizational Level

Like the literature on collective competences, the literature on inter-organizational competence is relatively undeveloped and recent. However, there is a very rich literature on inter-organizational relationships. It highlights forms of inter-organizational collaboration (Hardy et al., 2005; Sanders et al., 2011). In particular, it highlights the role of personal relationships (Gligor and Holcomb, 2013), the role of trust (Bachmann and Inkpen, 2011) in building this collaboration, as well as the growing role of electronic technologies in such working together (Sanders et al., 2011). On the other hand, the perspective of the competences that are built between organizations and that make it possible to create, maintain, and develop this inter-organizational collaboration is still not well studied.

The cross-sectoral collaboration literature is a subset of this literature on inter-organizational collaborations and networks (Cropper, 2008; Clarke and Fuller, 2010). It is in line with Beer et al. (2015), who encourage HRM to move beyond the boundaries of an organization, in order to rely on external stakeholders, particularly the territories (Mazzilli, 2016). This literature is particularly interesting because it does not limit itself to seeking the benefit of each of the companies participating in the network, in inter-organizational collaboration. Instead, it emphasizes that a cross-sectoral collaboration can also produce additional collective benefits (Bryson et al., 2015). It has mainly been used to think about complex public projects, rethink their governance, and attempt to articulate the contradictory objectives that run through public management (Selsky and Parker, 2005). It seems to us that this approach could also make it possible to think of inter-organizational competence as a shared product of inter-organizational collaboration between rather heterogeneous partners, who deal with innovative and multifaceted issues and who are actively involved in this collaboration. However, this literature is only at the very beginning of its development. It has mainly worked on how these relationships emerge and are constituted, the determinants and conditions for the success of these relationships, governance, or the sharing of inter-organizational resources (Selden et al., 2006; Tsasis, 2009). It would be useful to extend the analysis of competence in a way that would specifically address inter-organizational competence (Mazzilli, 2016).

1.4 Conclusion

This chapter has therefore taken us through the different concepts of competence that can be found on both sides of the Atlantic. While it is still a question of dealing with knowledge, skills, and other abilities (KSOAs) at the individual level, there are significant differences between the North American and European works. Competence can be considered innate, or on the contrary, it can develop throughout the lives of individuals, with the use of different levers such as learning by doing or training. The analysis of the importance of contexts also shows important differences, since concrete work situations can be considered as inseparable from competence in some European studies. Finally, it appears that European research has made a significant effort to understand the connections between the individual level of competence and other levels such as collective or inter-organizational competence. However, these differences do not constitute antagonisms but rather complementarities, especially since, on both sides of the Atlantic, the central aim is still to understand better the contribution of individual competences to the performance of organizations.

References

Arnaud, N., & Mills, C. E. (2012). Understanding interorganizational agency: A communication perspective. *Group & Organization Management*, *37*(4), 452–485.

Bachmann, R., & Inkpen, A. C. (2011). Understanding institutional-based trust building processes in inter-organizational relationships. *Organization Studies*, *32*(2), 281–301.

Bandura, A. (1986). *Social Foundation of Thought and Action: A Social Cognitive Theory*. Englewood Cliffs, NJ: Prentice-Hall.

Barney, J. (1991). Firm resources and sustained competitive advantage. *Journal of Management*, *17*(1), 99–120.

Beer, M., Boselie, P., & Brewster, C. (2015). Back to the future: Implications for the field of HRM of the multistakeholder perspective proposed 30 years ago. *Human Resource Management*, *54*(3), 427–438.

Boyatzis, R. E. (1982). *The Competent Manager: A Model for Effective Performance*. New York, NY: John Wiley & Sons.

Bryson, J. M., Crosby, B. C., & Stone, M. M. (2015). Designing and implementing cross-sector collaborations: Needed and challenging. *Public Administration Review*, *75*(5), 647–663.

Burgoyne, J. (1988). Management development for the individual and the organisation. *Personnel Management*, *20*(6), 40–44.

Capaldo, G., Iandoli, L., & Zollo, G. (2006). A situationalist perspective: To competency management. *Human Resource Management*, *45*(3), 429–448.

Charron, E., & Freyssenet, M. (1994). L'usine d'Uddevalla dans la trajectoire de Volvo. *Actes du GERPISA*, (9), 161–183.

Chédotel, F. (2004). Avoir le sentiment de faire partie d'une équipe: de l'identification à la coopération. *M@n@gement*, *7*(3), 161–193.

Chen, H. M., & Chang, W. Y. (2010). The essence of the competence concept: Adopting an organization's sustained competitive advantage viewpoint. *Journal of Management & Organization, 16*(05), 677–699.

Clarke, A., & Fuller, M. (2010). Collaborative strategic management: Strategy formulation and implementation by multi-organizational cross-sector social partnerships. *Journal of Business Ethics, 94*(1), 85–101.

Colin, T., & Grasser, B. (2009). Des compétences individuelles à la compétence collective : les apports d'une lecture en termes d'apprentissage dans un service d'urgence hospitalier. In Retour, D., Picq, T., & Defélix, C. (Coord.), *Gestion des compétences : nouvelles relations, nouvelles dimensions* (pp. 59–78). Paris, France: Vuibert.

Cropper, S. (2008). *The Oxford Handbook of Inter-organizational Relations.* Oxford University Press on Demand.

Defélix, C., Klarsfeld, A., & Oiry, E. (2006). Introduction. In Defélix, C., Klarsfeld, A., & Oiry, E. (Eds.), *Nouveaux regards sur la gestion des compétences* (pp. 1–9). Paris, France: Vuibert.

Delamare Le Deist, F., & Winterton, J. (2005). What is competence? *Human Resource Development International, 8*(1), 27–46.

De Montmollin, M. (1984). *L'intelligence de la tâche : Éléments d'ergonomie cognitive.* Berne Switzerland: Peter Lang.

Drejer, A. (2001). How can we define and understand competencies and their development? *Technovation, 21*(3), 135–146.

Dumont, A. (2000). Un individu devient compétent lorsque l'entreprise lui en donne les moyens. *Personnel, 412,* 25–29.

Eisenhardt, K. M., & Martin, J. A. (2000). Dynamic capabilities: What are they? *Strategic Management Journal, 21*(10–11), 110–1121.

Elkin, G. (1990). Competency-based human resource development: Making sense of the ideas. *Industrial and Commercial training, 22*(4), 20–26.

Forsyth, D. R. (2014). *Group dynamics* (6th edition). Belmont, CA: Wadsworth Cengage Learning.

Foss, N. J. (2007). Scientific progress in strategic management: The case of the resource-based view. *International Journal of Learning and Intellectual Capital, 4*(1–2), 29–46.

France Stratégie. (2017). Nouvelles formes du travail et de la protection des actifs. *Série «Stratégie, 2027.*

Freiling, J., Gersch, M., & Goeke, C. (2008). On the path towards a competence-based theory of the firm. *Organization Studies, 29*(8–9), 1143–1164.

Gallardo-Gallardo, E., Dries, N., & González-Cruz, T. F. (2013). What is the meaning of "talent" in the world of work? *Human Resource Management Review, 23*(4), 290–300.

Gligor, D., & Holcomb, M. (2013). The role of personal relationships in supply chains: An exploration of buyers and suppliers of logistics services. *The International Journal of Logistics Management, 24*(3), 328–355.

Grant, R. M. (1991). The resource-based theory of competitive advantage: Implications for strategy formulation. *California Management Review, 33*(3), 114–135.

Grant, R. M. (1996). Toward a knowledge-based theory of the firm. *Strategic Management Journal, 17*(S2), 109–122.

Håland, E., & Tjora, A. (2006). Between asset and process: Developing competence by implementing a learning management system. *Human Relations, 59*(7), 993–1016.

Hardy, C., Lawrence, T. B., & Grant, D. (2005). Discourse and collaboration: The role of conversations and collective identity. *Academy of Management Review, 30*(1), 58–77.

Helfat, C. E., & Winter, S. G. (2011). Untangling dynamic and operational capabilities: Strategy for the (N) ever-changing world. *Strategic Management Journal, 32*(11), 1243–1250.

Kim, W. C. (2005). Blue ocean strategy: From theory to practice. *California Management Review, 47*(3), 105–121.

Klarner, P., Sarstedt, M., Hoeck, M., & Ringle, C. M. (2013). Disentangling the effects of team competences, team adaptability, and client communication on the performance of management consulting teams. *Long Range Planning, 46*(3), 258–286.

Krasikova, D. V., Green, S. G., & LeBreton, J. M. (2013). Destructive leadership: A theoretical review, integration, and future research agenda. *Journal of Management, 39*(5), 1308–1338.

Lawler, E. E. (1994). From job based to competency based organizations, *Journal of Organizational Behavior, 15*(1), 3–15.

Lengnick-Hall, M. L., Lengnick-Hall, C. A., Andrade, L. S., & Drake, B. (2009). Strategic human resource management: The evolution of the field. *Human Resource Management Review, 19*(2), 64–85.

Leplat, J. (1990). Skills and tacit skills: A psychological perspective. *Applied Psychology, 39*(2), 143–154.

Lindberg, O., & Rantatalo, O. (2015). Competence in professional practice: A practice theory analysis of police and doctors. *Human Relations, 68*(4), 561–582.

Loufrani-Fedida, S., & Missonier, S. (2015). The project manager cannot be a hero anymore! Understanding critical competencies in project-based organizations from a multilevel approach. *International Journal of Project Management, 33*(6), 1220–1235.

Loufrani-Fedida, S., Oiry, E., & Saint-Germes, E. (2015). Vers un rapprochement de l'employabilité et de la gestion des compétences: grille de lecture théorique et illustrations empiriques. *Revue de Gestion des Ressources Humaines*, (95), 17–38.

Lorenz, E., & Valeyre, A. (2005). Les formes d'organisation du travail dans les pays. *Travail et Emploi, 102*, 91–105.

Mazzilli, I. (2016). Dans les rouages de la GPEC territoriale : surmonter les tensions pour élaborer une stratégie collaborative. *@GRH*, (1), 39–63.

McClelland, D. C. (1973). Testing for competence rather than for "intelligence." *American Psychologist, 28*(1), 1.

McClelland, D. C. (1976). *A Guide to Job Competency Assessment* (p. 178). Boston, MA: McBer.

McClelland, D. C. (1998). Identifying competencies with behavioral-event interviews. *Psychological Science, 9*(5), 331–339.

Melkonian, T., & Picq, T. (2010). Opening the "black box" of collective competence in extreme projects: Lessons from the French Special Forces. *Project Management Journal, 41*(3), 79–90.

Morgeson, F. P., DeRue, D. S., & Karam, E. P. (2010). Leadership in teams: A functional approach to understanding leadership structures and processes. *Journal of Management, 36*(1), 5–39.

Nordhaug, O. (1998). Competence specificities in organizations: A classificatory framework. *International Studies of Management and Organization, 28*(1), 8–29.

Nordhaug, O., & Gronhaug, K. (1994). Competences as resources in firms. *International Journal of Human Resource Management, 5*(1), 89–106.

OECD. (2017). Future of work and skills. In Paper Presented at the 2nd Meeting of the G20 Employment Working Group, 15–17 February, Hamburg, Germany.

Penrose, E. T. (1959). *The Theory of the Growth of the Firm*. New York, NY: Sharpe.

Ployhart, R. E., & Moliterno, T. P. (2011). Emergence of the human capital resource: A multilevel model. *Academy of Management Review, 36*(1), 127–150.

Porter, M. E. (1991). Towards a dynamic theory of strategy. *Strategic Management Journal, 12*(S2), 95–117.

Porter, M. E. (1985). *Competitive Advantage: Creating and Sustaining Superior Performance* (pp. 33–61). New York, NY: The Free Press,

Prahalad, C. K., & Hamel, G. (1990). The core competence of the corporation. *Harvard Business Review, 68*(3), 79–91.

Priem, R. L., & Butler, J. E. (2001). Is the resource-based "view" a useful perspective for strategic management research? *Academy of Management Review, 26*(1), 22–40.

Retour, D., & Krohmer, C. (2006). La compétence collective, maillon clé de la gestion des compétences. In Defélix, C., Klarsfeld, A., & Oiry, E. (Coord.), *Nouveaux regards sur la gestion des compétences* (pp.149–183). Paris, France: Vuibert,.

Rouvery, L., & Tripier, P. (1973). Une nouvelle problématique des qualifications : l'exemple italien. *Sociologie du Travail,* (2), 136–156.

Ruas, R., Defelix, C., Picq, T., & Retour, D. (2011). *Competências Coletivas. No Limiar da Estratégia* A. Porto legre, Brazil: Bookman.

Ruuska, I., & Teigland, R. (2009). Ensuring project success through collective competence and creative conflict in public–private partnerships–A case study of Bygga Villa, a Swedish triple helix e-government initiative. *International Journal of Project Management, 27*(4), 323–334.

Salas, E., Rosen, M. A., Burke, C. S., & Goodwin, G. F. (2009). The wisdom of collectives in organizations: An update of the teamwork competencies. In Salas, E., Goodwin, G. F., & Burke, C. S. (Eds.), *Team Effectiveness in Complex Organizations: Cross-Disciplinary Perspectives and Approaches* (pp. 39–79). New York, NY: Routledge.

Sanchez, R., & Heene, A. (1997). Reinventing strategic management: New theory and practice for competence-based competition. *European Management Journal, 15*(3), 303–317.

Sanchez, R., Heene, A., & Thomas, H. (1996). Introduction: Towards the theory and practice of competence-based competition. In Sanchez, R., Heene, A., & Thomas, H. (Eds.), *Dynamics of Competence-based Competition: Theory and Practice in the New Strategic Management* (pp. 1–35). Pergamon.

Sandberg, J. (2000). Understanding human competence at work: An interpretative approach. *Academy of Management Journal, 43*(1), 9–25.

Sandberg, J., & Pinnington, A. H. (2009). Professional competence as ways of being: An existential ontological perspective. *Journal of Management Studies, 46*(7), 1138–1170.

Sanders, N. R., Autry, C. W., & Gligor, D. M. (2011). The impact of buyer firm information connectivity enablers on supplier firm performance: A relational view. *The International Journal of Logistics Management, 22*(2), 179–201.

Selden, S. C., Sowa, J. E., & Sandfort, J. (2006). The impact of nonprofit collaboration in early child care and education on management and program outcomes. *Public Administration Review, 66*(3), 412–425.

Selsky, J. W., & Parker, B. (2005). Cross-sector partnerships to address social issues: Challenges to theory and practice. *Journal of Management, 31*(6), 849–873.

Singleton, W. T. (1978). *Study of Real Skills*. Edinburgh, UK: University Park Press.

Spencer, L. M. Jr., & Spencer, S. M. (1993). *Competence at Work, Models for Superior Performance*. New York, NY: John Wiley and Sons.

Spender, J. C. (1996). Making knowledge the basis of a dynamic theory of the firm. *Strategic Management Journal*, *17*(S2), 45–62.

Stokes, P., & Oiry, E. (2012). An evaluation of the use of competencies in human resource development: A historical and contemporary recontextualisation. *EuroMed Journal of Business*, *7*(1), 4–23.

Teece, D. J. (2007). Explicating dynamic capabilities: The nature and microfoundations of (sustainable) enterprise performance. *Strategic Management Journal*, *28*(13), 1319–1350.

Teece, D. J., Pisano, G., & Shuen, A. (1997). Dynamic capabilities and strategic management. *Strategic Management Journal*, *18*(7), 509–533.

Tether, B., Mina, A., Consoli, D. and Gagliardi, G. (2005). A Literature Review on Skills and Innovation. How Does Successful Innovation Impact on the Demand for Skills and How Do Skills Drive Innovation? *A CRIC Report for The Department of Trade and Industry* (124 pp.). Manchester, UK: ESRC Centre for Research on Innovation and Competition University of Manchester.

Toner, P. (2011). Workforce skills and innovation: An overview of major themes in the literature. *OECD* Education Working *Papers*, No. 55, OECD Publishing.

Tsasis, P. (2009). The social processes of interorganizational collaboration and conflict in nonprofit organizations. *Nonprofit Management and Leadership*, *20*(1), 5–21.

Wernerfelt, B. (1984). A resource-based view of the firm. *Strategic Management Journal*, *5*(2), 171–80.

White, R.W. (1963). Ego and Reality in Psychoanalytic Theory. *Psychological Issues*, *3*(3), 125–150.

Wright, P. M., McMahan, G. C., & McWilliams, A. (1994). Human resources and sustained competitive advantage: A resource-based perspective. *International Journal of Human Resource Management*, *5*(2), 301–326.

WTO (World Trade Organization) & ILO (International Labour Office). (2017). *Investing in Skills for Inclusive Trade* (188 pp.). Geneva, Switzerland: A Joint Study of the International Labour Office and the World Trade Organization.

Zarifian, P. (2001). *Le modèle de la compétence : trajectoire historique, enjeux actuels et propositions*. Paris, France: Editions Liaisons.

Chapter 2

Competence Management Tools: A Paradoxical Longevity

Dominique Bouteiller and Patrick Gilbert

Contents

2.1 Introduction

Tools for competence management are very often presented as innovations or disruptions. At the same time, many of them are rooted in a decades-old history and in a tradition. Sometimes they even keep the same names. Sometimes, this may change but without the structure or the purpose being seriously affected. In the same entity they therefore bring together innovation and tradition. This observation leads us to take an interest in the reasons why some tools for competence management have resisted the test of time. Let us begin with a commonsense explanation.

The idea of efficacity springs spontaneously to mind: the longevity of tools would have its source in the tried and tested efficacity of their uses. This hypothesis does not hold water. The history of competence management is certainly marked by a few success stories, but it also contains many frustrated hopes, like so many other managerial practices, such as re-engineering, ERP, and merger acquisitions. There is nothing strange about that: the effective contribution of management tools depends as much on the context in which they are deployed as on their own characteristics.

And this is the surprising fact: despite the observations just mentioned, some tools continue to exist, after a period when they were believed to have fallen victim to outmoded tradition; like the legendary phoenix, they arise from their own ashes. There may be a name change or a face-lift but they are, once again, hailed as innovations. What explains the longevity of a tool of competence management?

In order to address these questions, this chapter will concentrate on Strategic Workforce Planning known in France as "la gestion prévisionnelle des emplois et des compétences" – GPEC. It can be briefly defined as a method for managing human resources that aims at adapting jobs and competences in an organization according to the strategic choices made by the managers as well as the constraints of the environment. Strategic Workforce Planning covers only the quantitative dimension of workforce and job management and leaves aside the more qualitative dimension of jobs and people, i.e., their competences. The GPEC tries to integrate these two dimensions into the same concept. "GPEC" will be used throughout this text and will cover the quantitative dimension of job management and the qualitative dimension of competences management associated with them.

GPEC can be considered as the "major integrator" of competence management, conceived as the linchpin of renewed human resources management (HRM). It is based on a reference model in four stages:

- The analysis of current resources (in quantitative and qualitative terms)
- The forecasting of employment needs (in quantitative and qualitative terms)
- The diagnosis of the needs-resources gap for the forecast horizon (in quantity and quality)
- The drawing-up of an adjustment program (arrivals, departures, mobility, training, etc.)

The permanent nature of this model justifies it being qualified as a "reference model." Its origin is very ancient. We are going to focus this study on it without getting too involved in the successive names it has had but which have not changed the central structure. GPEC has not always had that name, but the reference model has been maintained throughout the successive shapes of forecast planning in HRM.

GPEC has known a number of failures. Forecasting for employment and competences has proved to be tricky (Stroobants, 1999), and many competences vital for success in a job have proved to be difficult to evaluate or even to identify (Ginsburger, 1992). Nevertheless, GPEC has constantly renewed itself, continuing to bear hope. In order to understand this paradox, we have first of all made use of two explanations based on the ideal and symbolic dimension of management tools: the managerial methodology and isomorphisms. We shall see that they do shed some useful, but inadequate, light for us. In order to go further, we propose two combined approaches, taking into account the materiality of management tools: the genealogical approach and the social approach. After having presented them, we will apply them to GPEC in order to understand them a little better.

2.2 From Ideal Approaches to Material Approaches

2.2.1 Competences Management Tools: Between Managerial Method and Rational Myth

To begin with, let us take note of the two well-established lines of research that provide us with keys that help us to understand the spread and the adoption of management tools: the theory of managerial methods and neo-institutionalism.

Considered from the angle of managerial innovations and the enthusiasm that they arouse, competence management instruments spontaneously evoke the phenomenon of managerial methods. According to Abrahamson (1996), the spread of managerial techniques can be explained by the phenomena of fashion, which are keen to appear both rational and progressive: "It is largely a cultural phenomenon shaped by norms of rationality and progress" (p. 261). Their spread does not only obey the technico-economic constraints which managers have to the face; they also respond to expectations of a socio-psychological kind.

The benchmark status of management competence tools also justifies analyses in terms of institutional isomorphisms (Di Maggio and Powell, 1983). In a context marked by the uncertainty of the environment, organizations imitate each other and, first of all, they copy those that they perceive as innovative (mimetic isomorphism). The GPEC is built up progressively as a professional norm for good management, via consultancies, university teachers, and quality norms (normative isomorphism). In France, pressure applied by the law, thorough employment law, and training legislation have also led to a homogenization of practices (coercive isomorphism).

In the neo-institutionalist perspective, the leaders of a company are obliged to put in place organizational practices, such as the management of competences, which are considered legitimate by the internal and external environments. The theory suggests in fact that managers are obliged to incorporate practices and procedures within the context of their own firms, taking inspiration from the norms which dominate in their sector of activity. Considering the analysis of competence management through this theoretical grid leads to a highlighting of their symbolic character. In this respect, the GPEC appears as a rational myth (Meyer and Rowan, 1977), to which many organizations pay lip service.

The theory of managerial methods and neo-institutionalism contribute most directly to understanding the dissemination of competence management models. But they only give a partial reply to our research question. While it is true that social representations of competences management bring together the criteria of rationality and progress, specific to managerial methods, as Abrahamson (1996) suggests, it is no less true that the audience for competences management tools has not lessened over time. The GPEC is not classified among these "massive phenomena of enthusiasm, limited over time," spoken of by Midler (1986, p. 74). It is difficult therefore to think that one is dealing with an affair of collective beliefs that are relatively transient, spread about by peddlers of fashion. As for the neo-institutional theory, it sheds some extra light on the dissemination of management tools by the convergence of practices. But it says nothing of the paradox which combines the feeble efficacity of tools and the persistence in their use. Moreover, these two approaches basically stress the ideal, symbolic, and discursive dimension of practices. However, while basing their development on rational discourses and myths, management models in general and those for the management of competences in particular have the particularity of combining them with material elements which we wish to highlight, in an approach that we qualify as a sociotechnical analysis.

2.2.2 Sociotechnical Analysis and "Invisible Technology"

Considering that material elements help to "solidify" beliefs and social representations are developed in a managerial model, we tackle GPEC at the meeting point of two approaches to management tools: the genealogical approach and the social analysis. Each approach, in its way, throws interesting light on the dual existence – both promising innovation and persistent tradition – of GPEC. Although it is entirely possible to combine the genealogical approach and the social analysis, we will dissociate them to facilitate the discussion of our results, with understanding being followed by analysis.

This perspective, opened up by Berry's seminal research (1987), takes its place in what has been qualified in recent years as the "material rotation of organisation theories," a research theme which reflects on the materiality of organizations and managerial techniques, without giving way to technological determinism (Mitev et al., 2018). It is about getting beyond the dichotomy between the social and the material by showing how they are linked in management tools or even by producing a new socio-technique (Chiapello and Gilbert, 2019).

2.2.2.1 The Genealogical Approach

This term of genealogy clearly refers to the works of the philosopher Michel Foucault, who was himself inspired by Nietzsche. But rather than referring to just a term, we are speaking of the approach which the philosopher is articulating: beginning from a problem in the terms in which it is posed in its current state, by leading a sort of enquiry: "It must record the singularity of events outside of any monotonous finality; it must seek them in the most unpromising places, in what we tend to feel is without history" (Foucault, 1977, p. 139).

The genealogical approach to management tools is the heir to Foucault (Aggeri and Labatut, 2010) and refers to the successive developments of the management tool, by placing these back in the theoretical and practical debates in which the tool was conceived and then disseminated. This approach also brings up to date the historical filiations of tools, which also still have relevance.

Following on this idea, we do not seek to inscribe GPEC in an uninterrupted tradition, where topicality would be the objective; rather, we shall show the discontinuous nature, the splits, and the breaks. We are particularly interested in deviations: the gaps between discourse and practice, first, and then the swerves between discourse and practices past and present.

2.2.2.2 The Social Analysis of Management Instrumentation

By the social analysis of management instrumentation (Chiapello and Gilbert, 2019), we mean an approach which is interested in the social fact that constitutes an instrumentation. This cannot be reduced to a strictly sociological analysis for it incorporates knowledge arising from other social sciences (economics, anthropology, political sciences, social psychology, and history). Adopting a social approach to instruments of competence management means considering these models not as purely technical products, where one can examine the finished character, nor as simple expressions of social relations, but rather as sociotechnical productions linking tools and actors in a given environment.

In this social analysis, the works by Michel Berry, who is considered to be the founder of a French school of management tools, have opened the way. His research was marked by the publication of a collective report from the Centre de Recherche en Gestion – CRG (the Centre for Research Management) at École Polytechnique on the role of management tools in complex social systems (Berry, 1983). This report, which defines management tools as conceptual or material means which aim to reduce the complexity of organizations, shook up the vision that organizations' behavior was essentially a question of strategy. It showed that, far from being a faithful servant, the tool orchestrates organizational action and that all of the tools form a technical system which is as fearsome as it is invisible (Berry speaks of "invisible technology"). This invisibility is linked to the fact that the collective imagination bestows a preponderant weight on the leaders' wills and on their talent, which the leaders can only be happy with as they are judged on their initiatives. However, Berry explains (1983, p. 4): "management tools are often the decisive elements in the structuring of the real, engendering choices and behaviours which escape men's clutches, and sometimes their awareness."

After these founding works, research first turned toward management control tools and those that measure performance, and then toward HRM and competences management in particular. The overwhelming presence of competences management in the social analysis of management tools (notably, Klarsfeld and Roques, 2003; Oiry, 2009; Bouteiller and Gilbert, 2011; Grimand, 2012) can be explained by the fact that, for several decades, competence was the key ingredient in the renewal of the instrumentation of human resources management.

We will start by proposing genealogy elements in the reference model which will help to provide a shared representation of it and supply a basis for the social analysis.

2.3 Genealogy of Forward Planning of Jobs and Skills

The reference model for the forward-looking planning of human resources has gone through many trials and tribulations. Successive criticisms have been leveled at its different embodiments, but from the 1960s to the present day, the reference model has hardly changed at all.

2.3.1 The 1960s and 1970s: Forecasting and Rational Approach to Personnel Management

The arrival of forecasting in personnel management in a way happened in the name of science, thanks to the progress made in operational research and the arrival of computer science. The first pieces of research were carried out in the American army, major industries, public administration, and airline companies. In France, as elsewhere, the first significant experiments in forecast management in human resources began in the 1960s, influenced by the technocratic paradigm: "the age of scientific management has begun," proclaimed R. Faure, J.-P. Boss and A. Le Garff (1967) in their publication on operational research, and they specified,

> thanks to methods in operational research and more specifically to those in simulation, the accumulation of figures has ended with a qualitative result: we will no longer be interested in precise numbers, but in their relative significance, on which choice orientation depends. Calculators

will therefore become means of forecast management. There is a fine future awaiting scientific management methods. (p. 126)

It seems that this message was heard by the specialists. In fact, a few years later, a book relating reflections on and experiences of forward management appeared. There is a direct link with operational research since "Approches rationnelles dans la gestion du personnel" (Rational approaches in personnel management) (Benayoun and Boulier, 1972) is the fruit of a working group from the Operational Research section of the AFCET (Association Française pour la Cybernétique Economique et Technique/French Association for Economic and Technical Cybernetics). This group was set up at the end of 1969 and was made up of personnel directors, operational researchers, computer scientists, and psychologists from large companies and administrations, as well as consultants. The working group was originally confined to forward staff planning but then extended its interests to other subjects (training and appreciation of staff, in particular).

The creation process for forward-looking management seems to have been similar in the Anglo-Saxon world. In Great Britain, initial thinking on "manpower planning" was worked out within the Operational Research Society (see Smith, 1970), as it was in the United States. At the end of the 1960s, the impressive bibliography compiled by C. G. Lewis (1969) contained no fewer than 706 entries. At that time, predictive management models were built on a purely numerical basis and were limited to what was calculable. They were mainly deployed in the long-term economic management of the workforce.

It can be noted that this quantitative period was a relative failure: leaders did not believe in it, the professionals in personnel management mastered the techniques poorly, certain aspects of workforce management, including some of the most critical, were forgotten, and above all, they presupposed a stable economic environment. The mechanistic principles on which the forecasts were built left aside the strategy and developments in the environment (changes in technology, in competition, in the labor market, in social legislation, etc.), as well as those in the internal social system (in particular the counter-power of trade union organizations).

2.3.2 The 1980s: Employment and the Company's Economic Strategy

In France, the renewal in human resource planning (HRP) began at the end of the 1970s, in response to the imbalances in the employment situation and the increase in unemployment combined with local or sectorial deficits in manpower. Companies no longer aimed at optimizing human resources management during a period of growth but turned to preventing crises following massive layoffs, in particular, in heavy industry (coal mining, steel).

Predictive employment management (gestion prévisionnelle de l'emploi – GPE) was developed in different circles of reflection among employers, which advocated the convergence of economic and social progress – (Institut de l'Entreprise/ Institute of the Enterprise, Institut Entreprise et Personnel/Institute of Companies and Personnel). Forward employment management is built on a critique of earlier conceptions of predictive HRP in relation to the emergence of the strategic management of human resources in North America.

Major industrial firms (BSN, Cogema, Framatome, Renault, Rhône Poulenc, etc.) were the first to deploy HRP. Experiments in the tertiary sector (mainly banks and insurance) companies came later. In other sectors such as trade, building, plastics industry, transports, and textiles, thinking about employment and the development of jobs were carried out by sectoral professional associations.

In the Anglo-Saxon world, simulation and optimization models, deemed to be too abstract and not easily mobilized in an increasingly uncertain environment, led to HR planning (Greer et al., 1989). But, above all, in the background, it was a search for harmonization between HR management practices and contingency factors (external and internal) that would likely have an effect on the HRM process and, in particular, on the strategic context (Fombrun et al., 1984; Schuler and Jackson, 1987), which brought about the development in forward management.

In France, the diagnosis was similar with the accent put on employment, linked with the rise in unemployment and with labor law that integrated the social and economic levels under a single economic leadership. In 1981, the association Développement et Emploi (Development and Employment) was set up, whose aim was to develop new approaches to employment. Following field research carried out for the association, its director, D. Thierry (1983), laid down the bases of "predictive and preventive workforce management," pleading for the integration of the variables "employment" and "human potential" in the definition of a company's strategy. At the same time, he proposed the updating of the very notion of a business plan (idem, p. 48).

Thinking along the same lines, G. Le Boterf (1988) declared:

> Forward planning of staff numbers is no longer sufficient (…). Projective and predictive approaches which "worked" well during times of sure and regular economic growth must now be completed by prospective thinking. "Hard" planning seeks to enter into the detail of each decision, often becoming counter-productive on account of its rigidity; it must give way to strategic management approaches. (p.19)

He proposed the blueprint of employment and human resources as a strategic management tool which, according to him, was adapted to an uncertain and unstable context.

GPEC became "an affair of state" when on September 27, 1988, the French prime minister declared before a forum of committees on hygiene, safety, and working conditions that it was a "burning obligation" for companies. Public authorities made an effort, by different methods, to encourage firms to internalize the costs associated with employment management. On December 7, 1988, in a cabinet meeting, the minister for Work, Employment, and Professional Training, M. Jean-Pierre Soisson, announced a package which would provide "help for the negotiated modernisation of companies." A few years later, this measure was translated by measures (notably increased financial aid) inciting companies to anticipate the handling of their industrial relations problems linked to technological and organizational developments. Among these measures, some have a direct bearing on the setting up of forward approaches: contracts for forecast studies signed with professional organizations in the sector and LIGE contracts (Ligne d'Innovation pour la Gestion de l'Emploi – Innovation Line for the Management of Employment), which help toward the financing of forward management actions which call on outside consultants.

The GPEC is thus inscribed within the framework of public authority thinking. Documents from the Ministry for Employment envisage it as

> an act of management which allows the company to increase its competences, its reactivity and its adaptability to the fluctuations in its environment, through an analysis of job content, the evolution in qualifications in relation to the organisation of work, the valorisation of skills and the individual and collective potential of the staff.

2.3.3 Since the 1990s: GPEC and the Qualitative Turn

At the start of the 1990s, in its turn, the GPEC became the subject of some criticism. It resisted poorly in an unpromising economic context. It is noted that, with the cyclical economic downturn, employment remained an "adjustment variable." "Predictive" studies rather more follow decisions than prepare them. In the Gestion Prévisionnelle et Préventive des Emplois et des Compétences approaches – GPPEC (Predictive and Preventive Management in Employment and Competences) – the "C" in the acronym (see Thierry, 1990) appears as if to set up a bridge between forecast studies and the preparation for actions of individual management. The HRP moves away from the quantitative and collective objective to return to a qualitative and individual approach.

Linked to the individualization movement in HRM, the notion of competence is taking up more and more space. The shift really happened at the beginning of the 1990s. Companies then seemed to be more attentive to job content than to the question of their volume. As V. de Saint Giniez and A. Bernard noticed (1996), the development of forecast management approaches was progressively accompanied by the notion of competence. Nevertheless, this development can only be interpreted from the point of view of progress: the management of jobs, despite the conceptual models which are still put forward, was no longer a question of forecast but of the short term, and human resources directors hardly had any control over the evolution of staff numbers. So they switched their focus. At the end of the 1990s the crisis in forecast management was clear, and researchers in HRM proposed to build a new representation (Defelix, Dubois et Retour, 1997).

In France, linked with the pursuit of industrial restructuring, it was no longer a question, as in the preceding period, of abandoning the logic of plans for layoffs but rather one of "managing uncertainty" concerning the evolution of the content of activities, including jobs. Companies sought instead to favor the adaptation to an environment perceived as turbulent in the long term and to develop the employ-ability of their workers:

■ internally, by the development of multitasking, an increase in functional mobility and the prevention of exclusion, and

■ externally, by accompanying the employee in the acquisition of recognized skills, appreciated on the labor market.

In relation to the theory of resources which renews the strategic analysis by basing it on internal organizational competences, a few companies try to identify those employees who possess strategic skills in order to optimize their functioning. But despite everything, the link between competences and strategy remains exceptional (Trépo and Ferrary, 1998). Moreover, firms find difficulties in defining the concrete modalities for the recognition of skills and in expressing, through this notion, the whole of the HRM processes (Pigeyre, 1994).

In the United States the qualitative shift was more marked, but unlike in France, HR applications based on skills were clearly inscribed in a logic of the evolution and improvement of HRM processes and not in a revolution in the paradigms and prac-tices already in place. What was at stake was essentially economic: the study carried out in 1996 by the American Compensation Association (Jones, 1997) showed, for example, that setting up competences management was mostly done in places that were trying to control costs, to improve client satisfaction, and to increase turnover. Since the 2000s the idea of talent (Michaels et al., 2001) has literally colo-nized competences management at the same time as reinforcing individualization in employment relationships. Let us nonetheless note that the instrumentation of the management of talents sometimes wholly borrows all the reasoning developed within skills management and that it is not rare to find talent benchmarks, where the distinction between talents and competences is hardly perceptible.

2.4 Social Analysis Reveals the Inner Workings of the Eternal Return of the Same Thing

To carry out this social analysis, we need to specify the GPEC in three dimensions, according to which the instrumentation of management is tackled in the special-ized literature:

■ Its structure (What is it made of?). This is about analyzing here the instrumentation in itself, its "anatomy," the elements which constitute it "physically," and the way they are arranged.

■ Its function (Of what use is it?). Whatever its object, a management instrumentation cannot be legitimate without having, in at least one of its manifestations, a link to organizational performance. But it would be simplistic to consider only this objective.

■ A company is not simply an organizational entity producing goods or services and the instrumentation it deploys serves other goals.

■ Its implementation process (How to use it?). This process needs an instruction manual on one hand independent of the context which will allow its dissemination, and on the other hand it should be indigenous, for generic instructions are always incomplete and to be accepted requires adaptation.

2.4.1 A Simple and Robust Representation (Structural Dimension)

From a structural point of view the reference model has no scientific foundation, but it answers fully to the needs for action, which impel the decision maker in a hurry. Its apparent simplicity gives it great advantages over other modes of expression. It facilitates the memorization of the model, naturalizes it by making it appear as something obvious, and thus facilitates also its acceptance and its dissemination, making it "pedagogical" and assuring that it is maintained over the long term.

2.4.1.1 Implicit Functions (Functional Dimension)

The existence of implicit functions makes up for the weakness of operational results (functional dimension); in other words, it is not because the GPEC does not produce the explicitly desired effects that it is not working, for it fills other roles than those which had been assigned to it by its designers. By considering the functional dimension, we note that the continuity of management tools is explained by many factors other than performance. In particular, they reaffirm professional identities and social statuses. Thus, the contribution of GPEC to the affirmation of the HR function is no small affair. Through its mediation, professionals have been able to both invite themselves to the strategy concertation and get close to those who are operational, creating objects upon which everyone will come to depend. It also participates in the rationalization of the social debate and in the emancipation regarding the exercise of power, by formulating the rules of the game which all actors have to obey.

Originally promoted by big name companies, GPEC received an *a priori* strong managerial legitimacy, which has favored its dissemination throughout a large slice of the economic fabric. This dissemination, in so far as it has engaged actors in interaction companywide and in particular HR and managers to whom it supplied a shared language, and sometimes all of society (in France, inscription of the GPEC in a legal framework), has been the source or organizational and institutional routines, creating an inertia which made contesting it difficult and favored its resilience. Interest from researchers, as initiators or analysts, has ensured it a kind of recognition via the numerous pieces of research and publications. The managerial and academic legitimacy of the GPEC has been maintained, taking into account the specific issues, permanent and obvious, to which it can claim to respond: to manage means to forecast (GPEC).

2.4.1.2 An Integrated Instruction Manual (Process-Based Dimension)

From the process-based perspective, the GPEC gives ready-to-use reasons, heuristics which indicate the path to follow and the steps to take. It thus participates in a cognitive economics of decision making. There is a narrow coupling between the structure of the reference model and the process by which it is implemented. In a way, the tool is its own instruction manual. Of course, we could say that in this lies a kind of illusion because, except for a few rare exceptions, the implementation process is incomplete: the GPEC can be interrupted at the collective studies stage. But, whatever the intensity of its application, the tool fixes a goal and pinpoints where managerial virtue lies. The simplified representation of the route to follow, incorporated in the reference model, facilitates taking charge of it and its reproduction (process-based dimension).

2.5 Contributions

The genealogical approach is a testimony to the flexibility of HRP, which has meant it has survived through several periods. The reference model that today we call GPEC has inherited strategic planning structure of human resources just as it descended from that of manpower planning itself. This flexibility has allowed the adaptation to the socio-economic context of each period.

Models of predictive staff planning were born in a period of growth, in a situation where employment was in workers' favor – shortage of labor – and when career development took place within one company. This trend was fed by scientific management. It benefited from operational research and information technology. The main problem for management at that time was to select and then to keep salaried workers.

HRP has been marked by the employment crisis, and its promoters would like to attenuate the effects of this and plan for future threats. More specifically, its rise accompanied the changes in employment structures linked to the growth in pressure, in international competitions and technological developments. It belongs to a search for arbitration between the economic and the social by companies described as "civic minded."

GPEC has prolonged the previous trend. It is less formalized than predictive employment management and adapts its tools rather more to the goals that are sought. The issues are linked to the renewal of the productive model and to the innumerable skills (customer service, self-checking of production operators, etc.) which have to accompany this transformation.

Although the reference model has not been affected by these developments, the HRP has adapted itself to the socio-economic contexts of the periods it has gone through, becoming the object of incremental innovations, which is what we hope we have shown. It remains for us to study the elements which have allowed the resilience of this model to be assured.

As a complement to an explanation in terms of the effects of fashion and isomorphisms, our genealogical and social analysis has brought some elements of response about the dissemination of management tools on competences over the long term, despite their partial effects. If these tools do not constitute the solutions dreamed of, they are nevertheless the reminder of obvious problems and help to orient the action in a direction favorable to their resolution.

Our study also contributes to the debate between competences management, in either French or American style (Bouteiller and Gilbert, 2005). It shows simultaneously the proximities and the differences. While it is true that in France the GPEC is inscribed in a law which has a planning orientation, in fact, the legislation leaves companies a great deal of freedom and does not prejudge any achievements (Gilbert et al., 2014; Oiry et al., 2013). On the other hand, if North America does not have the same inclination toward lawmaking, it does not shy away from planning practices.

Finally, it allows a certain detachment in relation to managerial methods, postulating that it is more important to orient effort toward handling the issues which competences management models face rather than toward new formulations, temporarily more pleasing, like those of talents, which far from soaring away may in fact constitute a stalemate (see Bouteiller and Gilbert, 2016).

References

Abrahamson, E. (1996). Management fashion. *Academy of Management Review, 21*(1), 254–285.

Aggeri, F., & Labatut, J. (2010). La gestion au prisme de ses instruments. Une analyse généalogique des approches théoriques fondées sur les instruments de gestion. *Finance Contrôle Stratégie, 13*(3), 5–37.

Benayoum, R., & Boulier, C.(1972). *Approches rationnelles dans la gestion du personnel.* Paris, France: Dunod.

Berry, M. (1983). *Une technologie invisible ? L'impact des instruments de gestion sur l'évolution des systèmes humains.* Cahier de recherche du CRG-École Polytechnique, http://hal.archives-ouvertes.fr/hal-00263141/fr

Bouteiller, D., & Gilbert, P. (2005). Intersecting reflections on competency management in France and in North America. *Relations Industrielles/Industrial Relations, 60*(1), 3–28.

Bouteiller, D., & Gilbert, P. (2011). La compétence numérisée: enjeux de validité et quête de sens. *Revue de Gestion des Ressources Humains, 79*(1), 56–71.

Bouteiller, D., & Gilbert, P. (2016). The dissemination of competency-based management tools in North America since David McClelland. *Relations Industrielles/Industrial Relations, 71*(2), 224–246.

Chiapello, È., & Gilbert, P. (2019). *Management Tools: A Social Sciences Perspective.* Cambridge, UK: Cambridge University Press.

Defelix, C., Dubois, M., & Retour, D. (1997). GPEC : une gestion prévisionnelle en crise. In Bouteiller, D. (Ed.), *GRH face à la crise: GRH en crise?* (pp. 83–99). Montréal, Canada: Presses HEC.

Di Maggio, P. J., & Powell, W. W. (1983). The iron cage revisited: Institutional isomorphism and collective rationality in organizational fields. *American Sociological Review, 48*(April), 147–160.

Faure, R., Boss, J.-P., & Le Garff, A. (1967). *La Recherche Opérationnelle*, PUF, coll. Paris, France: Que Sais-Je?

Fombrun, C. J., Tichy, N. M., & Devanna, M. A. (1984). *Strategic Human Resource Management.* Wiley.

Foucault, M. (1977). Nietzsche, genealogy, history. In Bouchard, D. F. (Ed.), *Language, Counter-Memory, Practice: Selected Essays and Interviews* (pp. 139–164). Ithaca, NY: Cornell University Press.

Ginsbourger F. (1992). Nouvelles compétences, rigidités sociales. In Linhart, D., & Perriault, J. (Ed.), *Le travail en puces* (pp. 221–233). Paris, France: PUF.

Gilbert, P., Baron, X., Bruggeman, F., & Chemin-Bouzir C. (2014). *Accords d'entreprises sur la GPEC: réalités et stratégies de mise en œuvre*, Rapport pour la Direction de l'Animation de la Recherche, des Etudes et des Statistiques (DARES).

Greer, C. R., Jackson, D. L., & Fiorito, J. (1989). Adapting human resource planning in a changing business environment. *Human Resource Management, 28*(1), 105–123.

Grimand, A. (2012). L'appropriation des outils de gestion et ses effets sur les dynamiques organisationnelles: le cas du déploiement d'un référentiel des emplois et des compétences. *Management & Avenir*, (4), 237–257.

Jones, R. G. (1997). Raising the bar: Using competencies to enhance employee performance/managing individual performance: An approach to designing an effective performance management system. *Personnel Psychology, 50*(2), 529.

Klarsfeld, A., & Roques, O. (2003). Histoire d'une instrumentation de gestion des compétences: entre rationalité contingente, rationalité limité et rationalité institutionnelle. In Klarsfeld, A., & Oiry, E. (Eds.), *Gérer les compétences. Des instruments aux processus* (pp. 171–190). Paris, France: Vuibert.

Le Boterf, G. (1988). *Le schéma directeur des ressources humaines. Un outil du management stratégique.* Paris, France: Editions d'Organisation.

Lewis, C. G. (1969). *Manpower Planning: A Bibliography.* London, UK: English Universities Press.

Meyer, J. W., & Rowan, B. (1977). Institutionalized organizations: Formal structure as myth and ceremony. *American Journal of Sociology, 83*(2), 340–363.

Michaels, E., Handfield-Jones, H., & Axelrod, B. (2001). *The War for Talent.* Boston, MA: Harvard Business School Press.

Midler, C. (1986). Logique de la mode managériale, Annales des Mines. *Gérer et Comprendre, 3*, 74–85.

Mitev, N., Morgan-Thomas, A., Lorino, P., de Vaujany, F.-X., Nama, Y. (Eds.). (2018). *Materiality and Managerial Techniques.* Cham, Switzerland: Palgrave Macmillan.

Oiry, E. (2009). *La dynamique des instruments de gestion: propositions pour un cadre d'analyse.* Sarrebrück, Germany: Editions Universitaires Européennes.

Oiry, E., Bellini, S., Colomer, T., Fayolle, J., Fleury, N., Fredy-Planchot, A., & Vincent, S. (2013). La GPEC : de la loi aux pratiques RH – identification de quatre idéaux-types. *Annales des Mines, Gérer et Comprendre, 112,* 4–16.

Pigeyre, F. (1994). La compétence : un nouvel outil pour la gestion de l'emploi? *La GRH, Science de l'action ?, 5ème Congrès de l'AGRH,* Montpellier (pp. 129–138).

Saint-Giniez, V., & Bernard, A. (1996). L'analyse des compétences et l'attribution du potentiel, deux modes de décision contradictoires dans la recherche d'une meilleure performance organisationnelle? In *Performance et Ressources Humaines* (pp. 130–144). Paris, France: Economica.

Smith, A. R. (1970). *Models of Manpower Systems.* London, UK: The English Universities Press.

Schuler, R. S., & Jackson, S. (1987). Linking-competitive strategies with human resource management practices. *Academy of Management Executive, 1*(3), 207–219.

Stroobants, M. (1999). Autour des mots "Gestion" et "Compétences". *Recherche & formation, 30*(1), 61–68.

Thierry, D. (Ed.). (1983). *L'emploi dans la stratégie socio-économique de l'entreprise.* Paris, France: FNEGE/DE.

Thierry, D. (1990). *La gestion prévisionnelle et préventive de l'emploi et des compétences.* Paris, France: L'Harmattan.

Trépo, G., & Ferrary, M. (1998). La gestion des compétences: un outil stratégique. *Sciences Humaines, 81,* 34–37.

Chapter 3

Competence as a Revelator of Blind Spots in the Talent Management Literature

Alain Klarsfeld and Sophie d'Armagnac

Contents

3.1 Introduction

In the *War for Talent*, Michaels et al. (2001) refer to an "old" HR model against which the "talent" model can be defined. This talent-based model is supposed to be the next step, beyond an HR-led management, based largely on supposedly rigid notions, among which is the notion of competence (Miralles, 2007). The supposed traditional HR model thus identified is criticized by promoters of the talent notion on several grounds: competence requirements are seen as rigid and addressing workers at large and not targeting the best performers, with the goal of matching resources to pre-defined needs. Competence is seen as an attribute of the worker which is decontextualized; competence is depicted as not concerned with the need to create a distinctive competitive advantage, but with the idea of reaching minimal requirements for everyone (Miralles, 2007; Dejoux and Thévenet, 2012). In short, according to these early promoters of talent on both sides of the Atlantic, competence is seen as an "old" notion, itself part of an outdated human resources management model, which the talent notion is expected to supplement. However, if it is true that competence is an established concept and that talent brings in new perspectives, we contend that the view of the promoters of talent on competence ignores the fact that competence had been given many meanings in various scientific fields in both France and the United States. Competence cannot be apprehended only by applying restrictive interpretations. While the notion of talent has been discussed both conceptually and empirically (as will be explained further), our contribution is to highlight how the richer scientific literature on competence may reveal blind spots and open up new perspectives to that of talent. While there may have been a talent turn at the end of the 1990s, we therefore argue in favor of a "return to competence" in talent management (TM). It must be highlighted that as we review definitions of both talent and competence and the reason for their emergence in various domains, our chapter is not devoted to talent (or competence) management *practices*, which may reveal a wide array of choices along the conceptual dimensions presented below. The focus of our chapter is conceptual rather than empirical. The chapter opens with a brief overview of the emergence of the talent concept. Then four characteristics of the talent concept borrowed to the talent literature are analyzed against the prism of the richer competence literature (sections 3.3, 3.4, 3.5, 3.6), leading to a synthesis of the main differences between the two concepts (section 3.7).

3.2 A History of the Emergence of the Talent Concept

Consultants working with McKinsey coined the term "talent" as part of the expression "war for talent" at the end of the 1990s (Michaels et al., 2001). At the time, the U.S. economy was booming and competition for skilled labor was becoming more and more intense with high levels of turnover and labor shortages. "The economy was burning white hot in the late 1990s and companies were scrambling to hire and retain the people they needed" (Michaels et al., 2001, p. 1). In relation to this context of scarcity, "talent" started out as an elitist notion targeting "highly skilled," "high potential," "high value," and "high performers" employees and "pivotal" positions (McKinsey, 2001; Iles et al., 2010; Berger and Berger, 2011) and was not meant for the rank and file. Consultants are there precisely to help firms attract and retain these scarce resources, and the narratives of talent management serve precisely the objective of persuading CEOs to have recourse to their services as witnesses the last page of the summary report presented by McKinsey, which specifies the talent management experts' contact data (McKinsey, 2001).

Talent, according to the founders of the notion, is "the sum of a person's abilities – his or her intrinsic gifts, skills, knowledge, experience, intelligence, judgment, attitude, character and drive" (Michaels et al., 2001, p. 12). Although this definition leaves the door open to the idea that talent is distributed across all segments of the workforce, what matters to early authors about talent and the contenders of "the war for talent" is "great managerial talent," which is "some [supposedly scarce] combination of sharp strategic mind, leadership ability, emotional maturity, communications skills, ability to attract others and inspire other talented people, entrepreneurial instincts, functional skills, and the ability to deliver results" (Michaels et al., 2001, p. 13). "Great managerial talent" characterizes "highly successful managers" (ibid.). Managers are invited to rank their workforce into "As," "Bs," and "Cs," namely high performers, average performers, and low performers, respectively. Talent is a characteristic of the "As" thus identified and therefore characterizes a tiny elite among employees. Talent is easily transferable. It is assumed that talent has to be fought for and poached in a "war" outside of the firm (Gardner, 2002). Talent management practices are presented in contrast with supposedly dominant "old HR practices." American firms acting along the "old way" presumably entrust the management of people to HR departments, rather than to the whole chain of command. In the "talent mindset," all practices as detection, hiring, promotion, compensation, and people development are owned primarily by the CEOs and cascaded down the managerial line. Another feature of the talent mindset is to shift the focus from financial figures to people, whereas "the old way" is supposedly obsessed with financial figures.

A more nuanced view of how talent adds value to competence and the other pre-existing concepts of expertise and high potential has been proposed in France (Dejoux and Thévenet, 2010; Miralles, 2007). Whereas competence refers to qualities necessary to meet a pre-set standard, talent implies being better at doing something than others. Where expertise also refers to some kind of excellence versus others, talent differs from it as it conveys a "bet on the future," whereas the notion of expertise is based on past achievements. Talent thus has a prophetic character, similar to the notions of high potential. However, unlike high potential, talent is not limited to filling top managerial positions but includes every employee facing challenges with success, be they managerial or technical (Peretti, 2009). In sum, talent (as theorized by French authors) is more unique than competence, more future-oriented than expertise, and less top executive–focused than the notion of high potential (Dejoux and Thévenet, 2012).

The rapid growth of talent literature seems to outshine the development of research on competence in the present days. If we examine the management literature in Business Source Complete in the past 19 years and search for the number of papers including "talent" in the title in May 2019, we observe that the tournament between competence and talent turns in favor of talent on the recent period, as far as growth is concerned. The hit count of the terms "talent" and "competence" in titles, for the non-academic sources of Business Source Complete, shows that talent is much more used in documents titles, and this superiority increases: for the last period (2015–2019), talent is up to ten times more cited than competence in titles of non-academic sources.

However, in academic journals, in contrast, competence is much more cited than talent, and this holds also for the most recent past. For the period 1990–1994, we found one academic paper including the word "talent" in the title for approximately ten including "competence"; for the period 2015–2019, the proportion still was one including "talent" for about three including "competence." Talent has been developing more quickly than competence in recent years and is prized by practitioners, but competence still largely dominates talent as a scientific concept (see Table 3.1 for a recap).

In short, the scientific foundations of talent notion remain weak. After having reviewed how the talent notion has been intended to supplement other pre-existing notions in use in HRM including competence, we will review some of the dimensions emerging from the talent and draw some parallels with the richer competence literature that allows to identify, in every instance, blind spots in the

Table 3.1   Citations of "Competence" and "Talent"

	All Business Source Complete resources except academic journals		Business Source Complete resources: Academic journals	
	Competence, Competency	Talent	Competence, Competency	Talent
1990–1994	63	168	185	17
1995–1999	211	810	396	41
2000–2004	356	1416	569	119
2005–2009	458	2678	863	295
2010–2014	264	1921	910	346
2015–2019, May 10	362	3030	1422	517

talent management: the inclusive/exclusive dimension of the talent and competence concepts, the role of the context in defining talent and competence, the meaning of the individual versus collective dimension for talent and competence, and the integration of social justice in the management of talent and competence. Some of these dimensions have already been identified previously as relevant in TM literature (Meyers and Van Woerkom, 2014; Nijs et al., 2014).

3.3 Inclusive versus Exclusive

3.3.1 *Talent*

Talent was originally carved out as an exclusive and elitist concept, where only "the best" have it (Michaels et al., 2001), certainly not everyone. The exclusive approach is rooted in psychological studies concerning gifted individuals and starting from the differences observed between them as far as abilities and resulting performances are concerned (Gagné, 2004; Ledford and Kochanski, 2004). Comparison between people is the rationale, and the scope is enlarged, not focused on a single organizational context. This approach is considered as fostering the claim for TM systems of identification, selection, and retention of talents on the enlarged labor market, with an elitist perspective. This is still the dominant approach adopted within the academic literature, be the articles conceptual or empirical, since they focus primarily on high performers and potential (Gallardo-Gallardo and Thunnissen, 2016; McDonnell et al., 2017), although there has been criticism of this elitist stance ever since the talent notion started to gain ground (Pfeffer, 2001). In a research recently conducted among large French firms about their talent management practices, exclusive approaches were overwhelmingly dominant as much as they were in North America (D'Armagnac et al., 2016). Here, compared to the inclusive approach, talent management relies strongly on the assumption that talent is not universal, inherent in mankind, but is rare, and that talent is not possessed by the individual, but is built according to a social perception within the organization.

Inclusive approaches of talent management are uncommon since they were developed in settings like small organizations (Valverde et al., 2013; Krishnan and Scullion, 2017), public organizations (Bolander et al., 2017), or cultural environments that favor the approach such as Germany or Sweden (Festing et al., 2013; Bolander et al., 2017). These approaches claim that everybody is potentially talented and that talent is a natural ability, contrary to exclusive approaches elaborated upon the scarcity of talent among people. The universality of talent is indeed now a debated issue, inviting to examine carefully where the opposition actually stands. According to Nijs et al. (2014), the inclusive approach is supported by an intrapersonal definition of talent whereas the exclusive approach is supported by an interpersonal approach. In the former, everybody would possess some strengths or innate abilities that an organization should identify and foster, in a search for better motivation and work climate (Nijs et al., 2014). Even in the early 2000s, a few unheard voices claimed that talent would be "inherent in each person" (Buckingham and Vosburgh, 2001) and that the organization would have to get the best of all individuals rather than just the best individuals (Pfeffer, 2001). HR's challenge is to "focus on the unique talents of each individual employee and the right way to transform these talents into lasting performance" (Buckingham and Vosburgh, 2001, p. 18). Empirically, Festing et al. (2013) documented the adoption by German SMEs (small and medium size enterprises) of an inclusive approach, encompassing almost all the employees, which they consider preferable to being engaged in the war for talents seen as rare.

3.3.2 Competence

Reminding of inclusive approaches of talent, early on, competence had been conceptualized (in linguistics) as a universally held human attribute. Linguistic competence is the set of rules that enable the speaker to creatively turn the deep abstract structure into statements as we hear them, even statements unpronounced to the present day. For Chomsky, the study of this linguistic competence is the ultimate purpose of the study of language, which he considers as a mirror of the mind (Chomsky, 1977, 1980). Chomsky separates competence and ability, which falls within the cognitive sphere itself, from all of the other factors that can have an influence on performance: one can be linguistically competent, without which this translates into a corresponding performance (Chomsky, 1977). A sole focus on performance does not do justice to the linguistic competence, a universally held attribute, a common heritage of mankind. Therefore, the "new" inclusive focus on talent echoes a very old and well-established branch of the competence literature. Outside of linguistics, as we shall see below, authors from disciplines such as ergonomics or occupational psychology contend that all workers can develop competences in order to meet what is expected from them in the workplace. However, competence scholars disagree about whether competence is context-free or context-bound.

3.4 Context-Free versus Context-Bound

3.4.1 Talent

The dominant implication of the early talent literature is not only that the talented employee is a member of a small elite of high performers. Talent management was elaborated upon the assumption of high transferability of a selected few talents from one work context to another. This paradoxical view of talented employees as objects to be managed is reinforced by the lexical ambiguity of the term "talent": it could mean the knowledge, skills, or attitude of a person, but in practice it means the person himself or herself (Gallardo-Gallardo et al., 2013), irrespective of context.

Talent was only recently acknowledged as the result of a social, situated construction, rather than being seen as a context-free "object" to be chased and cuddled. The awareness of the need to develop their labor force prompts regions of the world to reinforce their economies through regional TM policies (Khilji et al., 2015; Tarique and Schuler, 2018). The effort made in Asia and Europe toward talent development programs indicates the prevalence of the notion at the government and societal levels. This is indicative of some degree of contextualization of talent albeit at a very high level (Khilji et al., 2015).

3.4.2 Competence

Where talent appears predominantly as a context-free notion and an object to be managed, competence is an attribute of the worker, an attribute that appears context-free or context-bound, depending on the scientific discipline.

3.4.2.1 "Competency" as a Context-Free Notion

If talents are a selected few employees that are high performers regardless of the context, then competencies, a plural derived from "competency" (McClelland, 1973), could be said to be the personal attributes of talented persons. In the early 1970s, the objective behind the emergence of the notion of competency was to provide more valid and fair recruitment testing tools in order to hire the best performers (McClelland, 1973). Competency is defined as an individual underlying characteristic, which is in causal relation with effective or superior performance (Spencer and Spencer, 1993). "Competency" is a characteristic of the individual rather than of the job context. There are five types of competencies: aspirations ("motives"), i.e., things which a person thinks, or that he or she wishes, and which are at the origin of his or her action; traits, i.e., physiological characteristics such as eyesight and hearing; self-concept, namely the attitudes, values, and self-image; knowledge; and know-how, defined as the ability to perform a physical or mental task. The relationship with work performance is predictive in nature: competence is a person's attribute that pre-exists work performance and can be described independently from the latter.

If one refers to competency as conceptualized by Boyatzis (1982), McClelland (1973), and Spencer and Spencer (1993), one can draw parallels with the concept of talent as popularized by Michaels et al. (2001): it is all-encompassing, including motivation; it ranks high-performing versus average- and low-performing individuals, much as the notion of talent does. It is unevenly distributed rather than universally held. It can be appraised and transferred outside of a specific work context. The major difference is in the goals pursued: where McClelland's main concern upon promoting competency was to help firms adopt more inclusive selection practices,

McKinsey's emphasis in the early 2000s was on helping them overcome labor short-ages and the chase of the best performers, possibly by taking their distances with inclusive policies as will be seen below. However, not all researchers on competence agree that competence is context-free. Many contend that it is context-bound.

3.4.2.2 Competence as a Situated Notion

Long ago, the concept of competence was introduced in ergonomics in France as a context-dependent notion in addition to the already existing concept of *activity* (De Montmollin, 1986). The ergonomist tries to understand the activity in the specific context where it takes place, in order to improve working conditions, reduce occupa-tional hazard, and improve performance and well-being – if necessary, through the implementation of training and development actions. However, observing workplace behavior proves insufficient to understand work itself: workers manifest an activ-ity which cannot be captured only as a succession of snapshots (of gestures, behav-iors), but which implies something like already available structures (De Montmollin, 1986). These available structures (pretty much like with Chomsky's linguistic com-petence), although implemented in action, are not a simple "copy and paste" of these actions, which are potentially in infinite numbers. The notion of competence pro-vides a deeper level of understanding which takes into account the existence of some-thing that is already there within each worker. But unlike linguistic competence that is innate, this competence is built throughout working life: competences are sets of knowledge and know-how and procedures that can be mobilized without new learning (De Montmollin, 1986). While for Chomsky there is a universal and innate linguistic competence, independent of the contexts of use, ergonomics stresses the importance of context and the unique responses workers invent to face its multiple requisites. Professional competence is accessible to anyone but is learned at the work-place rather than innate. Ergonomists reject any attempt to equate competence with a fixed attribute of the person, let alone of mankind, independent from work context.

In the international management literature, the relational perspective on com-petences, the situationalist perspective on knowledge and competences (Lave and Wenger, 1991; Brown and Duguid, 1991; Capaldo et al., 2006), and the under-standing approach (Sandberg, 2000; Sandberg and Pinnington, 2009) resemble that of the French ergonomists: person and work cannot be disentangled. Competence is socially constructed by people in a work context according to the colleagues engaged with them (Sandberg, 2000). However, the relational approach does not deny an existence of knowledge, skills, and attitudes *per se*: what matters is their integration in performing activities, and this is what competence means. Competence depends on people's understanding of work situations and self. Beyond knowledge, skills, and attitude, competence refers to ways of being at work (Sandberg and Pinnington, 2009). For the purpose of clarification, Hayton and McEvoy (2006) suggested using the term competence in relation to the individual performance of someone and competency when referring to interactional constructs. In a perspective similar to the French ergonomists', competency modeling can be contrasted with job analysis, according to Sanchez and Levine (2009): job analysis is focused on job activities, attempting to account for the content of work and measure the performance achieved. Competency modeling would be now substituting to job analysis in HR management practices, putting the interaction between the worker and the context of work at the core (Sanchez and Levine, 2009).

3.5 Individual versus Collective

3.5.1 Talent

Talent management refers to a perspective of individual human beings as strategic differentiators, providing a sustainable competitive advantage (Lewis and Heckman, 2006; Collings and Mellahi, 2009). Talent management is thus rooted in an individualistic approach of the resource-based view of the firm that valued rare and valuable assets (Barney, 1991) and supported by the implicit assumption that the performance of all talented individuals will add up to form corporate performance, with no concern for organizational-level capabilities. The underlying assumption is that firms have to attract and retain the best people in order to be the best in their market segment. But talented individuals actually differ in their personal goals and the understanding of corporate issues (Thunnissen et al., 2013): the definitions of situations and the activities to set up differ. All types of distances between individuals are a potential source of dysfunction or conflict which could undermine the talent performance unless a proper diversity climate is created. Cognitive distance is one issue, but talented employees may also be culturally distant from each other and have different ways of conceiving interactions, status, and hierarchy (Peltokorpi, 2006). A company consisting in a collection of very good individual talents is thus not immune to under-performance, if appropriate steps are not taken to best tap this diversity in order to turn it into a competitive advantage (Klein and Harrison, 2007).

In addition to ignoring differences among individuals' strategies, the early talent management literature ignored the role of individual perceptions (Hoglund, 2012). It is questionable whether people labeled as "talents," and being recognized as such, results in additional motivation (Hoglund, 2012; Dries, 2013). But if someone understands he/she is not identified as talent, his or her motivation decreases (Dries, 2013), which is not bearable in SMEs in particular (Krishnan and Scullion, 2017). Therefore, talent management is not free from the shortcomings resulting from individualization. Neither is of course competence, which has been found (mainly in France) to be potentially usable in order to fragment the collective and individualize performance management and the employment relationship (Dugué, 1994; Vidaillet, 2013; Gilbert and Yalenios, 2017). But such usage did not figure among the intentions of its early promoters.

3.5.2 Competence

Although competence is generally defined as an individual attribute (Gilbert and Parlier, 1992; Malglaive, 1995) and can thus be used as a vehicle for individualization (Rozenblatt, 2000), more often than not it is not introduced with this intent by scientists, as has been explained in previous sections. In one branch of management, strategic management, authors even propose a collective perspective on competence. Indeed, in the wake of resource-based view of the firm, a successful company can be seen as a collection of individuals collectively creating a competitive advantage (Barney, 1991). The firm cannot be regarded as a simple portfolio of individuals, activities, technologies, products, prices, and markets (Prahalad and Hamel, 1990). Core competence has a collective, integrative dimension comprising know-how and technologies, in sharp contrast with talent. Competence is *a set* of knowledge and technologies, rather than an isolated technology or a piece of knowledge (Hamel and Heene, 1994): any single know-how, any single technology, is not a core competence. Similarly, recent perspectives on talent management consider key positions or strategic jobs rather than outstanding performers (Cappelli and Keller, 2014; Sparrow and Makram, 2015). The focus on the value associated with key positions tends to de-personalize talent management and put the emphasis on a value approach (Sparrow and Makram, 2015). Still, this renewed talent approach remains based on an individualistic view of how people contribute to competitive advantage, even if the focus has shifted from persons to jobs.

The strategic approach based on core competences has at least one merit within the strategic management literature: to restore the focus on internal analysis as recommended by early authors (Penrose, 1959). The mere introspection effort implied by this approach has the advantage of raising essential and relevant questions – what do we know and what do we want to do better than others? Identifying core competences is the corner stone of any dynamic capability aiming to permanently reinvent competitive advantage (Teece et al., 1997).

In France, scholars have attempted to link individual approaches implicit in traditional HRM approaches of competence, with the strategic management-driven collective approach, and their attempt to define a notion of collective competence has met with some success (Défélix et al., 2006; Retour et al., 2009). Such collective competences are not purely based on company requisites and emerge continuously among teams, organizations, and communities, when managed properly. The lesson for talent management is plain: hiring the best does not produce competitive advantage unless talents are managed in such a way as to tap the best out of them and of everyone else.

3.6 Socially Just or Not

3.6.1 Talent

Beyond fostering potentially damaging rivalry among employees, the talent notion may actually be used as a subtle vehicle for re-legitimizing discrimination against disadvantaged groups. Indeed, a risk of adverse impact surfaces in the founding contribution that established the notion of talent, The *War for Talent* (Michaels et al., 2001). There was a pro-middle-aged bias in this seminal work. It is assumed that "the demographic segment that will supply companies with their future leaders" (Michaels et al., 2001, p. 4) is the 25–44-year olds. That older employees could fill the gap is dismissed based on the assumption that the retirement age will remain stable in the future and that people will not work longer (ibid., p. 5). This is contradicted by the recent trend toward longer working lives evidenced in most Organisation for Economic Co-operation and Development (OECD) countries since 2000 (OECD, 2017). Tapping more into the 44–62-year olds is not even discussed in the *War for Talent*. Tapping more into women, ethnic minorities, and migrant groups is not discussed either.

What is more, the *War for Talent* studies (1997 and 2000) used 5960 and 6900 respondents, respectively: corporate officers, senior managers, and middle managers. It is remarkable that in the methodology section, no statistics or even vague statements are available as regards the gender and/or age and/or ethnic make-up of the sample, a rare occurrence in cross-sectional science research produced in social science. Of the 80 interviewees quoted in the book, 69 are men and 11 are women, which confirms the existence of a pro-male bias, be it involuntary. On another troubling note, we find that the focus of the *War for Talent* is supposedly on the for-profit sector, according to the methodology section (page xxiii); it appears that the authors have deviated from this limitation: three not-for-profit organizations are included in the study. Alas, the not-for-profit organizations chosen by Michaels et al. are far from gender-balanced: the Royal Air Force, the Marine Corps, and the McCallie School, a boys high school. When diversity is mentioned, and considered a possibility, as talent shortages are on the rise, it is as a constraint rather than as an opportunity. "[Companies] are being forced to hire people who do not have the traditional background" (Michaels et al., p. 81). It is also evident that diversity, as understood by the authors of the *War for Talent*, is not the demographic diversity that David McClelland and his associates had in mind in the United States in the 1970s (i.e., gender and ethnic diversity), or the one that most French training and development specialists had in their own minds in the 1970s and 1980s, when they wanted to open up occupational mobility to low- and medium-level professionals by introducing the notion of competence.

Half-way through the *War for Talent*, Michaels et al. (2001) tackle the diversity issue and give two examples of how the talent pool can be made more "diverse." For a big consulting firm, where elite MBA graduates are depicted as the norm, "non-traditional" audiences are defined as undergrads, lawyers, doctors, physicists, and experienced business managers, but not women or minorities or non-traditional age groups. For an electronics retailer, where electronic sales graduates are the norm, "non-traditional" means prize winners of "small colleges" sales contest, salespeople from other industries, former members of the military, and engineers from fields other than electronics. Never are women, the young, the aging, the disabled, or minorities considered as "diverse" talent pools that could be tapped.

There is even explicit demeaning of "legal" forms of diversity criteria as favored by equal employment opportunity laws: Michaels et al. (2001, p. 81) contend that diversity is "not just [underscored by us] more women and more visible minorities" but "people with different experiences, education, ways of thinking, problem-solving styles." The authors clearly express their preference for "this" kind of diversity when they conclude: "diversity of this kind builds the strength of an organization" (p. 81). It is of little wonder that later authors (Festing et al., 2015) have warned against the biases inherent in the notion of talent, as this bias was ingrained in its first mass-dissemination effort.

3.6.2 Competence

As for competence, the preoccupation of its early promoters for universality, or equality, or the collective, or society, looks a much stronger preoccupation than it is for talent's early promoters.

The concept of competence emerged on both sides of the Atlantic over the last 50 years in many different scientific and social contexts. We propose that it appears to address some "invisible" or not-considered-before attribute that "underlies" a more visible concept that the notion of competence purports to complement. This concept against which that of competence is defined varies from discipline to discipline. In linguistics, what the listener hears (and therefore what is apparent to him or her) is linguistic "performance." Linguistic "competence" is an invisible and universal trait that underlies linguistic performance and that cannot be accounted for by the mere study of performance (Chomsky, 1977, 1980). In ergonomics, what the ergonomist sees first is behaviors and technical activities. Yet, competence, an invisible set of pre-existing cognitive structures derived from prior learning, underlies the relevance and quality of these behaviors and technical activities (De Montmollin, 1986). Traditional education systems, for practical and cultural reasons, rely on knowledge, written essays, or multiple-choice questionnaires as a cheap way to assess knowledge. However, "competences" are those characteristics that are typically "left out" and invisible in traditional, knowledge-based education systems (Malglaive, 1995; Gilbert and Parlier, 1992). In the U.S. occupational psychology, the same social concern for fairness (but with an elitist perspective), under the pressure of non-discrimination legislation, leads consultants to seek those "underlying characteristics" that lead to "superior performance," beyond what was readily visible under the form of standard academic testing procedures: knowledge and general abilities. These "underlying characteristics" are presumably less race- and class-sensitive than academics abilities, as assessed through standard academic tests (McClelland, 1973). In strategic management, core competences are a hidden root system, while the more traditional products, markets, business portfolio, and business units, supported by this root system, are of course highly visible flowers and leaves (Prahalad and Hamel, 1990).

Our argument is that among reasons that motivated the adoption of the notion competence, the notion of social justice/equity is prevalent across a range of scientific disciplines: linguistics and occupational psychology in the United States and ergonomics and education science in France. Of course, this should not overshadow the possibility that competence might be used with power-laden, anti-social agendas, targeted against trade unions' and workers' rights (Dugué, 1994; Rozenblatt, 2000). We just point that the concerns that motivated the early promoters of the notion included concerns for society at large and social justice.

As suggested by the use of the competence notion, more diversity-friendly views of talent management are possible. "At its heart, talent management is simply a matter of anticipating the need for human capital and setting out a plan to meet it" (Cappelli, 2008, p. 1). Talent management aims at filling pivotal roles (Boudreau and Ramstad, 2005; Collings and Mellahi, 2009) and can be promoted using rearing metaphor rather than a war metaphor: to win in a competitive environment, firms have breed champions. Talent management can even be conceptualized as inclusive as there are now alternative philosophies available (Meyers and Van Woerkom, 2014). However, only if associated with a conscious diversity message and consciously inclusive HRM practices can talent management include more women and minorities (Ng and Burke, 2005; Warren, 2009; Festing et al., 2015).

3.7 Conclusion

When compared to the varied and multiple definitions of the notion of competence and its multiple anchoring across various scientific disciplines, countries, and social actors, that of talent appears to be in sharp contrast, concerning their origin, the inclusive or exclusive dimension, the role of the context, the individual or collective dimension, and the importance of social justice (see Table 3.2). The notion of talent mainly originated in only one country, the United States, even though it was subsequently exported across the world, whereas the notion of competence emerged independently in both France and the United States and in both practitioner and scientific fields, making it unlikely that the diffusion of competence would result from pure mimicry. Talent is mainly concerned with the supply of labor rather than with the development and recognition of work and the workers, whereas the notion of competence is used not only in recruitment, but in educational and employment policies, in research about linguistics, in ergonomics, in applied psychology, and in strategic management. The notion of competence has a strong and rich scientific grounding in multiple disciplines, where the notion of talent lacks a strong scientific base and has been studied by scholars only in recent years. Talent approaches have a narrow focus principally driven by strategic HRM considerations and ignore the talented person's agency and the work context (i.e., its organizational and institutional embeddedness), contrary to competence that, at least in some approaches such as ergonomics, includes and elaborates upon these dimensions. The notion

Table 3.2 Talent and Competence

	Talent	*Competence*
Origination	United States	Multiple countries
Science versus practitioner	Practitioner-driven	Science-driven
Inclusive/exclusive	Exclusive	Inclusive
Context-free/bound	Context-free	Context-free/bound depending on discipline
Individual/collective	Individual	Individual/collective depending on discipline
Social justice preoccupation	Non-existent	Strong

of talent appears to be mainly management-driven whereas the notion of competence is carried forward by a larger coalition of actors: human resource managers, recruitment consultants but also strategic management consultants, and beyond managerial stakeholders, by linguists, ergonomists, education scientists and practitioners, occupational psychologists, training and employment specialists, trade union officials, and other stakeholders. Where the introduction of talent management rests on a caricatured representation, supposedly rigid pre-existing human resource function with a view to improving managerial processes, the notion of competence is put in place not only to improve managerial processes, but in order to achieve larger societal goals of employability, equity, well-being at work, and/or the enhancement of disadvantaged groups. Possibly thanks to the notion of competence, talent management can be reinterpreted, as suggested by some management scholars (Thunnissen et al., 2013; Meyers and van Woerkom, 2014; Bolander et al., 2017), with a view to promote similar, long-term societal goals of inclusion, people development, and well-being.

References

Barney, J. (1991). Firm resources and sustained competitive advantage. *Journal of Management, 17*(1), 99–120.

Berger, L. A., & Berger, D. D. (2011). *The Talent Management Handbook*. New York, NY: McGraw Hill.

Bolander, P., Werr, A., & Asplund, K. (2017). The practice of talent management: A framework and typology. *Personnel Review, 46*(8), 1523–1551.

Boudreau, J. W., & Ramstad, P. M. (2005). Talentship, talent segmentation, and sustainability: A new HR decision science paradigm for a new strategy definition. *Human Resource Management, 44*(2), 129–136.

Boyatzis, R. E. (1982). *The Competent Manager*. New York, NY: Wiley.

Brown, J. S., & Duguid, P. (1991). Organizational learning and communities-of-practice: Toward a unified view of working, learning, and innovation. *Organization Science*, *2*(1), 40–57.

Buckingham, M., & Vosburgh, R. M. (2001). The 21st century human resources function: It's the talent, stupid! *Human Resource Planning*, *24*(4), 17–23.

Capaldo, G., Iandoli, L., & Zollo, G. (2006). A situationalist perspective to competency management. *Human Resource Management*, *45*(3), 429–448.

Cappelli, P. (2008). Talent management for the twenty-first century. *Harvard Business Review*, *86*(3), 74–81.

Cappelli, P., & Keller, J. R. (2014). Talent management: Conceptual approaches and practical challenges. *Annual Review of Organizational Psychology and Organizational Behavior*, *1*, 305–331.

Chomsky, N. (1977). *Réflexions sur le langage*. Paris, France: François Maspéro.

Chomsky, N. (1980). *Règles et représentations*. Paris, France: Flammarion.

Collings, D. G., & Mellahi, K. (2009). Strategic talent management: A review and research agenda. *Human Resource Management Review*, *19*(4), 304–313.

D'Armagnac, S., Klarsfeld, A., & Martignon, C. (2016). La gestion des talents: Définitions, modèles, pratiques d'entreprises. *@GRH*, (3), 9–41.

Defélix, C., Klarsfeld, A., & Oiry, E. (2006). *Nouveaux regards sur la gestion des compétences*. Paris, France: Vuibert.

Dejoux, C., & Thévenet, M. (2012). *Talent Management*. Paris, France: Dunod.

De Montmollin, M. (1986). *L'intelligence de la tâche*. Berne, Switzerland: Peter Lang (reprinted in 1994, *Sur le travail, choix de textes du même auteur*. Toulouse: Octarès).

Dries, N. (2013). The psychology of talent management: A review and research agenda. *Human Resource Management Review*, *23*(4), 272–285.

Dugué, E. (1994). La gestion des compétences: les savoirs dévalués, le pouvoir occulté. *Sociologie du travail*, *36*(3), 273–292.

Festing, M., Schäfer, L., & Scullion, H. (2013). Talent management in medium-sized German companies: An explorative study and agenda for future research. *The International Journal of Human Resource Management*, *24*(9), 1872–1893.

Festing, M., Kornau, A., & Schäfer, L. (2015). Think talent – think male? A comparative case study analysis of gender inclusion in talent management practices in the German media industry. *The International Journal of Human Resource Management*, *26*(6), 707–732.

Gagné, F. (2004). Transforming gifts into talents: The DMGT as a developmental theory. *High Ability Studies*, *15*(2), 119–147.

Gallardo-Gallardo, E., Dries, N., & González-Cruz, T. F. (2013). What is the meaning of "talent" in the world of work? *Human Resource Management Review*, *23*(4), 290–300.

Gallardo-Gallardo, E., & Thunnissen, M. (2016). Standing on the shoulders of giants? A critical review of empirical talent management research. *Employee Relations*, *38*(1), 31–56.

Gardner, T. M. (2002). In the trenches at the talent wars: Competitive interaction for scarce human resources. *Human Resource Management*, *41*(2), 225–237.

Gilbert, P., & Parlier, M. (1992). La compétence: du mot-valise au concept opératoire. *Actualité de la Formation Permanente*, *116*, 14–18.

Gilbert, P., & Yalenios, J. (2017). *L'évaluation de la performance individuelle*. Paris, France: La Découverte.

Hamel, G., & Heene, A. (1994). *Competence-based Competition*. Chichester, UK: Wiley.

Hayton, J. C., & McEvoy, G. M. (2006). Guest editors' note. *Human Resource Management, 45*(3), 291–294.

Hoglund, M. (2012). Quid pro quo? Examining talent management through the lens of psychological contracts. *Personnel Review, 41*(1–2), 126–142.

Iles, P., Preece, D., & Chuay, X. (2010). Talent management as a management fashion in HRD: Towards a research agenda. *Human Resource Development International, 13*(2), 125–145.

Khilji, S. E., Tarique, I., & Schuler, R. S. (2015). Incorporating the macro view in global talent management. *Human Resource Management Review, 25*(3), 236–248.

Klein, K. J., & Harrison, D. A. (2007). On the diversity of diversity: Tidy logic, messier realities. *Academy of Management Perspectives, 21*(4), 26–33.

Krishnan, T. N., & Scullion, H. (2017). Talent management and dynamic view of talent in small and medium enterprises. *Human Resource Management Review, 27*(3), 431–441.

Lave, J., & Wenger, E. (1991). *Situated Learning: Legitimate Peripheral Participation.* Cambridge, MA: Cambridge University Press.

Ledford, G., & Kochanski, J. (2004). Allocating training and development resources based on contribution. In Berger, L. A., & Berger, D. D. (Eds.), *The Talent Management Handbook* (pp. 218–229). New York, NY: McGraw Hill.

Lewis, R. E., & Heckman, R. J. (2006). Talent management: A critical review. *Human Resource Management Review, 16*(2), 139–154.

Malglaive, G. (1995). Compétences et ingénierie de formation. In Minet, F., Parlier, M., & De Witte, S. (Eds.), *La compétence: mythe, construction ou réalité?* (pp. 153–167). Paris, France: L'Harmattan.

McClelland, D. (1973). Testing for competence rather than for intelligence. *The American Psychologist, 28*(1), 1–14.

McDonnell, A., Collings, D. G., Mellahi, K., & Schuler, R. (2017). Talent management: A systematic review and future prospects. *European Journal of International Management, 11*(1), 86–128.

McKinsey. (2001). *The War for Talent, Organization and Leadership Practice.* Boston, MA: McKinsey.

Michaels, E., & Handfield-Jones, H., & Axelrod, B. (2001). *The War for Talent.* Boston, MA: Harvard University Press.

Meyers, M. C., & Van Woerkom, M. (2014). The influence of underlying philosophies on talent management: Theory, implications for practice and research agenda. *Journal of World Business, 49*(2), 192–203.

Miralles, P. (2007). La gestion des talents: émergence d'un nouveau modèle de management. *Management & Avenir, 1*(11), 29–42.

Ng, E. S., & Burke, R. J. (2005). Person–organization fit and the war for talent: Does diversity management make a difference? *International Journal of Human Resource Management, 16*(7), 1195–1210.

Nijs, S., Gallardo-Gallardo, E., Dries, N., & Sels, L. (2014). A multidisciplinary review into the definition, operationalization, and measurement of talent. *Journal of World Business, 49*(2), 180–191.

OECD. (2017). Ageing and Employment Policies – Statistics on average effective age of retirement, http://www.oecd.org/els/emp/average-effective-age-of-retirement.htm retrieved June 7, 2019.

Peltokorpi, V. (2006). Knowledge sharing in a cross-cultural context: Nordic expatriates in Japan. *Knowledge Management Research & Practice, 4*(2), 138–148.

Penrose, E. T. (1959). *The Theory of the Growth of the Firm*. New York, NY: Wiley.

Peretti, J. M. (1994). *Tous DRH*. Paris, France: Eyrolles.

Peretti, J. M. (2009). *Tous Talentueux*. Paris, France: Eyrolles.

Pfeffer, J. (2001). Fighting the war for talent is hazardous to your organization's health. *Organizational Dynamics, 29*(4), 248–259.

Prahalad, C. K., & Hamel, G. (1990). The core competence of the corporation. *Harvard Business Review, 68*(3), 79–91.

Retour, D., Picq, T., & Defélix, C. (2009). *Gestion des compétences: Nouvelles relations – Nouvelles dimensions*. Paris, France: Vuibert.

Rozenblatt, P. (2000). *Le mirage de la compétence*. Paris, France: Syllepse.

Sanchez, J. I., & Levine, E. L. (2009). What is (or should be) the difference between competency modeling and traditional job analysis? *Human Resource Management Review, 19*(2), 53–63.

Sandberg, J. (2000). Understanding human competence at work. An interpretive approach. *Academy of Management Journal, 43*(1), 9–25.

Sandberg, J., & Pinnington, A. H. (2009). Professional competence as ways of being: An existential ontological perspective. *Journal of Management Studies, 46*(7), 1138–1170.

Sparrow, P. R., & Makram, H. (2015). What is the value of talent management? Building value-driven processes within a talent management architecture. *Human Resource Management Review, 25*(3), 249–263.

Spencer, L., & Spencer, S. (1993). *Competence at Work*. New York, NY: Wiley.

Tarique, I., & Schuler, R. (2018). A multi-level framework for understanding global talent management systems for high talent expatriates within and across subsidiaries of MNEs: Propositions for further research. *Journal of Global Mobility, 6*(1), 79–101.

Teece, D. J., Pisano, G., & Shuen, A. (1997). Dynamic capabilities and strategic management. *Strategic Management Journal, 18*(7), 509–533.

Thunnissen, M., Boselie, P., & Fruytier, B. (2013). Talent management and the relevance of context: Towards a pluralistic approach. *Human Resource Management Review, 23*(4), 326–336.

Valverde, M., Scullion, H., & Ryan, G. (2013). Talent management in Spanish medium-sized organisations. *The International Journal of Human Resource Management, 24*(9), 1832–1852.

Vidaillet, B. (2013). *Évaluez-moi. Évaluation au travail: les ressorts d'une fascination*. Paris, France: Le Seuil.

Warren, A. K. (2009). *Cascading Gender Biases, Compounding Effects: An Assessment of Talent Management Systems*. New York, NY: Catalyst.

Chapter 4

Developing Soft Skills through Social Learning: A Model Implemented at a Canadian Business School

Pénélope Codello and Delphine Theurelle-Stein

Contents

4.1 Introduction

In 2017, the Adecco Group published *The Soft Skills Imperative*.* The authors of this white paper concluded that so-called soft skills are in higher and higher demand in the current socioeconomic context. This context is characterized by factors such as the end of the hierarchical organization of work, the development of the project management approach, and the acceleration of technological change. In the United States and Europe, soft skills are attracting the interest, not only of business enterprises and the business press (Devaney and Moroney, 2018) but also of academic researchers (Baron and Tang, 2009; Berg et al., 2017). This is because studies prove that soft skills boost performance, both at the individual level (Borghans et al., 2008) and at the group level (Pauget and Wald, 2013). This has led important global organizations, such as the Organisation for Economic Co-operation and Development (OECD) (Martin, 2018) and the European Union, to attempt to define the soft skills that are essential for success in the 21st century.

---

* Consulted at https://www.adeccogroup.com/wp-content/themes/ado-group/downloads/the-adecco-group-white-paper-the-soft-skills-imperative.pdf.

Yet the notion of soft skills remains vague. Indeed, they are mainly defined by default (soft skills are different from "hard skills" that depend on knowledge and expertise) or by lists that bring together a diversity of points of view, without indicating any clear connection between them (Bellier, 2004, p. 1).

The aim of this chapter is to provide a more accurate conceptualization of soft skills. We will begin by examining some relevant French literature on social and relational skills. This literature states that these skills, which eventually came to be called "soft skills" even in French, have a strong connection to the context in which they are developed. The French studies show that this connection exists, but they do not fully conceptualize it; therefore, we intend to draw on Bandura's (1986) social cognitive theory, whose explicit goal is to conceptualize the connection between individuals and their environment. We will then present the case of a soft skills development program, created and implemented at a Canadian business school. This generative case (Siggelkow, 2007) will allow us to analyze in detail how Bandura's (1986) theory can be incorporated into soft skills development practices. This will lead to a conceptualization of soft skills that shows how they are structured around three dimensions (the intrapersonal, the interpersonal, and the contextual dimensions). Using this more accurate conceptualization, we will then be able to lay the ground for a model of soft skills development.

4.2 The Analysis of Soft Skills as Social and Relational Skills within the French Literature

The term "soft skills" is used today in Europe to refer to a vast array of non-technical competences related to areas such as communications, leadership, and interpersonal relations (Riggio and Saggi, 2015). It has been imported from the United States, but in France, in particular, researchers initially focused on social and relational qualifications and/or skills.

4.2.1 Research on Social and Relational Competences

In 1955, the French sociologist Alain Touraine showed that in addition to "technical" qualifications, there are also "social" qualifications in existence. The latter are the skills that allow employees to be recognized by the management of an enterprise as intelligent agents with the capacity to think.

This "soft" dimension is very frequently discussed in the French literature on skills that began to emerge in the 1980s. The metaphor of the iceberg proposed by Spencer and Spencer (1993) is widely embraced in this literature (Oiry, 2004). This metaphor suggests that the technical skills described as "hard" merely represent the less complex part of competence, the smallest part above the surface, and that it is essential to also take into consideration the soft skills, the submerged part of the iceberg, because they are crucial to employee performance.

In the French literature, competences are very often defined using the conceptual triad of knowledge (*savoir*), expertise (*savoir-faire*), and interpersonal skills (*savoir-être*), which is very close to the three-part distinction between knowledge, skills, and abilities (KSA) used in the American literature. However, the research in French is largely centered on the technical dimensions of competences. Interpersonal skills receive much less analysis, in particular, because evaluating them appears to be a delicate task with a high risk of bias (Courpasson and Livian, 1991; Gilbert and Yalenios, 2017).

In the French literature on skills, Bellier (2004) is the first to make an explicit effort to analyze interpersonal skills. She proposes a multidimensional definition of the concept of interpersonal skills. According to this definition, this concept covers (1) moral qualities that are either acquired (honesty) or natural (intrinsic authority); (2) character (calm, authoritarian); (3) personality traits; (4) abilities that make it possible to understand an individual's career choices; and (5) behavior.

4.2.2 The Learning Mechanisms for Social and Relational Competences

Bellier's (2004) typology makes it clear that in both the French and the American literature, the definition of soft skills grants an important place to personality traits (Boyatsis et al., 2002). On the other hand, it also highlights a difference between the French and the American approaches. At first, French researchers preferred to use the term "social and relational competences" (*compétences sociales et relationnelles*), but the term "soft skills" is now widely used in French. In the literature in French, there has been a consensus that at least a part of what are called "social and relational competences" is learned (Le Boterf, 2000). This work is strongly influenced by educational theories.

Nevertheless, in this work, it was understood that the development of social and relational competences occurs through modes of training that are necessarily different from classic teaching, for these competences are mainly acquired through action. Thus Zarifian (2001) states that it is impossible to develop social attitudes outside of the professional situations that solicit them. Indeed, experiential learning is a way of developing soft skills that is advocated by Mintzberg (1990). The most efficient training programs begin by analyzing the tasks performed in work situations, and then, they favor learning through work simulations at training sessions (role play, project development at a business simulation center, etc.) (Laal and Ghodsi, 2012).

4.2.3 The Importance of Context for the Development of Social and Relational Competences

This perspective explains why Bellier's (2004) typology underscores the importance of work situations for the definition and the development of social and relational competences. Like other competences, social and relational competences are contextualized. Their existence and their development depend not only on the individual but also on the work situations and the organizational contexts in which the individual has to function. Thus, Le Boterf (2000) defines social and relational competences as abilities that are useful for behaving or conducting oneself in specific professional contexts. It is the variety and the multiplicity of the social contexts that make it possible to acquire these competences (family upbringing, community life, academic and extracurricular activities, etc.). Bellier (2004) adopts the same perspective, maintaining that these competences must be analyzed in terms of the relationship between the individual and the organization, since this relationship shapes the modes of management as well as the work culture. In this, the French research differs from the American research, which tends to aim toward the construction of non-contextual reference systems for soft skills.

Thus, it appears that French researchers have been conceptualizing social and relational competences for a long time and that, like their American counterparts, they have emphasized the importance of personality traits. However, they have also been interested in the fundamental role that context plays in those skills' development.

Finally, although European researchers have traditionally used the term "social and relational competences," they have gradually come to accept the term "soft skills." The same applies within the United States. Therefore, in the rest of the chapter, we will respect this convention by using the term "soft skills."

4.3 The Contribution of Social Cognitive Theory to Research on the Development of Soft Skills

The French literature on the development of soft skills raises the question of the most favorable learning environment. However, the link between the two is not clearly conceptualized in this literature. The work of Bandura (1986), in particular his cognitive social theory, questions the role of the social environment in human development and suggests that individuals are both the producers and the products of their social environment. This theory is extremely useful for conceptualizing the link between soft skills and social environments.

4.3.1 Agency and the Self-Efficacy in the Service of Soft Skills Development

Agency is one of the central concepts in social cognitive theory. Bandura (2001, p. 1) defines it as the control that persons exercise over their lives, and he maintains that "the capacity to exercise control over the nature and quality of one's life is the essence of humanness." Four essential factors structure agency (see

Figure 4.1   The characteristics of agency (adapted from Bandura, 2001).

Figure 4.1): *intentionality* (the will to act); *forethought* (the anticipated result of action); *self-reactiveness* (the definition of criteria for action); and *self-reflectiveness* (the subject's self-evaluation of its abilities, its motivation, and its values).

   The concept of self-efficacy is also central to social cognitive theory. Bandura (1997) defines self-efficacy as an individual's belief in his or her ability to adopt a line of conduct that will lead to a desired result. He identifies four sources of the sense of self-efficacy that operate with decreasing impact (see Figure 4.2): *lived*

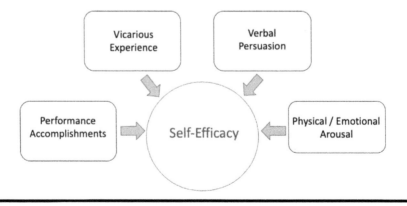

Figure 4.2   The sources of self-efficacy (adapted from Bandura, 1997).

experiences (the subject's successes and failures); *vicarious experience* (other persons' successes and failures as observed and interpreted by the subject); *verbal persuasion* (the discourse of other persons); and the *physical, psychological, and emotional arousal* of the subject.

4.3.2 Triadic Reciprocal Causation: The Framework for the Development of Skills

Agency and self-efficacy operate through a *triadic reciprocal causation* involving three types of factors: (1) personal factors (events experienced at the biological, the cognitive, and the emotional level, and the perception of these events by the subject); (2) behavioral factors (actions performed and behavioral patterns); and (3) environmental factors (the constraints and opportunities of the social and organizational environment).

In this model (see Figure 4.3), the three types of factors are in constant interaction with each other, but their influence varies with the circumstances and the activities of the subject.

According to social cognitive theory, the environment (the set of social structures) interacts with personal factors, such as agency and the sense of self-efficacy, in ways that produce and modify behaviors.

In the next section, we show how we mobilized this conceptual framework to create a course on soft skills development at a Canadian business school.

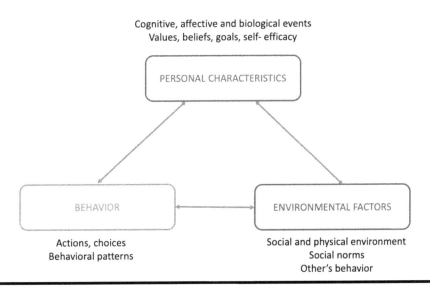

Figure 4.3   Triadic reciprocal causation (adapted from Bandura, 1997, and Carré, 2004).

4.4 A Soft Skills Development Course at a Canadian Business School

4.4.1 Methodology, Data Collection, and Data Analysis

The phenomenon under study is complex, poorly understood, and difficult to analyze. From a methodological perspective, this is why it seemed best to approach it using a case study. As for the specific type of case study, we adopted the generative model (Siggelkow, 2007), the goal of our case study being to produce new knowledge. We were particularly interested in the way that soft skills are developed through interaction with the social environment and in the question of whether Bandura's (1986) social cognitive theory is able to structure the link between soft skills and the social environment.

Collecting data related to these issues is difficult. We decided to use the action research method (Baskerville and Myers, 2004), because it is recommended when the research settings are complex and constantly evolving and when they reflect ambiguous social phenomena. For this type of cases, the researcher must be physically present in the field on an ongoing basis; and action research is one of the most suitable methodologies for conducting this type of field research (Lewin, 1946). Action research revolves around introducing changes in the organizational setting and observing the impact of these changes in order to enrich theoretical understanding (Baskerville and Myers, 2004). In other words, it entails moving back and forth between practices, data, and theory to deepen the analysis of a complex phenomenon progressively.

One of the authors of this chapter created a course on soft skills development at a Canadian business school. During this action research project, we collected all the documents produced in the context of the course and we took intensive field notes to take account of the exchanges that occurred during the learning activities (Burgess, 2002).

We applied thematic coding to the data (Miles and Huberman, 1994). The main codes came from theory (in particular, Bandura's (1986) social cognitive theory and the French theories of social and relational competences). For example, we had a main code for agency, one for self-efficacy, and one for each of the elements in the triadic relation. However, some codes emerged from the data. For example, this was the case for the code for the inspirational character of an encounter or an experience. The data analysis allowed us to explain the creation and the implementation of this course on soft skills development. This is the topic of the next section.

4.4.2 A Course on Soft Skills Development

Offered at the undergraduate level, the course that was created had the explicit goal of helping students to develop soft skills. It was designed as a two-semester course (six classes during the fall, six classes during the winter) so that a longitudinal follow-up was possible.

The main course objectives were defined as follows:

> Developing soft skills requires reflexivity and self-knowledge. Accompanying students in this process, the course will allow them, not only to acquire soft skills that are useful in employment contexts, but also to facilitate their university studies by clarifying their academic choices and increasing their agency.

(**course plan**)

The course used key concepts from social cognitive theory. Particular attention was given to the development of personal factors (especially agency and self-efficacy) and also to the creation of a supportive learning environment. Thus, to favor the development of their soft skills, students were encouraged to analyze their personal and interpersonal abilities and to improve their understanding of their environment.

The course was structured around three blocks of learning objectives: (1) the development of increased self-knowledge and a greater ability for self-management; (2) the development of a deeper awareness of others and an improved ability to manage relationships with others; and (3) the development of a greater understanding of social environments and a higher level of adaptability to them. Seven specific pedagogical tools (see 1–7 in Figure 4.4) were set in place to ensure that the learning objectives of each block were met. Three cross-disciplinary pedagogical tools (see 8–10 in Figure 4.4) were used as modes of evaluation for the course. Figure 4.4 provides an overview of the course structure.

4.4.3 Three Cross-Disciplinary Tools for Reflexivity and Coursework Evaluations

The three tools in the vertical boxes in Figure 4.4 – the self-reflection log (8), the action plan (9), and the expert colloquium (10) – support the overall approach used in the course. In addition, they are also the three evaluation tools used in the course. The self-reflection log encourages students to engage in self-reflection on a regular basis. Among other factors, the development of soft skills depends on self-reflectiveness, it being one of the characteristics of agency (see Figure 4.1). Self-reflectiveness allows students to engage in the self-evaluation of their abilities, motivations, and values. Therefore, the self-reflection log provides the central support for this part of the learning process.

The action plan provides a basis for defining relevant experiences and choosing them. The students must create their action plans before they begin their relevant experiences so that the latter are as consistent as possible with their behavioral preferences, their motivations, and the types of activities that they wish to participate in. They must also define the factors of success for their relevant experiences so that they can evaluate these experiences after they have gone through them. Creating an action plan allows students to develop a new awareness of all the dimensions

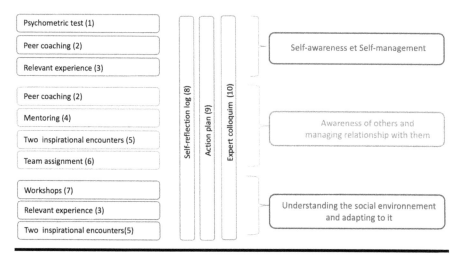

Figure 4.4 Pedagogical tools used in the soft skills development course.

of their agency (intentionality, forethought, self-reactiveness, and reflexiveness). The action plan is constructed after the students have done an assignment on self-awareness and its motivations. It allows them to make the most informed choices concerning the workshops (7) that they are offered (see below for more details).

Finally, the expert colloquium is a seminar offered at the end of year to give students the opportunity to present their relevant experiences and, most importantly, to review what they have learned during the course.

4.4.4 Developing the Three Dimensions of Soft Skills

4.4.4.1 Self-Awareness and Self-Management

A psychometric test (1) was used to anchor the work of self-reflectiveness. This type of test allows students to develop a better understanding of their actions, their needs, and their motivations (personal factors connected to triadic reciprocal causation). It helps them become aware of the dynamics of triadic causation and thus of the role that personal factors play in their behavior. It also helps them become aware of the role of their actions in their conception of themselves, particularly with respect to their sense of self-efficacy.

Guided peer-coaching sessions* (2) have the same objective. The students have to work in pairs or in groups of four. First, they are asked to discuss the role played by their past experiences in the development of their self-representation and

---

* During these sessions, the professors frame the exercise by giving precise instructions on the role of each participant in the client-coach relationship, and they offer a simple discussion guide to orient the exchanges and ensure that they do not turn into unstructured conversations.

particularly in the development of self-efficacy. Then, the discussion with peers allows them to question their relationship to failures. For some, failures have had a devastating effect on their self-efficacy, but others have experienced failures as ways of learning that have helped them develop their self-efficacy. This being the case, peers can help transform perceptions of failure into motivational factors. Verbal persuasion is in fact an important source of self-efficacy (see Figure 4.2).

In the instructions for the self-reflection log, students are asked to continue their reflection from the peer-coaching session by combining what they learned in the session with the results of the psychometric test (1). Their goal is to develop a better understanding of the relation between their personal factors and their behavior and to determine how these two dimensions influence the social environment while being constantly influenced by it in turn. This reflection is important because it serves as a guide for choosing the relevant experience that the students wish to have. This experience consists in putting oneself into a specific learning context. For this purpose, any type of experience is accepted (for example, an internship or shadowing a person with interesting skills) as long as the student can demonstrate that it favors his or her development. The experiences are not imposed by the teaching team. On the contrary, in line with the principle of agency, students must use their self-awareness to define their goals and the main lines of their approach to personal development.

In their action plan, students must demonstrate that their goals and their approach to personal development are consistent with each other. This self-directed learning (Knowles, 1975) gives them another opportunity to exercise their agency fully. The psychometric test, the peer coaching, and the relevant experience allow students to enter into an intrapersonal dialogue and to understand the constant interactions between personal, behavioral, and environmental factors. As a result, students develop a much higher degree of self-awareness and they improve their self-management skills.

4.4.4.2 The Awareness of Others and the Management of Relationships with Them

To develop soft skills related to the awareness of others and the management of relationships with them, teaching methods based on social interactions were adopted. This type of teaching seeks to make the most of the environmental factors in triadic reciprocal causation (see Figure 4.3).

Peer coaching (4) and mentoring (5) (professional support from graduates from the previous year) are mobilized to stimulate students' curiosity about other possibilities and to help them develop the skills and qualities that facilitate relationships with others (harmony, respect, the ability to listen, and empathy).

Moreover, each student is asked to set up meetings with two inspirational persons (6) in order to explore a field of work or a specific individual profile. These meetings should nourish students' inspiration in ways related to their personalities, their skills, and their aspirations.

Eventually, the course provides students with support in their team assignments in the other classes, which is another way to develop self-reflection. Students must observe their team, the overall way it functions, and their own role as team members. To do so, they can use the "team profile" created through the psychometric test (1). This allows them to become aware of the abundant complementarity on a team, but also of the risks connected to a team's diversity (misunderstandings, conflicting motivations, etc.). This self-reflective work can be quite rewarding. For example, it may bring to light coping strategies that facilitate relationships with other persons. Students may also come to understand that developing better self-management skills helps improve their ability to manage relationships with other persons.

This is not to say that socio-cognitive conflicts (Jenny, 2005) are eliminated. Such conflicts occur spontaneously (with varying intensity) in any group relationship, and they can be used as a learning tool. The peer coaching, the mentoring, the relevant experience, and the analysis of the team assignment make it possible for students to develop soft skills that are based on their social environment. *Lived experience* (whether acquired individually or through teamwork) and *vicarious experience* (whether acquired through peers, mentors, or inspirational persons) both increase self-efficacy, which is the main driver of personal development (see Figure 4.2).

4.4.4.3 Understanding the Social Environment and Adapting to It

The final dimension of the teaching approach is to help students develop the ability to understand the social environment and adapt to it. Four pedagogical tools are used to meet this objective.

The first one is the relevant experience (3) that students are required to undertake. This experience offers them the chance to confront environmental constraints and to take advantage of opportunities (see Figure 4.3) while continuing their self-reflective work. Before this experience takes place, the meetings with inspirational persons (6) aim at putting students into contact with new social environments. Besides interpersonal relationships, this second pedagogical tool also involves having students do research, ask questions, create networks, and discern the norms followed at a specific organization or in a particular context. During this learning process, students must continually update their self-reflection log in order to reexamine the actions that they have undertaken. The third pedagogical tool relies on the thematic workshops (7) offered by internal service providers at the school. These workshops cover themes such as exam-related anxiety, time management, stress management, and networking. Altogether, there are ten workshops, and students must choose the four that they believe will best respond to their needs. Triadic reciprocal causation shows the important role that environmental factors play in the development of soft skills. This is the reason that our teaching approach involves encouraging students to use their self-reflection log (8) to analyze their way of interacting with the various social and organizational environments in their lives.

The last pedagogical tool, the expert colloquium (10), is more cross-disciplinary and brings the course to a close. Taking place at the beginning of the following academic year, the colloquium gives students the opportunity to do a presentation involving a poster for their expert project. The goal of this event is twofold. First, it encourages students to communicate their experiences and draw lessons from them. Second, it fosters them to do networking. Indeed, persons from the school's academic community are invited to attend the seminar (professors, students from other programs, etc.), as are persons from the outside (partners, guests invited by students, etc.). Thus, the students are fully engaged in practical interactions with other persons in a range of different settings. For this final evaluation, the professors observe their performances and their posters. For newly admitted students, it is the first opportunity to do some networking and the time to choose a mentor from among the students presenting their posters.

4.5 Discussion

Confronting our case study with the literature on soft skills shows that it falls within the French research tradition that highlights the interaction between soft skills and social contexts. Our case study reinforces and extends this research tradition by taking into consideration Bandura's (1986) social cognitive theory and by making two important contributions. First, we improve our understanding of soft skills by identifying the three dimensions that structure them. Second, we lay the ground for a model of soft skills development.

4.5.1 The Three Dimensions That Define Soft Skills

4.5.1.1 The Intrapersonal Dimension of Soft Skills: Self-Awareness and Self-Management

The literature in English on soft skills sees them as mainly structured by intrapersonal factors. The literature in French shares the notion that soft skills are constructed by individuals; however, it also highlights a contextual dimension, for French researchers tend to attribute an important role to the work environment in the development of soft skills.

The results of our case study make it possible to analyze in detail the intrapersonal dimension, but they also show that it is necessary to examine closely the interaction between the interpersonal and the contextual dimensions. A psychometric test can be used to identify the characteristics of individuals, but it has to be used in conjunction with other investigative tools. Peer coaching, where interaction with others allows individuals to become aware of their own personal characteristics, is a good example. Soft skills are linked to self-knowledge, to abilities connected to self-image, and to the ability to put oneself into question, but their development is favored by interaction with others.

4.5.1.2 The Interpersonal Dimension of Soft Skills: The Awareness of Others and the Management of Relationships with Them

Bandura's (1986) conceptual framework has received little or no attention in the literature in English on soft skills. However, combined with our results, it indicates that interpersonal relationships play a fundamental role in the development of soft skills. In our course on soft skills development, we saw that in addition to peer coaching, mentoring and teamwork are also key activities for structuring soft skills. These two tools are indispensable for the development of soft skills such as relational and communicational abilities (the ability to listen and the ability to communicate orally or in writing), social adaptability, the willingness to cooperate, and the knowledge of relational norms. Among the social skills that are useful for managing relationships with others, it is also important to mention empathy but having the ability to influence others, to lead others to respond favorably to requests can be important too. In addition, managing relationships with others also requires a sense of direction, an awareness of change, and mediation skills. These relational skills are an integral part of organizational stewardship, where recognition has to be forged in relationships with persons who are substantially different from oneself or even inconsistent and unpredictable. Accepting difference and otherness makes fortuitous learning possible in encounters with other persons, and it is one of the foundations of soft skills.

4.5.1.3 The Contextual Dimension of Soft Skills: Understanding the Environment and Adapting to It

Finally, it is important to recall that the literature in French stresses the important role played by the contextual dimension of soft skills. The latter are useful abilities that orient individuals when they behave or conduct themselves in specific professional contexts (Le Boterf, 2000). Bandura's (1986) social cognitive theory makes it possible to conceptualize this link between soft skills and the social environment. Our case study shows how this theory can be incorporated into a soft skills development program, for our course on soft skills development makes use of tools (for example, relevant experiences and inspirational encounters) whose presence in several of the dimensions of soft skills ensures that there is a strong link and significant interaction between these dimensions.

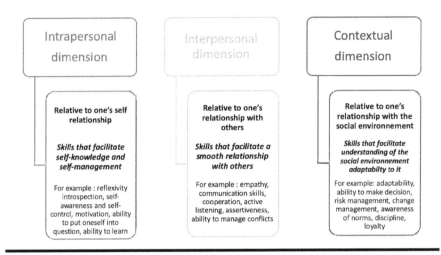

Figure 4.5   The three dimensions of soft skills.

Using Bandura's (1986) conceptual framework and the results of our case study, it is possible to provide a more precise definition of soft skills by structuring them around three dimensions: the intrapersonal, the interpersonal, and the contextual dimensions. Figure 4.5 presents these three dimensions.

4.5.2 A Model of Soft Skills Development Based on Bandura's Social Cognitive Theory

The course on soft skills development, which was created and implemented at a Canadian business school, also provided strong evidence to confirm that each of the dimensions of soft skills develops by way of the triadic reciprocal causation that characterizes the constant interaction between personal, behavioral, and environmental factors. This suggests that a soft skills development program should be based on activities that are mainly experiential and self-reflective in order to bring into play the three dimensions of soft skills:

■ The intrapersonal dimension through self-reflection on the triadic dynamic, a process that allows individuals to mobilize their agency and make choices and to understand how these choices impact their conception of themselves – especially their self-efficacy – and the image of themselves that they project in social environments.
■ The interpersonal dimension through social interaction in which vicarious experience and verbal persuasion allow individuals to develop soft skills (for example, empathy and the ability to communicate) that facilitate relationships with others.

■ The contextual dimension of projects that placed the students in our course in real situations, so that they could discover new environments and adapt to them by developing their ability to decode the relevant social norms and to understand the specific coping strategies used in these environments.

It is important to note that although these three dimensions are developed through mechanisms linked to triadic causation, they are also strongly interconnected, so that the development of one of them has an effect on the others. For example, the development of aspects of the intrapersonal dimension, such as reflectiveness, has an important impact on relationships with others and on the ability to adapt to social environments.

Thus, in addition to identifying the three dimensions of soft skills, our case study yielded results that make it possible to propose a model of soft skills development.

4.6 Conclusion

Our objective has been to provide a more accurate conceptualization of soft skills. To meet this objective, we have mobilized the literature in French in which the concept of social and relational skills is used to highlight the fact that the development of soft skills requires significant interaction with social environments. Our conceptualization of soft skills indicates that they are not merely characteristics of individuals. This conceptualization was reinforced both by our use of Bandura's (1986) social cognitive theory, which stresses the link between individuals and their social environment, and by our application of this theory in a course on soft skills development at a Canadian business school. The results of our case study led to two main conclusions: (1) soft skills are structured around three dimensions (the intrapersonal, interpersonal, and contextual dimensions) and (2) the interactions between these three dimensions provide the basis for a model of soft skills development.

The limits of our research are ones shared by all case studies. It is necessary to replicate our results in other contexts and situations in order to move closer to establishing their external validity. It would be particularly interesting to mobilize the three dimensions of soft skills and a model of soft skills development that is based on them at an industrial firm or at a business in the service sector.

References

Bandura, A. (1986). *Social Foundations of Thought and Actions: A Social Cognitive Theory.* Englewood Cliffs, NJ: Prentice Hall.

Bandura, A. (1997). *Self-efficacy: The Exercise of Control.* New York, NY: W. H. Freeman.

Bandura, A. (2001). Social cognitive theory: An agentic perspective. *Annual Review of Psychology, 53,* 1–26.

Baron, R. A., & Tang, J. (2009). Entrepreneurs' social skills and new venture performance: Mediating mechanisms and cultural generality. *Journal of Management, 35*(2), 282–306.

Baskerville, R. L., & Myers, M. D. (2004). Special issue on action research in information systems: Making IS research relevant to practice – foreword. *MIS Quarterly, 28*(3), 329–335.

Bellier, S. (2004). *Le savoir-être dans l'entreprise*. Paris, France: Vuibert.

Berg, J., Osher, D., Same, M., Nolan, E., Benson, D., & Jacobs, N. (2017). *Identifying, Defining, and Measuring Social and Emotional Competencies: Final Report*. Washington DC: American Institutes for Research.

Borghans, L., Weel, B. T., & Weinberg, B. A. (2008). Interpersonal styles and labor market outcomes. *The Journal of Human Resources*: Special Issue, *Noncognitive Skills and Their Development, 43*(4), 815–858.

Boyatzis, R. E., Stubbs, L., & Taylor, S. (2002). Learning cognitive and emotional intelligence competencies through graduate management education. *Academy of Management Journal on Learning and Education, 1*(2), 150–162.

Burgess, R. G. (2002). *In the field: An introduction to field research*. London, UK: Routledge.

Carré, P. (2004). Bandura: une psychologie pour le XXIème siècle ? *Savoirs*, HS 5, 9–50.

Courpasson, D., & Livian, Y. F. (1991). Le développement récent de la notion de compétence: Glissement sémantique ou idéologie? *Revue de Gestion des Ressources Humaines, 1*, 3–10.

Devaney, E., & Moroney, A. E. (2018). *Social and emotional learning in out-of-school time*. Charlotte, NC: Information Age Publishing.

Gilbert, P., & Yalenios, J. (2017). *L'évaluation de la performance individuelle*. Paris, France: La Découverte.

Jenny, R. (2005). *Les traces de l'apprendre: un autre regard sur les salariés d'entreprise*. Paris, France: L'Harmattan.

Knowles, M. (1975). *Self-directed Learning: A Guide for Learners and Teachers*. New York: Association Press.

Laal, M., & Ghodsi, S. M. (2012). Benefits of collaborative learning. *Procedia-social and Behavioral Sciences, 31*, 486–490.

Le Boterf, G. (2000). *Construire les compétences individuelles et collectives*. Paris, France: Éditions d'Organisation.

Lewin, K. (1946). Action research and minority problems. *Journal of Social Issues, 2*(2), 34–46.

Martin, J. P. (2018). Skills for the 21st Century: Findings and policy lessons from the OECD survey of adult skills. OECD Working Paper, 166. Paris, France: OECD Publishing.

Miles, M. B., & Huberman, A. M. (1994). *Qualitative Data Analysis: An Expanded Sourcebook*. New York, NY: Sage Publications Ltd.

Mintzberg, H. (1990). *Mintzberg on Management: Inside Our Strange World of Organizations*. New York, NY: Free Press.

Oiry, E. (2004). *De la qualification à la compétence, rupture ou continuité ?* Paris, France: L'Harmattan.

Pauget, B., & Wald, A. (2013). Relational competence in complex temporary organizations. The case of a French hospital construction project network. *International Journal of Project Management, 31*(2), 200–211.

Riggio, R. E., & Saggi, K. (2015). Incorporating "soft skills" into the collaborative problem-solving equation. *Industrial & Organizational Psychology, 8*(2), 281–284.

Siggelkow, N. (2007). Persuasion with case studies. *Academy of Management Journal, 50*(1), 20–24.

Spencer, L. M. Jr., & Spencer, S. M. (1993). *Competence at Work: Models for Superior Performance*. New York, NY: John Wiley and Sons.

Touraine, A. (1955). La qualification du travail: Histoire d'une notion. *Journal de Psychologie Normale et Pathologique, 13*, 97–112.

Zarifian, P. (2001). *La logique compétence*. Paris, France: Éditions Liaisons Sociales.

Chapter 5

Competences-Based Assessment of Employability: How to Deconstruct a Variety of Interpretations and Articulations?

Eve Saint-Germes

Contents

5.1 Introduction

Even if employability is an old concept that appeared in the beginning of the 20th century and matured progressively with at least seven different versions (Gazier, 2003), its integration in human resources management (HRM) is somehow recent, during the 1990s. Numerous debates remain in the literature about its definitions and determinants, and in particular, supply side and demand side approaches coexist and structure the field, with a focus either on individual factors of employability or on contextual factors (De Grip et al., 2004; Fugate and Kinicki, 2008). In the middle of the 2000s, a competence-based approach to employability emerged (De Vos et al., 2011; Froehlich et al., 2015; Fugate and Kinicki, 2008; Fugate et al., 2004; Haasler, 2013; Redmond, 2013; Scholarios et al., 2008; Thijssen et al., 2008; Van Der Heijde and Van Der Heijden, 2006; Wittekind et al., 2010). This approach defines employability as a form of work-specific active adaptability along with individuals' career potential that derives from their specific capital of competences (De Cuyper et al., 2011; De Vos et al., 2011; Forrier et al., 2015; Fugate and Kinicki, 2008; Fugate et al., 2004; Redmond, 2013; Scholarios et al., 2008; Van den Broeck et al., 2014; Van Der Heijde and Van Der Heijden, 2006; Wittekind et al., 2010). "On a labor market segmented by competence," employability of individuals, attractiveness of employers, and competitiveness of companies are interrelated (see Chapter 9). By creating a link between competence and employability, the competence-based approach enriches the previous definitions of employability and offers new research avenues on the link between these two central concepts of contemporary HRM. The emergence of the competence-based approach to employability is finally a form of institutionalization of the concept of employability in HRM: beyond its economic origins and its link with the labor market, it integrates the field of HRM and its articulation with competences management reinforces this integration. It is then explicitly placed at the interface with human resources management, new career forms, and more recently talent management, and it is through the articulation with the notion of competence that this interface is established.

In the competence-based approach of employability, the portfolio of individual competences is rarely sufficient by itself to assess employability: potential competences, i.e., those that an individual may develop in the future, are central (Van Der Heijde and Van Der Heijden, 2006). Most authors agree that willingness to develop new competences or to change jobs has become a key variable for employability, even if many different attitudes are theorized (De Grip et al., 2004; De Vos et al., 2011; Fugate et al., 2004; McQuaid and Lindsay, 2005; Van Dam, 2004; Wittekind et al., 2010; see also Chapter 4, about the soft skills). Within this variety of interpretations and theorizations of employability, it can be difficult to identify how to assess employability. Convention Theory (Boltanski and Thévenot, 1999, 2006; Eymard-Duvernay, 2002; Favereau and Lazega, 2002; Gomez and Jones, 2000) is thus useful to shed new light on this diversity of ways of assessing employability: using and applying the quality convention concept to employability enable to identify and to map the legitimate ways of assessing employability in the HRM literature (i.e., the quality convention of employability in the research in the field).

This chapter aims to investigate competences-based assessment of employability and to offer an integrative framework to understand theoretically and operationally how employability is assessed from competences. *How to identify a variety of interpretations of employability from competences with the help of quality conventions and how to shed light on the diverse articulations between employability and competences embedded in the assessment practices?*

Drawing on the competence-based approach to employability, it presents a conceptual framework that integrates quality conventions of employability and different types of competences. We underline and demonstrate the contribution of this framework to study the infrastructure of representations in each operational interpretation of employability from competences. We then investigate the relevance and suitability of this conceptual framework by one emblematic case study: reclassification of victims of layoffs due to the business closure of an airline company – Air Littoral (AL) (856 layoffs, the implementation of a reclassification cell with more than 500 adherents accompanied). Finally, we discuss the contribution and the limits of the conceptual framework to study multiple interpretations of employability in a competences-based approach, with special focus on the dominant convention of projective employability and potential competences, with ongoing debates around transferability of competences and specific competence in career enactment and job search.

5.2 Competences-Based Quality Conventions of Employability

5.2.1 The Competences-Based Approach of Employability

The concept of employability appeared in the beginning of the 20th century, but it integrates recently into the HRM: in the 1990s and in the 2000s; with the emergence of the boundaryless career approach, numerous debates have been initiated in the literature about its definitions and determinants. At that time, employability appears as a potential substitute to security in the psychological contract of employment (Nicholson, 1996) in a post-corporate approach of careers (Peiperl and Baruch, 1997, Rousseau, 1995, Van Burren, 2003, Waterman et al., 1994). But the concept is also under debate because of its duality (individual vs. contextual level of analysis and factors, De Grip et al., 2004; Fugate and Kinicki, 2008) and of the coexistence of different versions of employability. Supply side and demand side approaches coexist and structure the field, and definitions of employability can be stratified at three levels (De Grip et al., 2004): core definitions (focused on individual potential), enlarged definitions (enlarging individual factors considered), and generalized ones (adopting a dual or relative approach that integrates the non-individual factors also).

In the middle of the 2000s, a competence-based approach to employability emerged (De Vos et al., 2011; Froehlich et al., 2015; Fugate and Kinicki, 2008; Fugate et al., 2004; Haasler, 2013; Redmond, 2013; Scholarios et al., 2008; Thijssen et al., 2008; Van Der Heijde and Van Der Heijden, 2006; Wittekind et al., 2010). More precisely, in research on modeling and measuring perceived employability (De Cuyper et al., 2011; Fugate et al., 2004; De Vos et al., 2011; Forrier et al., 2015; Van den Broeck et al., 2014; Van Der Heijde and Van Der Heijden, 2006; Wittekind et al., 2010), or on the conditions of individual competences and career management with a view to employability (Fugate and Kinicki, 2008; Redmond, 2013; Scholarios et al., 2008), employability is defined as "the continuous fulfilling, acquiring or creating of work through the optimal use of competences" (Van der Heijde and Van Der Heijden, 2006, p. 453). By creating a link between competence and employability, the competence-based approach enriches the previous definitions which focused on "the chance for employment on the internal or external labor market" (Forrier and Sels, 2003, p. 106) and on "a form of work-specific active adaptability that enables workers to identify and realize career opportunities" (Fugate et al., 2004, p. 16). The emergence of the competence-based approach to employability is finally a form of institutionalization of the concept of employability in HRM: beyond its economic origins and its link with the labor market, it integrates the field of HRM and its articulation with competences management reinforces this integration. It is then explicitly placed at the interface with human resources management, new career forms and more recently talent management, and it is through the articulation with the notion of competence that these interfaces are established and interpreted. Moreover, the competence-based approach to employability is a way to reconcile the stratified approaches of the concept of employability and to overcome its duality: individual and collective employability factors can be linked through the mediation of the concept of competences that offers milestones for each level of definition of employability (core, enlarged or generalized). In the end, the competence-based approach to employability reconciles the different visions of the concept and creates a fruitful interface for HRM with the labor market.

This competence-based approach to employability articulates the importance of individuals' adaptability to negotiate and promote the value of their accumulated individual competences (Scholarios et al., 2008; Van der Heijde and Van Der Heijden, 2006; Wittekind et al., 2010). Employees build their employability on the basis of their personal flexibility and their capacity to anticipate job changes and careers outcomes but also when they enact their individual competences with personal qualities, such as motivation, personality, and attitudes (De Vos et al., 2011; Van Der Heijde and Van Der Heijden, 2006). On a labor market segmented by competences, accessing embodied competence in individuals is strategic for competitiveness (see Chapter 9). But the portfolio of individual competences is rarely sufficient by itself. Most authors agree that willingness to develop new competences or to change jobs has become a key variable for employability, even if many different attitudes are theorized (De Grip et al., 2004; De Vos et al., 2011; Fugate et al., 2004; McQuaid and Lindsay, 2005; Van Dam, 2004; Wittekind et al., 2010). In a renewed approach to careers, the competences-based approach to employability offers new opportunities to design more active career management and more attentive talent management in line with the labor market.

5.2.2 Analyze Employability in Terms of Quality Conventions

As noted above, the literature offers very diverse definitions of employability. These have resulted in a huge diversity of how employability can be assessed and the factors that are supposed to be part of this assessment process. To organize the literature on assessment employability, we use Convention Theory (Boltanski and Thévenot, 1999, 2006; Eymard-Duvernay, 2002; Favereau and Lazega, 2002; Gomez and Jones, 2000). This provides meaning and order to the heterogeneity and diversity of assessing employability.

According to Gomez and Jones (2000, p. 700), "a convention is a social mechanism that associates a rational void, i.e., a set of non-justified norms, with a screen of symbol, i.e., an interrelation between objects, discourses and behaviors." In a pragmatist view, Convention Theory, an original neo-institutional approach, focuses on coordination dynamics and analyzes situated efforts for identifying, interpreting, and coping with complexity, uncertainty, and limited rationality (Gkeredakis, 2014; O'Reilly et al., 2014). Conventions are explicit cognitive representations actors use "to gain confidence that their interpretations can be found valid by others over time and across physical boundaries" (Gkeredakis, 2014, p. 1478). A convention is stable and has extended validity because it is based on models, formalizations, or standards. It creates equivalences and stable associations among situations, objects, or problems (ibid.). It can be viewed as a screen of symbols or information enabling actors to rationalize their decisions and justify their behavior (Gomez and Jones, 2000).

A quality convention is a specific application of the concept, corresponding to a coherent conception of the quality of a product and/or of work (among the different ways of evaluating quality; see Eymard-Duvernay, 2002). Each quality convention is related to socially legitimate rules and principles for evaluating an object (their number is thus limited): actors use them to interpret the object and construct their assessment. To understand and study the equivalences and associations used in the assessment process, it is useful and necessary to draw maps of the "theories of action" among which agents must choose (ibid.). One of our key proposals is thus to clarify and deepen our understanding of the link between employability and competences. To do this, we present a typology of the quality conventions of employability as a basis for analyzing employability assessment practices. The typology is based on a deepen literature review of works on employability. In other words, we break them down in order to identify how employability and competences are interpreted and linked, both by researchers and practitioners.

5.2.3 Typology of Competences-Based Quality Conventions of Employability

The theoretical framework of Loufrani-Fedida et al. (2015, *cf.* Figure 5.1) allows to assess employability from competences. It integrates the typology of Saint-Germes (2007) on the quality conventions of employability and the typology of Retour (2005) on the figures of individual competences. Two axes (static/dynamic and individual/organizational) structure the theoretical framework and define four specific registers for interpreting employability and competences (see figure 5.1). The choice of these axes is the result of the research of structuring criteria, representations, beliefs, and ideology, allowing to contrast visions and to structure, in a general way, large theoretical categories. Quality conventions are based on models, standards, and formalizations: their legitimacy (stability and validity) rely on the equivalences and stable associations they create between objects, situations, and problems. For employability, an extensive literature review is conducted to legitimate two structuring dimensions to assess employability from competences: the assessment factors taken into account can be at an individual or an organizational level, and they can be static or dynamic in nature. Crossing these two axes reveals four types of conventions for assessing employability that are underpinned by four types of competences. The conventions of employability assessment rely on the types of individual competences that are identifiable and distinct.

Based on the definitions of employability, four quality conventions of employability are described (extending Saint-Germes, 2007) and articulated to a figure of competence of Retour (2005).

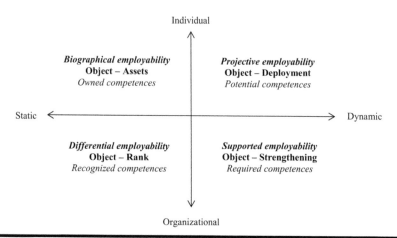

Figure 5.1 Typology of competences-based quality conventions of employability.

Biographical employability and owned competences. In this specific register for interpreting employability and competences, assessment practices are essentially based on descriptions of experience and professional achievements (curriculum vitae, application forms, and biodata questionnaires). Psychometrics tests (intelligence, ability, aptitude, and attainment tests), simulations, and personality tests may also complete the assessment (Armstrong, 2006). Asset based and individualized, the *biographical employability* convention is focused on the individual's portfolio of capital (human, social, cultural, and career capital), including initial capital and that which is accumulated during professional and personal experience. This convention corresponds to employees' *owned competences* whatever the work (or non-work) situation in which they were developed. The transferability of these assets remains uncertain, but the competence is considered here as a combination of resources, set in motion to respond in a pertinent way to a work situation. Work situations may be very numerous because they include the whole set of work situations that employees have experienced at any time. The biographical employability is assessed from owned competences, as the portfolio of assets owned by the individual.

Differential employability and recognized competences. The assessment criteria used here are depersonalized: a logic of profiling based on various competence frameworks is applied; these may be job descriptions, competence modeling, and/ or probabilities of failure and success of various statistical profiles (in reclassifying or supporting the unemployed, for example). Biodata questionnaires or typologies may also be used to identify talents and high potential employees using sociodemographic variables. The 360° method is another way to audit and demonstrate the competence of professionals (Ulrich, 1997), with a high validity (Hagan et al., 2006). This assessment logic places the individual in a hierarchy of qualifications, each of which gives access to different collective resources (De Grip et al., 2004; Gazier, 1998). The depiction of *recognized competences* corresponds to this assessment logic that is based on classification, profiling, and ranking: only individual competences recognized and approved by the hierarchy and the organization are taken into account. The differential employability is assessed from recognized competences, as the rank in a collective hierarchy of competences.

Supported employability and required competences. Formal or informal interviews, observation, and interaction practices provide the means to evaluate the required competences. More generally, assessment practices develop an evaluation of the quality of work organization, HR, and management in the company: the "active" career management practices ("active management" and "active planning" Baruch, 2004) and the degree of sophistication of the career management system (Scholarios et al., 2008) are central in this convention of *supported employability*. The logic to assess employability corresponds here to the environment's dynamic support of the individual's position. It combines various factors and refers to the strengthening (or weakening) of employability linked to the company's situation and economic outlook and its HR and employment policies. In this register, we find all organizational management policies for developing individual competences (De Cuyper et al., 2011; De Vos et al., 2011; Scholarios et al., 2008; Van den Broeck et al., 2014). The corresponding depiction of individual competences is that of *required competences*, the competences that are really necessary for the employee to accomplish his/her job. The supported employability is assessed from organizational required competences, as the support of the organizational environment and HRM policies.

Projective employability and potential competences. In this register for interpreting employability and competences, numerous practices available for attributing potential are to be found. Armstrong (2006) identifies several methods of selection that measure fairly different elements with different accuracy, which cannot therefore all be put at the same level: traditional methods (competence profiles, psychological and psychometric tests, role-plays exercises, or even managerial diagnosis), biographical methods (especially biodata questionnaires and bio typologies), qualitative methods (360° interviews with experts or peers), quantitative methods (personality tests and attitude scales), synthetic methods (combining various methods such as assessment centers), and even "esoteric methods" (astrology, graphology, etc.). Auditing potential competences relies on various data: self-assessments, quantitative assessments of traits on the survey form, focus groups, or interviews (Ulrich, 1997). Assessment relies on how the individual acts in the context, on potential or observed behavior. The proactive aspect of personality (in particular, self-confidence, adaptability, capacity to learn, and capacity to watch for job opportunities) is at the heart of the *projective employability* convention. The assessment logic seeks to appreciate the individual's capacity to adapt, transfer, promote, and develop competences in a different job and other professional situations: the *potential competences*, i.e., those that could be developed by a given employee in the future, are associated with projective employability. They are the most complicated to conceptualize in the field of HRM because they are not situated in time or space, and their relationship to the organizational situation is more elastic (the work situation that is supposed to develop the competences does not really exist yet). In sum, the projective employability is assessed from individual potential competences, as the potential deployment of the individual into employment and career.

This framework needs now a confrontation with empirical data to demonstrate its coherence and its contribution: a longitudinal case study of assessment practices of employability offers such a confrontation. We have chosen to study the reclassification of victims of downsizing, in the Air Littoral emblematic case.

5.3 Air Littoral Emblematic Case Study: Competences-Based Employability and Assessment Practices along a Reclassification Process

Our empirical research relies on one "representative" case study, as an emblematic field for the problem under investigation (Eisenhardt, 1989; Eisenhardt and

Graebner, 2007; Siggelkow, 2007; Yin, 2008). More specifically, for this research, we selected Air Littoral case as being representative of one context of effective rapprochement between assessing employability and individual competences. The Air Littoral group has encountered very serious economic difficulties and finally declared bankruptcy in August 2003. Despite four potentially serious offers, the liquidation was pronounced in February 2004, resulting in the loss of over 850 jobs in two successive plans to safeguard employment (PSEs): 256 in December 2003 then 600 in February 2004. The context is that of support immediately after job loss, specifically in the context of reclassification cells working on PSE. The PSE set up on the liquidation of Air Littoral is representative of a context where reclassification support procedures were developed to assess and develop the competences and employability of those laid off, thus to help them in their search for a new job or career plan.

After the first layoffs, a reclassification unit was set up by a private consultant chosen by personnel representatives. It was managed by a monitoring committee bringing together PSE stakeholders: French Regional Labor Institution, elected employee representatives, trade union delegates, ANPE (government job centers), region council, heads of consulting firm, and members of the reclassification unit. For 12 months, the reclassification unit worked on how to best support employees' reclassification (for those who chose to be included in the process, as this was not obligatory). This support depended on the means and procedures of the PSE.

At the time of its liquidation, the Air Littoral group had 856 employees, including 444 for the airline company, AL, and 156 for the maintenance entity, AL Industry (ALI). The company's activity was spread over three main geographical areas: Montpellier (44% for AL, nearly 80% for ALI), Nice (47% for AL, 10% for ALI), and a third area grouping all the presence on stopovers and qualified as Other Areas (nearly 9% for AL and 10% for ALI). Finally, there are three main categories of staff: STS (specialized transport staff, 27% of the total number of staff at the time of liquidation), UTS (user transport staff, 17%), and SAS (support and administrative staff, almost 56%); the latter category being characterized by a great diversity and variety of the professions carried out. We can highlight the high proportion of managers, in general and in the AL company, and on the contrary, the high proportion of technicians in the maintenance subsidiary ALI.

In general, the staff is very diversified technically, administratively, and statutorily and geographically fragmented. Despite a wide variety of age and seniority situations by occupational category and entity, it should be noted that the company's personnel were particularly old and with seniority, especially transport staff. Employees to be reclassified had atypical and highly diverse profiles: they were on average middle aged with long seniority in the company (over 15 years for 27% of the executives); they were mostly highly qualified and experienced but with individual competences specific to regional air transport, thus difficult to transfer.

We conducted a longitudinal case study, partly retrospectively, of the employability assessment practices implemented in the reclassification cell. In this research under convention with a French Regional Labor Institution,* four sources of data ensure the richness of the findings (Yin, 2008): interviews (almost 20 semi-directive interviews, lasting on average 1 h 30 min), documents, observation, and informal dialogues.

5.4 Results and Findings: Projective Employability and Dominant Quality Convention of Employability

The study of the assessment practices of employability is operated at the central interfaces of coordination between those that accompany and the reclassification cell and that between the cell and its monitoring committee. The three moments of the reclassification process (preparation and entry into the cell, implementation of support for reclassification, and results and exit of the cell) lead to six different assessment practices of employability: the first three are at the interface between the cell and the monitoring committee (cell's specifications, reports to the monitoring committee, and the reclassification rate and number of valid job opportunities) and the other three are at the interface between the cell and the individuals (membership form, employment project, and typology of situations).

The cell–individual interface was central in the beginning and in the end of the process: with more than 850 laid offs and more than 600 adherents to the cell, the entry into the cell and the exit of the cell are phases during which information management about the former employee was central. The membership form and the typologies of situations are the two assessment practices developed to articulate individual employability and collective employability. During the implementation of support for reclassification, several interpretations exist. The employment project is the mean or artifact of translation of the individual employability and competences. The practices identified here show that the dominant assessment convention is that of projective employability. Nevertheless, other employability conventions and types of competences are present, but only in secondary practices or conditioned by the dominant register.

The reclassification unit set up a two-step process. The first step involves meeting with employees, informing them, and preparing them for change. In the Air Littoral case, the different stakeholders were alerted to the psychological suffering of many employees embarking on reclassification. Indeed, certain employees, "who had not digested the liquidation," proved to be highly negative toward all actors of the reclassification process. They were determined to contest everything and had a "bad mentality" (employee representative). The employees' traumatic experience

* C. Fabre (coord.), I. Bories-Azeau, P. Chappelier, A. Loubès, Saint-Germes et A. Briole (2006) « *L'accompagnement social des restructurations d'entreprises: étude des plans de sauvegarde de l'emploi et des démarches d'anticipation* », Rapport DRTEFP-LR (327 p.), juillet 2006.

blocked their capacity to project themselves onto the job market, and this had an impact on setting up support practices:

> It was hard to set up the reclassification unit because of the way employ-ees experienced the layoffs. People were bitter from the start, they had been taken advantage of, and up to the end they believed it would never happen (…). Because of this, our everyday work was really hard.

(reclassification cell consultant)

This difficulty was only overcome with the support of certain personnel represen-tatives, who took on the role of expert consultants and made it possible to take account of psychological and personal factors affecting those to be reclassified. Effective psychological support was then given by consultants from the field: they listened to and followed up the former employees in their mourning process (a very difficult process with multiple losses – losing a comfortable job in a well-respected company, a job they loved and a potential radical change in their way of life). As well as the initial appraisal and reclassification plan that were systematic for each person in the program, there were also numerous sessions preparing former employ-ees for change (individual interviews, group meetings, and speech groups). The employability assessment was above all based on employees' potential competences for job seeking and their reclassification depending on their progress in dealing with their mourning process. Projective employability underlies psychological sup-port, with the assessment of competences focused on personal, psychological, and sociological adaptability.

The second step consisted of a personal and professional review for each former employee. This review aimed to formulate and validate a reclassification project and coordinate and define subsequent individual action. This appraisal was the central pivot of the plan, influencing prospection in the environment and potential relations with companies. During these assessments, employability was centered on the transferability of owned competences as well as on potential competences that could be anticipated. However, even if an "assets" approach was used to draw up individuals' portfolio of competences accumulated over their whole career (profes-sional and personal), this was not the main goal of the assessment, and the "owned competences" were not the main object of evaluation. The assessment aimed above all to construct a reclassification plan based on employees' capacity to project their accumulated competences into other situations. In this way, even if the initial assessment could be associated to biographical employability, the above practice relates rather to projective employability.

Two other practices of the reclassification unit also relate to projective employ-ability. First, the process of "(proactive) revitalization" or psychological coach-ing that offered individual interviews – but only to those who had achieved an approved, realistic reclassification plan; second, training to develop and master the necessary job seeking techniques to implement that plan. This training took the form of group sessions for job seeking techniques and individual support once the job search was under way. This was almost systematic for those receiving unit support. In Air Littoral, support for reclassification was thus mainly based on projective practices of assessment and the development of former employees' projective employability from their potential competences. Nevertheless, other employability conventions and other types of competences were also present in this reclassification process.

First, and as already explained, projective employability requires the prior identification of owned competences by laid off employees. Biographical employability is therefore also present in the Air Littoral case, but only to the extent that previously accumulated competences appear as a preparatory support for projective employability. Next, given the number of laid off employees followed (over 500), the assessment of employability quickly gave way to an initial profiling to direct them toward different reclassification paths. This diagnosis was based on individual psychological and sociological factors (psychological state and experience of the PSE, personal situation, and professional identity, respectively). It allowed to orient individuals toward different support paths: they might be directed immediately toward job search or embark upon a step-by-step process including phases for mourning, "(proactive) revitalization"/"psychological coaching," and job search support; other possibilities included training or working out their project. These practices ranked individuals with regard to collective criteria such as obstacles to reclassification. In particular, they evaluated individuals' rank and capacity to seek employment or their risk of being long-term unemployed: this is related to the differential employability convention.

Besides, a set of support practices – relevant to supported employability – were deployed to help implement employees' career plans, even those whose project needed time to mature or who took a long time to recover from their loss. In particular, a great number of training sessions were financed; these were mainly in the technical domains of air transport and in English to facilitate reclassification in this rapidly changing sector of activity. The reclassification unit also developed systematic targeted prospection of employment offers in the air industry as well as other employment opportunities in the local area. Although few offers resulted from this prospection, this support aimed to maintain individuals' employability so that it still belongs to the convention of supported employability. Table 5.1 summarizes our data from the Air Littoral case, starting with practices for supporting reclassification and going toward the employability assessment conventions.

To conclude this case, we can affirm that projective employability is the dominant convention in support of the reclassification of the Air Littoral employees. The assessment processes try to recognize into which new contexts the employees' professional competences can be projected. Many different practices are used to achieve this: personal assessment, job search, training, etc. Biographical employability appears as a prior support for employees' projective employability.

Table 5.1   Data Structure in the Air Littoral Case

Practices for supporting the reclassification	Type of competence	Object of assessment	Employability convention
Psychological support from consultants/preparation for change	Potential competences	Deployment	Projective employability
Initial personal/professional appraisal			
Individual reclassification plan			
Job-search training			
"(Proactive) revitalization" and individual interviews			
Personal and professional review/portfolio of competences accumulated over their whole career	Owned competences	Assets	Biographical employability
Systematic targeted prospection of employment offers	Required competences	Strengthening	Supported employability
Funding for training (technical and English)			
Initial profiling for direction toward different reclassification paths	Recognized competences	Rank	Differential employability

The assessment of the capital of owned competences is one useful ingredient for effective projective employability. In the same way, supported employability (the reclassification unit prospecting employment offers, training, etc.) and differential employability (the reclassification unit classifying employees according to their supposed risk as long-term unemployed, etc.) appear as a support for the predominant projective employability.

5.5 Discussion and Contributions

This work aims at the proposition of a conceptual framework to study multiple interpretations of employability in a competences-based approach and to apply it to an emblematic case study, such as the support for reclassification of victims of layoffs with Air Littoral liquidation. It reveals some interesting findings and avenues for future research we present now. Our focus here is on the dominant convention of projective employability and potential competences, with on-going debates around transferability of competences and specific competence in career enactment and job search.

The projective convention of employability associated with potential competences appears as central and dominant in the reclassification process, even if other conventions appear in the process. The potential competences (i.e., those that could be developed by a given employee in the future), associated with projective employability, are the most complicated to conceptualize in the field of HRM, because they are not situated in time or space and their relationship to the organizational situation is more elastic (the work situation that is supposed to develop the competences does not really exist yet). As a result, assessment practices are reinforced and partly translated from other conventions and figures of competences. For instance, biographical and differential employability convention are used at the first moment of the reclassification process, during the personal and professional review, to elaborate the path of reclassification. A profiling logic is used to choose the project and the level of support and thus to translate levels of biographical and differential employability into projective employability assessment: the profiles with high risk of unemployability were oriented to a psychological support before starting job search; the profiles with lower risk of unemployability were conducted to a support for job search concretization.

In our case, the employability assessment was above all based on employees' potential competences for job seeking and their reclassification depending on their progress in dealing with their mourning process. Projective employability underlies psychological support, with the assessment of competences focused on personal, psychological, and sociological adaptability. We find here the proactive aspect of personality at the heart of the projective employability convention, as the potential deployment of the individual into employment and career. The competences for job search appeared as central for reclassification process, but the ability to deploy oneself in a new employment project relies above all on the enactment of the career, on the capacity to transfer its future into new professional situations, and as a consequence, to transfer its competences in a different job and other professional situations. The ability to monitor job opportunities, job search, and career competences are central competences for projective employability. As Air Littoral case study shows, psychological, sociological, and cultural dimensions are of a high importance for these abilities and competences.

One perspective of research would be to deepen the question of the transferability of individual competences to explore their nature and the assessment of potential individual competences. These are core elements for determining opportunities for professional evolution and thus of employability. The Air Littoral case suggests that above all, individual psychological and personal factors enable the assessment of an individual's capacity to transfer his/her individual competences and project himself/herself into a new professional situation. The role of factors linked to the individual converges with career management practices and mobility support that often propose processes to support spouses, children, or even find accommodation. Finally, when confronted with a large number of potential professional situations that are fuzzy and ill-determined, the individual situation becomes the reference for assessment, and subsequent decisions about the level of support are required. A second promising research perspective would aim to better understand how, over space and time, the different employability conventions and types of underlying individual competences complete and combine with each other in other emblematic cases of competence-based employability assessment. This idea could also feed into other inter-organizational dimensions of competence management, like the territorial competence (see Chapter 8). The framework we propose could then offer tangible elements to draw these two notions together, especially by focusing on logics of assessment and the main practices associated with different steps of the networked HRM process.

5.6 Conclusion

To conclude, we hope that our study has contributed to a better understanding of the difficult and incomplete links between employability and individual competences using an integrative framework and a methodology with the help of quality conventions of employability. While the emergence of a competences-based approach to employability corresponds to an institutionalization of concept in the field of HRM, it also corresponds to a reaffirmation of the employer's (or a network of actors') responsibility in terms of career and talent management to maintain and develop employability and individual competences. The competences-based approach of employability legitimates the active role and support of the employer and the necessity to coordinate efforts and assessments of the different stakeholders around competences and employability. Specifically, projective employability convention, which is dominant in international research and in our case study, is focused on the deployment of an individual into new job opportunities through its potential competences: a permanent duality of the assessment practices is identified here. The dialectic and the articulation between the employment situation and potential situations are at the heart of the question of the transferability of competences. In both employability and competences fields, these debates contrast European and American approaches, but the competences-based approach to employability could be a way to bring these visions closer together.

References

Armstrong, M. (2006). *A Handbook of Human Resource Management Practice* (10th edition). London, UK: Kogan Page.

Baruch, Y. (2004). *Managing Careers: Theory and Practice*. Harlow, UK: FT-Prentice Hall/Pearson.

Boltanski L., & Thevenot L. (1999). The sociology of critical capacity. *European Journal of Social Theory*, 2, 359–377.

Boltanski, L., & Thévenot, L. (2006). *On Justification: Economies of Worth*. Princeton University Press.

De Grip, A., Van Loo, J., & Sanders, J. (2004). The industry employability index: Taking account of supply and demand characteristics. *International Labour Review*, 143(3), 211–233.

De Vos, A., De Hauw, S., & Van Der Heijden, B. (2011). Competency development and career success: The mediating role of employability. *Journal of Vocational Behavior*, 79(2), 438–447.

Eisenhardt, K. M. (1989). Building theories from case study research. *Academy of Management Review*, 14(4), 532–550.

Eisenhardt, K. M., & Graebner, M. E. (2007). Theory building from cases: Opportunities and challenges. *Academy of Management Journal*, 50(1), 25–32.

Eymard-Duvernay, F. (2002). Conventionalist approaches to enterprise. In: Favereau, O., & Lazega E. (ed.), *Conventions and Structures in Economic Organization: Markets, Networks and Hierarchies*, Cheltenham: Edward Elgar, 60–78.

Favereau, O., & Lazega, E. (2002). *Conventions and Structures in Economic Organization: Markets, Networks and Hierarchy*, Cheltenham: Edward Elgar.

Forrier, A., & Sels, L. (2003). The concept of employability: A complex mosaic. *International Journal of Human Resources Development and Management*, 3(2), 103–124.

Forrier, A., Verbruggen, M., & De Cuyper, N. (2015). Integrating different notions of employability in a dynamic chain: The relationship between job transitions, movement capital and perceived employability. *Journal of Vocational Behavior*, 89, 56–64.

Froehlich, D. E., Beausaert, S. A. J., & Segers, M. S. R. (2015). Age, employability and the role of learning activities and their motivational antecedents: A conceptual model. *International Journal of Human Resource Management*, 26(16), 2087–2101.

Fugate, M., & Kinicki, A. J. (2008). A dispositional approach to employability: Development of a measure and test of implications for employee reactions to organizational change. *Journal of Occupational & Organizational Psychology*, 81(3), 503–527.

Fugate, M., Kinicki, A. J., & Ashforth, B. E. (2004). Employability: A psycho-social construct, its dimensions and applications. *Journal of Vocational Behavior, 65*, 14–38.

Gazier, B. (1998). *Employability: Concepts and Policies*. Berlin, Germany: European Employment Observatory.

Gazier, B. (2003), « L'employabilité », in Allouche, J. (coord.), *Encyclopédie des Ressources Humaines*, Paris, Vuibert, 418–427.

Gkeredakis, E. (2014). The constitutive role of conventions in accomplishing coordination: Insights from a complex contract award project. *Organization Studies, 35*(10), 1473–1505.

Gomez, P. -Y., & Jones, B. J. (2000). Crossroads-conventions: An interpretation of deep structure in organizations. *Organization Science, 11*(6), 696–708.

Haasler, S. R. (2013). Employability skills and the notion of "self." *International Journal of Training and Development, 17*(3), 233–243.

Hagan, C. M., Konopaske, R., Bernardin, H. J., & Tyler, C. L. (2006). Predicting assessment center performance with 360-degree, Top-down, and Customer-based competency assessments. *Human Resource Management, 45*(3), 367–390.

Loufrani-Fedida, S., Oiry, E., & Saint-Germes, E. (2015). Vers un rapprochement de l'employabilité et de la gestion des compétences: Grille de lecture théorique et illustrations empiriques. *Revue de Gestion des Ressources Humaines, 97*(2), 17–38.

McQuaid, R. W., & Lindsay, C. (2005). The concept of employability. *Urban Studies, 42*(2), 197–219.

Nicholson H. (1996). Career system in crisis: Change and opportunity in the information age. *Academy of Management Executive, 10*, 50–60

O'Reilly, J., Nazio, T., & Roche, J. M. (2014). Compromising conventions: Attitudes of dissonance and indifference toward full-time maternal employment in Denmark, Spain, Poland and the UK. *Work, Employment and Society, 28*(2), 168–188.

Peiperl, M., & Baruch, Y. (1997). Back to square zero: The post-corporate career. *Organizational Dynamics, 25*(4), 6–22.

Redmond, E. (2013). Competency models at work: The value of perceived relevance and fair rewards for employee outcomes. *Human Resource Management, 52*(5), 771–792.

Retour, D. (2005). Le DRH de demain face au dossier compétences. *Management & Avenir, (2)*, 187–200.

Rousseau, D. (1995). *Psychological Contracts in Organizations* (246 p.). Thousand Oaks, CA: Sage Publications.

Saint-Germes, E. (2007). *L'employabilité, un enjeu pour la GRH: Contribution à l'analyse du concept et de sa pratique en contexte de gestion*. Thèse de Doctorat en Sciences de Gestion, Université de Montpellier 2.

Scholarios, D., Van Der Heijden, B., Van Der Schoot, E., Bozionelos, N., Epitropaki, O., Jedrzejowicz, P., Knauth, P., Marzec, I., Mikkelsen, A., & Van Der Heijde, C. (2008). Employability and the psychological contract in European ICT Sector SMEs. *The International Journal of Human Resource Management, 19*(6), 1035–1055.

Siggelkow, N. (2007). Persuasion with case studies. *Academy of Management Journal, 50*(1), 20–24.

Thijssen, J. G., Van der Heijden, B. I., & Rocco, T. S. (2008). Toward the employability—link model: Current employment transition to future employment perspectives. *Human Resource Development Review, 7*(2), 165–183.

Ulrich, D. (1997). Measuring Human Resources: An overview of practice and a prescription for results. *Human Resource Management, 36*(3), 303–320.

Van Burren, H. J. (2003). Boundaryless careers and employability obligations. *Business Ethics Quaterly, 13*(2), 131–149.

Van den Broeck, A., De Cuyper, N., Baillien, E., Vanbelle, E., Vanhercke, D., & De Witte, H. (2014). Perception of organization's value support and perceived employability: Insights from self-determination theory. *International Journal of Human Resource Management, 25*(13), 1904–1918.

Van Der Heijde, C., & Van Der Heijden, B. (2006). A competence-based and multi-dimensional operationalization and measurement of employability. *Human Resource Management, 45*(3), 449–476.

Van Dam, K. (2004). Antecedents and consequences of employability orientation. *European Journal of Work and Organisational Psychology, 13*(1), 29–51.

Waterman, R. H., Waterman J. A., & Collard, B. A. (1994). Toward a career resilient workforce. *Harvard Business Review, 72*, 87–95.

Wittekind, A., Raeder, S., & Grote, G. (2010). A longitudinal study of determinants of perceived employability? *Journal of Organizational Behavior, 31*, 566–586.

Yin, R. K. (2008). *Case Study Research: Design and Methods* (Vol. 5, 4th edition). London, UK: Sage Publication.

Chapter 6

Together, Do We Go Further? The Dynamic between Rules and Collective Competence

Frédérique Chédotel and Cathy Krohmer

Contents

6.1 Introduction

Working in teams has become pervasive, with a "plethora of research (…) attempting to explain teamwork and the conditions surrounding its success or failure" (Salas et al., 2015, p. 599). Within this body of research, the concept of collective competence, defined as a group's recognized ability to cope with a given situation (Bataille-Chédotel, 2001), has given rise to a number of studies in the literature published in English (e.g., Hager and Johnsson, 2009; Kitto et al., 2015; Ruuska and Teigland, 2009; Shuffler et al., 2018) and in French (e.g., Retour and Krohmer, 2006; Chédotel and Krohmer, 2014). These studies have shown that creation and mobilization of collective competence are not self-evident in teams whose members may be unable to compare their representations, or get bogged down pursuing contradictory objectives. It is thus important to identify the levers that support the development of this competence (Retour and Krohmer, 2006; Chédotel and Krohmer, 2014; Hass and Mortensen, 2016; Brulhart et al., 2019).

Two differing attitudes to collective competence coexist. The first looks for universal solutions to facilitate development of what is called generic teamwork skills (e.g., Cannon-Bowers et al., 1993; Ellis et al., 2005). The second sees competence as a situated dynamic that cannot be separated from practice (e.g., Sandberg and Pinnington, 2009; Lindberg and Rantatalo, 2014) and considers levers of competence management as a framework that constrains people's action, but empowers them to take it, and that action in return reinforces and/or transforms those levers (Havard and Krohmer, 2008; Oiry, 2011; Ragaigne et al., 2014; Krohmer and Bretesché, 2013).

Although the first of these attitudes has led to significant contributions, identifying intervention methods that can strengthen collective competence (e.g., Shuffler et al., 2018; Lacerenza et al., 2018), the results remain ambiguous, since teamwork is a dynamic construct and interventions take time to build, leaving a gap between theory and practice (Salas et al., 2018). The study presented here takes a more dynamic, situated approach, with the objective of advancing the understanding of the dynamics between collective competence and its levers. The questions addressed are as follows: *What are the dynamics between competence and managerial levers? And how do those dynamics evolve over time?* To answer these questions, the study's central focus is on one managerial lever: team rules (Hackman, 1987; Brown and Eisenhardt, 1998; Jolivet and Navarre, 1996). This chapter primarily draws on research concerning collective competence and the role of rules. It then presents the abductive research method used and analyzes two cases of teams in the medical/social sector: GERON and SOLIDAR. This chapter enhances understanding of the specific dynamics that form between collective competence and rules and makes recommendations for team management.

6.2 Developing Collective Competence

After presenting the origins of the concept, collective competence is then considered in connection with one particular managerial lever, namely team rules.

6.2.1 Collective Competence: The Origins of a Concept

This section looks at the definition of this multifaceted concept and presents the two attitudes that have developed in parallel.

6.2.1.1 Collective Competence: A Multifaceted Concept

Many authors (e.g., Retour and Krohmer, 2006; Ruuska and Teigland, 2009; Klarner et al., 2013) have worked to conceptualize collective competence, defined as a group's recognized ability to cope with a given situation (Bataille-Chédotel, 2001). The summary review drawn up by Chédotel and Pujol (2012) reports on the multifaceted nature of competence.

First, collective competence needs team members to construct *a common* set of rules and language (Bataille-Chédotel, 2001; Retour and Krohmer, 2006; Boreham, 2004; Kitto et al., 2015), i.e., a unified vision of the situation and a shared vocabulary that enable them to work together and respond to the situation. English-language research has shown that the quality of these rules plays a decisive role (Cannon-Bowers et al., 1993; Mathieu et al., 2005; Salas et al., 2009), and it may be the case that they are biased or of poor quality.

Next, collective competence is founded on *comparison of individuals' representations*, in order to identify and discuss the various options in the situation at hand (Bataille-Chédotel, 2001; Retour and Krohmer, 2006). This comparison takes place through discursive activities (such as meetings and conversations) and written texts (such as management dashboards) that are channels for interaction between practitioners (Arnaud, 2008). In situations involving uncertainty and time pressure, comparison of representations builds mutual understanding and fosters sensemaking (Weick, 1995).

Finally, mobilizing collective competence leads to a *collective decision*, made in a given situation (Pantin, 2006; Ruuska and Teigland, 2009). Before the final decision is made, it is debated in the team so that all opinions can be aired (Chédotel and Pujol, 2012). It may happen that a team has a common set of rules, and an opportunity to compare its members' knowledge, and yet, ultimately, the final decision does not result from collective debate (e.g., when the decision had already been made before the team was set up).

6.2.1.2 From Generic Teamwork Skills to Collective Competence as a Dynamic

Identifying levers of development has become a major aim of current research into collective competence (Retour and Krohmer, 2006; Retour et al., 2009), in which two different approaches are observed.

The first belongs to the KSAs (Knowledge, Skills, and Abilities) approach and considers competence as a set of human properties (Boyatzis, 1982; Spencer and Spencer, 2008). After long concentrating on the individual competence, the research adopting this approach has more recently focused on KSA teams, examining what it calls "team skills" or "collective skills" (Shuffler et al., 2018). By definition, such team skills are KSAs which are considered critical for team members to interact with one another interdependently and effectively, in a way that leads to positive team-based outcomes (Salas et al., 2009). Generic skills are classified into three broad categories (Shuffler et al., 2011): attitudes (e.g., cohesion or team efficiency), behaviors (e.g., communication, coordination, or shared leadership), and cognitions (e.g., shared mental models or situation awareness). To strengthen team skills, certain authors recommend "team development interventions," i.e., actions taken to alter the performance trajectories of organizational teams (Shuffler et al., 2018), such as team building, team training, leadership, or coaching (Lacerenza et al., 2018). The general aim of this stream of research is to conduct systematic empirical studies in order to understand which team development intervention (TDI) methods and tactics are appropriate and which are not and to build a "team intervention science" (Shuffler et al., 2011) of relevance to practitioners (Salas et al., 2018).

As collective competence is not context-free, many authors have criticized the one-size-fits-all nature of this first approach (e.g., Boreham, 2011; Lingard, 2012). A second approach, more relational and situated, considers competence as an open entity that is socially distributed inside teams and communities of practice (e.g., Häland and Tjora, 2006; Sandberg and Pinnington, 2009; Fauré and Rouleau, 2011; Lindberg and Rantatalo, 2014). In this approach the aim is to study relations of mutual constitution (Feldman and Orlikowski, 2011) between levers of management and collective competence. These levers both constrain and empower people (Ragaigne et al., 2014), whether they remain broadly incomplete (Oiry, 2011) or whether they are extended or put to different uses by the employees themselves (Havard and Krohmer, 2008; Krohmer and Bretesché, 2013). Collective competence is thus shaped by a set of rules and is the outcome either of going further than those rules or of combining them (Chédotel and Krohmer, 2014).

6.2.2 Combining Rules and Collective Competence

To understand the relations of mutual constitution between collective competence and its managerial levers, this chapter focuses on one of those levers that have been widely studied in the literature: team rules. Analyzing these rules is equivalent to asking the essential question of what makes an appropriately malleable framework to develop and support collective competence over time.

6.2.2.1 Organizational Metarules and Team Rules

Two types of team rules can be distinguished (Pinto et al., 1993): rules that apply to all hierarchical levels (organizational metarules) and rules that guide a team's action locally (team rules).

Metarules are overarching, simple rules which provide an overall view of a situation and guide action, while also allowing teams to redefine their priorities if necessary and "auto-organize" to deal with complex situations rapidly (Le Bris et al., 2019). Such rules have essentially been studied through cases of innovative project teams (Brown and Eisenhardt, 1998; Jolivet and Navarre, 1996; Chédotel, 2012; Tatikonda and Rosenthal, 2000). These rules can be adapted locally: each team can interpret the metarules and organize itself for a specific situation. Meanwhile, following the pioneering work of Hackman (1987), research has been undertaken to study the "design" of teams. Designing a team aims to satisfy three questions (Wageman et al., 2005): (1) Is it a "real team"?*; (2) Does the team have a compelling direction?[†] And (3) does the team have an enabling structure and a supportive organization?[‡]

6.2.2.2 Toward a Dynamic Approach

While research concerning these two types of rules (team rules and organizational metarules) does not directly consider them as levers for development of collective

---

* Real teams have clear boundaries, and team members are interdependent for some common purpose. They also have at least moderate stability of membership.

[†] A compelling direction involves clear, challenging, and consequential specification of the team's overall purposes and resources and emphasize on the direction setters.

[‡] An enabling structure needs a task design that mobilizes complementary KSAs in a small team and definition of core norms of conduct for team members' behavior. A supportive organization provides the team with the necessary resources (information, training, technical assistance, coaching, etc.) and recognition.

competence, the metarules can still supply pointers for working in a team, by being a guide for action, a channel for comparing representations, and a framework for collective decision-making. Research has also explored the levers that foster development of collective competence (Retour and Krohmer, 2006). The composition of teams, which is one dimension of team design rules, requires consideration of how individual skills complement each other, but also seeks a well-balanced combination of talents by putting together a range of profiles and experiences. Setting clear, precise, accessible objectives is another dimension of team design.

Taking this research as a springboard, it is possible to go further and study the dynamic of mutual constitution between rules and collective competence in order to answer our research questions. Team design rules, for example, are intended to govern action in a way that encourages development of collective competence. But they can also be resources that team members can interpret, mobilize, and combine in a situation to develop collective competence. As such, they can be extended, transformed, or put to different uses by people (Havard and Krohmer, 2008). Also, they may be associated with the team's capacity for auto-organization (Retour and Krohmer, 2006), with the development of a team that gives its members responsibility based on the collective dynamic and with a management mode that allows autonomy and initiative taking. This context is favorable for implementation of metarules, adapted into local sets of rules.

6.3 Two Illustrative Cases

In the two cases studied (see panel 1), rules played a decisive role in developing (or failing to develop) collective competence over time. In the first case (GERON), the rules were in the end a driving force in this development, while in the other case (SOLIDAR), disruption of the rules weakened the foundations of the collective competence.

PANEL 1: RESEARCH METHODOLOGY

Two cases of teamwork were studied in two different social/medical organizations, selected for their theoretical representativeness (Eisenhardt, 1989). The first case, GERON, studied by Cathy Krohmer, concerns a team of 21 people (hospital doctors, nurses, auxiliary nurses, physiotherapists, occupational therapists, healthcare managers, social workers, hospital support staff) belonging to a follow-up care and rehabilitation section of a local hospital that specializes in geriatrics. Between March 2010 and July 2010, 18 semi-structured interviews were conducted with medical and management staff, internal and external documents were collected, and observations of meetings and work took place. The second case, SOLIDAR, studied by Frédérique Chédotel, concerns an NGO project team consisting of 15 people, who specialize in management of humanitarian emergencies and took action after the earthquake that hit Haiti on January 12, 2010. Between January 2010 and May 2011, 27 semi-structured interviews were conducted with members of the emergency team, their contacts in the management and support staff, internal and external documents were collected, and one-time observations took place. The data were analyzed under an abductive process, aiming to progressively categorize data based on research questions and iterative examinations oscillating between the literature review and results from the field.

6.3.1 The GERON Case: Constructing the Rules and Collective Competence

The GERON team consists of 21 people and is in charge of preventing or limiting the functional, physical, cognitive, psychological, and social consequences of patients' diminished abilities and promoting their rehabilitation and return to normal life. This first case shows how a collective competence dynamic, associated with the design of rules, can develop over time in a hospital setting.

6.3.1.1 The Emergence of Collective Competence

In 2009, a hospital doctor was hired for a full-time post in the GERON team, which until then had operated with a part-time doctor. The new doctor, a specialist in geriatrics and addiction treatment, which was not one of the team's specialist areas at the time, was the impetus for new modes of operation with a high teamwork component. From small beginnings, the team's collective competence gradually improved until it could provide patients with coordinated, individually tailored care:

> If it's about discharging someone or something, everyone has to give their opinion. We don't just discharge people without thinking. The auxiliary nurse says, "in my opinion, for washing, he's able to wash himself, or eat by himself." The physio will say "he can walk, he can go back home." What support should the social worker set up? Should the occupational therapist go and do a home visit? Now, everyone gets coordinated well before we consider a discharge.
>
> **(auxiliary nurse)**

In this case, development of the three dimensions of collective competence was identified during the observation periods. First, the common language and references evolved to incorporate care of patients being treated for addictions. In particular, the purpose of hospital treatment changed: treating the patient meant technical acts (injections, dressings, washing the patient, etc.) and/or addressing the addict's personal situation (considering the possibility of support for the family, the general state of health, etc.).

> The addiction patients are usually young – well, when I say young I mean 40 to 50 – who aren't necessarily sick, don't need any special medical care, but do need a lot of listening to because they're unhappy. So they need a specific type of contact with us.
>
> **(nurse)**

Next, patient treatment became genuinely collective, and comparison of team members' representations grew more frequent during the day and in "handover summaries," as appropriate to the situation. At these meetings, for example, the team now examines each patient's records together and makes discharge decisions jointly:

> I see it like this, there's the patient and we all gravitate around him in our respective roles. As far as I can see everyone has about the same gravitational orbit … what I mean is, there's lots of information around the patient, from the physio, the auxiliary nurse, the nurse … all that info surrounds the patient. There are times where decision-making and treatment draws us closer to the patient, and then we go back to our gravitational orbit.
>
> **(hospital doctor)**

Finally, where decisions used to be mostly made by the nurses, they are now more collective. However, this does not mean there is no arbitration, and when that happens, the medical opinion takes priority: "The medical decision often overrules the others, so that's how it is (…). I think communication work is crucial, but sometimes in an emergency, the decision can be authoritarian" (hospital doctor).

6.3.1.2 Introduction of Rules That Create a Dynamic

Regarding the organizational framework which contributes to this dynamic, practices in hospital, particularly the work of the medical teams, are generally under very strict control. This is reflected in the existence of a number of procedures and protocols for treatment. But the teams also have their own metarules that correspond specifically to the principles of a public hospital service: equality of treatment for all patients, continuity of treatment, and communication – which is fundamental to healthcare work. The principles of responsibility are also clearly defined. Each function has its own scope of responsibility within the patient's treatment. For example, prescribing medicine must be done by a doctor, while administering the same medicine can be done by a nurse or doctor.

Bearing in mind the metarules, the team rules are interpreted by team members in a way that enables them to mobilize their collective competence in response to situations, putting the patient first. For example, task evolution is frequent, and the nurse(s) or doctor may help the auxiliary nurses in their everyday tasks, especially in physically handling patients. The rules may also be broken sometimes. Decisions that are the doctor's responsibility may be made by the auxiliary nurses when necessary:

> The auxiliary nurses sometimes take initiatives for the use of an anti-bedsore mattress. An experienced auxiliary nurse who's used to this sort of situation and has worked with sick people for years, well she just does it, she tells me and in general I approve it.
>
> **(hospital doctor)**

The doctor has a key role here, participating in and managing this "rule-breaking," which has become more transparent inside the team.

This doctor also introduced design rules for the team. The primary reason for achieving the collective competence dynamic after one year was that the team was stable in time. Its members realized that each person's work influenced the work of the other team members, and the mission of the team became clear to everyone: working together to take care of the patients admitted to their section of the hospital, under the authority of the doctor. From the outset, the new doctor encouraged consideration of every medical worker's opinion, whatever their function (nurses, auxiliary nurses, healthcare managers, etc.), through regular informal discussions of the patients and setting up weekly handover meetings, which are an important time in the team's work.

6.3.2 The SOLIDAR Case: When Collective Competence and the Rules Are Weakened

The SOLIDAR team consists of 15 experienced humanitarian emergency specialists who manage projects involving urgent action to help vulnerable populations. In January 2010, this team was responding to the Haiti earthquake disaster, with two phases of intervention: in January 2010, immediately after the earthquake (phase 1) and then in October 2010, when the team was called back to address a cholera outbreak (phase 2). The team dynamic was initially created in the same way as in the GERON case, but as the case study shows, it remained fragile and crumbled in phase 2.

6.3.2.1 Phase 1 of the Haiti Emergency: Collective Competence in Action

At the beginning of the study, collective competence enabled the team to take decisions collectively in an extreme situation: an estimated 80,000 people had died, around 300,000 were injured, and up to 1.3 million people had been displaced to some 1,300 camps, while 50 hospitals and health centers were unusable. As the head of the emergency desk explained:

> We ask the teams to put forward problems, reflections, solutions, their preferred solution. It's the team's responsibility. And it's easier: in 90% of cases, we agree, but this means we can see whether the subject has been given due consideration.

Collective competence played a driving role in analyzing needs and accelerating the action. The team thus worked together to send out two initial surgery teams and several charter planes full of medical equipment and medicines and set up dispensaries in five days.

In practice, all the dimensions of collective competence were in place. First, all the team members shared the vocabulary of emergency action. They knew that every hour matters when lives are to be saved. They were very experienced, and all shared the same representation of the principle of humanitarian action, which came to form the basis of a shared set of rules to respond to the situation: "We're all one team, everyone's singing from the same hymn sheet" (program leader). Next, comparison of representations was facilitated by personal interactions (in the open-plan office, at ad hoc meetings, etc.), the actors' experience, and using their network of contacts:

> Communication is essential, it means you can act fast, monitor things. The [emergency team] is what makes contacts systematic. They want to be informed as soon as possible about anything concerning the department's response (...) Once we have the info, things move very fast.

> **(a logistics officer)**

Finally, decisions inside the team were made collectively, although if there was any doubt, the final decision was made by the people working in the stricken area: "We analyze together, we take corrective measures together, and we take responsibility together" (program leader).

6.3.2.2 Phase 2 of the Haiti Emergency: The Collective Competence Weakens

In early October, when the situation seemed to be growing more stable and the emergency team had handed over to specialist humanitarian development teams,

Haiti was hit by an almost unprecedented epidemic of cholera. The management of SOLIDAR's NGO decided to call in the emergency team again. At this point, medical supplies had almost run out and all the NGOs working in Haiti were in difficulty as the cholera spread extremely quickly. The SOLIDAR team could no longer work collectively to cope with the exponential rise in the number of patients:

> In Haiti I felt extremely alone. We were working like crazy but nothing was getting done (…) We got no support, even though the teams were doing everything they could in Haiti.
>
> **(an emergency worker)**

This translated into a deterioration of the collective competence. Although everyone's main aim was to save lives, there were several different representations of the cholera emergency: while the coordinators on site in Haiti needed enormous amounts of resources to cope with the massive influx of patients, the team members at the head office were faced with the question of the limits to the team's intervention capacity (it had the biggest budget ever allocated in the NGO's history, at a time when there were four other emergencies requiring attention). The comparison of representations thus hit a block, despite daily emails:

> It's the end of internal communication, there's a general fog and everyone's redefining their own role (…) Out here, we don't know who can help us any more. The communication channels are unclear.
>
> **(program leader)**

In the end, decisions were no longer collective: the team members in Haiti sometimes made decisions that went against the recommendations from the program leaders at the head office, so they could treat the patients flooding in:

> When there was a disagreement between the head office and the on-site team, the team found a way of getting what they wanted.
>
> **(program leader)**

6.3.2.3 The Dynamic Runs Out of Steam: Why?

Definition of simple metarules plays a major role for action in emergencies, which by nature are always new situations. The social aim (e.g., the rule of non-discrimination between patients), the principle of communication, safety and security, internal rules, and guidelines (strategic priorities, budget limit, and resources available) constitute a basic set of rules that is adapted in the project team for each individual mission. Given the extreme conditions of emergency intervention, these rules can also be modulated or even broken when necessary, according to the priorities on each mission, thanks to the extensive autonomy and experience of the teams mobilized:

> In this place, the teams have a lot of autonomy, a lot of NGOs have more rules. Whatever's structured is structured in response to demand from the emergency site. We're here to help the on-site workers.
>
> **(member of the management committee)**

Initially, this adaptation of the metarules for intervention in Haiti took place at a crisis committee meeting held the day after the earthquake:

> We met from 8 to 9.30 in the morning using the fast-track process. The principle is, we say "yes, we'll take the risk of intervention for at least x months and at least x amount of money, for such and such a type of work." Then we consider who we're going to send, and with what equipment. We also check that it's a matter for the emergency desk. We make fast decisions about major points of strategy, involving dialogue.
>
> **(team manager)**

But in October 2010 in phase 2, three emergency doctors in key posts (team manager, general on-site coordinator, and program leader) left the NGO, and this affected the fast-track process. The generic rules that made it possible for the emergency team to operate autonomously were no longer in operation.

The initial team design rules also disintegrated. Until this point, the team had been clearly defined and stable, with boundaries set for its authority (team members in Haiti could act autonomously, with the support of members in the head office). The structure was facilitating (job descriptions, well-defined roles, and expected behaviors). But the roles became vague in the autumn of 2010:

> It was all very foggy regarding who does what – and who's responsible
>
> **(team member at the head office)**

The objectives were no longer clear: the team was being required to respond to an emergency that needed enormous resources just as the budget for Haiti 2010 – the biggest budget in the NGO's entire history – was being finalized. This situation had major consequences: the team had considered itself effective after the earthquake, but now it was under intense stress and an excessive workload (three members declared they were suffering from burnout).

6.3.3 The Dynamics between Rules and Collective Competence

These two illustrations show the extent to which team rules and collective competence are related through specific dynamics that are always fragile.

6.3.3.1 Links between Rules and Collective Competence

In the two cases studied, rules and competence are closely linked (see Table 6.1). The GERON team follows the rules of hospital organizations (equality of patient treatment, continuity of care, etc.) and the rules of the team members' professions. These metarules enabled the team to develop a shared language and set of rules. Comparison of representations was reinforced when the new doctor arrived, as he adapted the interaction rules at team level and introduced handover summaries. Finally, identification of each healthcare professional's responsibilities at team level, and establishing rules about who has the final decision, encouraged development of collective decision-making. All of these team design rules are resources that team members can use if required by the situation, and they facilitate development of collective competence.

In the SOLIDAR team, every member knew the guidelines for emergency intervention (social mission, equal treatment, etc.) from experience. These metarules, which were laid down at the beginning of the mission, guided the construction of the team design, since everyone shared the same representation of the objectives. Also, the NGO's principle of communication, combined with the team's adaptation of interaction rules (e.g., the frequency of emails), made it easy for team members to compare their representations. Finally, clear boundaries to the team's autonomy, and the rules for collective decision-making, enabled the team to make collective decisions fast.

Consequently, in both cases the rules are directly linked to the various dimensions of collective competence. Through an analysis of the links between rules and collective competence over time, it is possible to describe their dynamics.

6.3.3.2 Specific Dynamics between Collective Competence and Rules

Analysis of our two cases over a period of time shows the specific dynamics between collective competences and rules. The GERON case reveals a dynamic that operates at the level of design rules and collective competence, while the metarules remain unchanged. The metarules that set the general framework for hospital organizations shape the GERON team's collective competence, but they do not evolve and the professionals in the team can only follow them or break them. The team's design rules and collective competence, however, evolve jointly and mutually reinforce each other. The newly introduced practice of handover meetings was adjusted as the team gained experience. For example, new team members were invited to take part: "now, we try to get the occupational therapist to participate in the handovers, even though she can't always come, we still try to have her information about the patients" (nurse). In this case, the design rules shaped the collective competence to provide tailored treatment for each patient, which itself reinforced and recreated these design rules.

Table 6.1   Links between Collective Competence and Rules

		Metarules	*Design rules*
Common language and set of rules	GERON	Guiding principles for medical treatment (equality of treatment and continuity of care) and the scope of responsibility of the different professionals involved in the treatment	Meaning of treatment for this team (treating by medical acts and through talking) Roles of the professionals in the team and the collective mode of operation
	SOLIDAR	Guiding principles for emergency action (resource limits, social mission, and equality of treatment)	Autonomous adaptation of the objective and available resources for the Haiti emergency
Comparison of representations	GERON	Rule of communication and interdependence	Organization of collective interactions in relation to the individualized treatment of the patient
	SOLIDAR	Generic rule of communication in the whole NGO	Adaptation of interaction modes for each emergency event (frequency of emails, meetings, etc.)
Collective decision-making	GERON	Clear rules for final decisions (the doctor's decision has priority)	Each healthcare professional's responsibility is identified
	SOLIDAR	Clear rules for final decisions (priority for the local population's interests, "fast-track" project planning)	Collective responsibility and adaptation of decision-making modes to each mission

In the SOLIDAR case, metarules, design rules, and collective competence evolve in conjunction over time. The metarules lay down the guiding principles for interventions, while the design rules adapt the team's objective on site, using a local interpretation: "We only concentrate on what's useful on site, so we can't be too inflexible. If a rule doesn't apply, we can get rid of it, that's decided in the management committee" (member of management). The weakening of the collective competence in phase 2 also reflects this dynamic. A disintegration of the metarules triggered a joint dynamic of disintegration of the design rules and weakening of the collective competence. The lack of clear objectives and clear roles then generated different sets of rules (What are the priorities?) and made comparison of representations and collective decision-making difficult (Who does what? What are the resources? Who has the final say?). This weakening of the collective competence then accentuated the disintegration of the metarules and design rules. In the absence of a common set of rules, the distribution of roles was redefined as and when necessary: for example, a program leader was able to unofficially take on the role of head of the emergency desk, and a coordinator occupied several key posts in Haiti.

6.4 Conclusion

This chapter has shown that studying the dynamic between collective competence and rules is a relevant angle for better understanding how teams work and increasing their chances of success (Boreham, 2011; Ruuska and Teigland, 2009). In practice, this dynamic between collective competence and rules is initiated once a system of design rules and metarules, which are interpretable and adaptable according to the context, and nourishes and are nourished by collective competence. This raises the question of consistency and contradictions between these rules: design rules are largely an adaptation of metarules, but due to team contingencies, the metarules may be temporarily changed or given priority if necessary. In the cases studied, despite their differences, defining clear, shared guiding principles, introducing an enabling structure, and having a clear distribution of roles played a decisive part, but that was not enough in itself, and the dynamic remains specific and permanently fragile (Krohmer and Bretesché, 2013). Importantly, our cases raise the issue of plasticity (the SOLIDAR case) versus inflexibility (GERON) in rules that ultimately turn out not to be a decisive factor in the development of collective competence. This understanding of the dynamic between collective competence and the work framework, here the team rules, extends reflection beyond the ambiguous results reported in the current literature (e.g., Salas et al., 2018). What if effective teamwork is more than an intervention science and is necessarily associated with sensitive team management and genuine commitment by the highest levels of organizations to more socially responsible management?

References

Arnaud, N. (2008). Construction et management des compétences collectives dans le cadre des relations inter-organisationnelles: une approche communicationnelle. *Finance Contrôle Stratégie*, *11*(1), 9–39.

Bataille-Chédotel, F. (2001). Compétence collective et performance. *Revue de Gestion des Ressources Humaines*, *40*, 66–81.

Boreham, N. (2004). A theory of collective competence: Challenging the neo-liberal individualisation of performance at work. *British Journal of Educational Studies*, *52*(1), 5–17.

Boreham, N. (2011). Competence as collective process. In Catts, R., Falk, I., & Wallace, R. (Eds.), *Vocational Learning* (pp. 77–91). Dordrecht, Netherlands: Springer.

Boyatzis, R. E. (1982). The Competent Manager: A Model for Effective Performance. New York, NY: John Wiley & Sons.

Brown, S. L., & Eisenhardt, K. M. (1998). *Competing on the edge: Strategy as structured chaos*. Cambridge, MA: Harvard Business School Press.

Brulhart, F., Favoreu, C., & Loufrani-Fedida, S. (2019). L'influence de la compétence collective sur la performance d'équipe : analyse du rôle modérateur du leadership partagé et du coaching. *Management International*, *23*(4), 149–164.

Cannon-Bowers, J. A., Salas, E., & Converse, S. (1993). Shared mental models in expert team decision making. In Castellan, N. J. (Ed.), *Current Issues In Individual and Group Decision Making* (pp. 221–246). Hillsdale, MI: Taylor & Francis.

Chédotel, F. (2012). Comment intervenir en temps réel à l'autre bout du monde? *Revue Française de Gestion*, *7*, 151–163.

Chédotel, F., & Krohmer, C. (2014). Les règles, leviers de développement d'une compétence collective–deux études de cas. *@GRH*, *12*(3), 15–38.

Chédotel, F., & Pujol, L. (2012). L'influence de l'identité sur la compétence collective lors de prises de décision stratégique. *Finance Contrôle Stratégie*, *15*(1), 87–107.

Eisenhardt, K. M. (1989). Building theories from case study research. *Academy of Management Review*, *14*, 532–550.

Ellis, A. P., Bell, B. S., Ployhart, R. E., Hollenbeck, J. R., & Ilgen, D. R. (2005). An evaluation of generic teamwork skills training with action teams: Effects on cognitive and skill-based outcomes. *Personnel Psychology*, *58*(3), 641–672.

Fauré, B., & Rouleau, L. (2011). The strategic competence of accountants and middle managers in budget making. *Accounting, Organizations and Society*, *36*(3), 167–182.

Feldman, M. S., & Orlikowski, W. J. (2011). Theorizing practice and practicing theory. *Organization Science*, *22*(5), 1240–1253.

Hackman, J. R. (1987). The design of work teams. In Lorsch, J. W. (Ed.), *Handbook of Organizational Behaviour*. Englewood Cliffs, NJ: Prentice Hall.

Hager, P., & Johnsson, M. C. (2009). Working outside the comfort of competence in a corrections centre: Toward collective competence. *Human Resource Development International*, *12*(5), 493–509.

Håland, E., & Tjora, A. (2006). Between asset and process: Developing competence by implementing a learning management system. *Human Relations*, *59*, 993–1016.

Hass, M., & Mortensen, M. (2016). The secrets of great teamwork. *Harvard Business Review*, *94*, 70–76.

Havard, C., & Krohmer, C. (2008). Création et articulation des règles dans le cadre d'un management des compétences. *Revue de Gestion des Ressources Humaines*, *70*, 88–101.

Jolivet, F., & Navarre, C. (1996). Large-scale projects, self-organizing and meta-rules: Towards new forms of management. *International Journal of Project Management*, 14(5), 265–271.

Kitto, S., Marshall, S. D., McMillan, S. E., Shearer, B., Buist, M., Grant, R., . . . & Wilson, S. (2015). Rapid response systems and collective (in) competence: An exploratory analysis of intraprofessional and interprofessional activation factors. *Journal of Interprofessional Care*, 29(4), 340–346.

Klarner, P., Sarstedt, M., Hoeck, M., & Ringle, C. M. (2013). Disentangling the effects of team competences, team adaptability, and client communication on the performance of management consulting teams. *Long Range Planning*, 46(3), 258–286.

Krohmer, C., & Bretesché, S. (2013). Fragilités et modes de régulation des figures de la compétence. *Finance, Contrôle, Stratégie*, 16(2), https://journals.openedition.org/fcs/1362.

Lacerenza, C. N., Marlow, S. L., Tannenbaum, S. I., & Salas, E. (2018). Team development interventions: Evidence-based approaches for improving teamwork. *American Psychologist*, 73(4), 517.

Le Bris, S., Madrid-Guijarro, A., & Martin, D. P. (2019). Decision-making in complex environments under time pressure and risk of critical irreversibility: The role of meta rules. *M@n@gement*, 22(1), 1–29.

Lindberg, O., & Rantatalo, O. (2014). Competence in professional practice: A practice theory analysis of police and doctors. *Human Relations*, 68, 561–582.

Lingard, L. (2012). Rethinking competence in the context of teamwork. In Hodges, B. & Lingard, L. (Eds.), *The Question of Competence: Reconsidering Medical Education in the Twenty-First Century* (pp. 42–69). Ithaca, NY: Cornell University Press.

Mathieu, J, Heffner, T, Goodwin, G, Cannon-Bowers, J., & Salas, E. (2005). Scaling the quality of teammates' mental models: Equifinality and normative comparisons. *Journal of Organizational Behavior*, 26(1), 37–56.

Oiry, E. (2011). Usages imprévus et dynamique des instruments de gestion. Réflexions à partir du cas d'un instrument de gestion des compétences. *Management International*, 15(2), 11–22.

Pantin, F. (2006). L'internationalisation: un défi pour les compétences de l'équipe dirigeante? *Gestion*, 31(1), 77–87.

Pinto, M. B., Pinto, J. K., & Prescott, J. E. (1993). Antecedents and consequences of project team cross-functional cooperation. *Management Science*, 39(10), 1281–1297.

Ragaigne, A., Oiry, E., & Grimand, A. (2014). Contraindre et habiliter: la double dimension des outils de contrôle. *Comptabilité-Contrôle-Audit*, 20(2), 9–37.

Retour, D., & Krohmer, C. (2006). La compétence collective, maillon clé de la gestion des compétences. In Defélix, C., Klarsfeld, A., & Oiry, E. (Eds.), *Nouveaux regards sur la gestion des compétences*. Paris, France: Vuibert, 149–183.

Retour, D., Picq, T., & Defélix, C. (2009). *Gestion des compétences: Nouvelles relations, nouvelles dimensions*. Paris, France: Vuibert.

Ruuska, I., & Teigland, R. (2009). Ensuring project success through collective competence and creative conflict in public–private partnerships: A case study of Bygga Villa, a Swedish triple helix e-government initiative. *International Journal of Project Management*, 27(4), 323–334.

Salas, E., Reyes, D. L., & McDaniel, S. H. (2018). The science of teamwork: Progress, reflections, and the road ahead. *American Psychologist*, 73(4), 593.

Salas, E., Rosen, M. A., Burke, C. S., & Goodwin, G. F. (2009). The wisdom of collectives in organizations: An update of the teamwork competencies. In Salas, E., Goodwin, G. F., & Burke, C. S. (Eds.), *Team Effectiveness in Complex Organizations: Cross-disciplinary Perspectives and Approaches* (pp. 39–79). New York, NY: Routledge.

Salas, E., Shuffler, M. L., Thayer, A. L., Bedwell, W. L., & Lazzara, E. H. (2015). Understanding and improving teamwork in organizations: A scientifically based practical guide. *Human Resource Management, 54*(4), 599–622.

Sandberg, J., & Pinnington, A. H. (2009). Professional competence as ways of being: An existential ontological perspective. *Journal of Management Studies, 46*, 1138–1170.

Shuffler, M. L., DiazGranados, D., & Salas, E. (2011). There's a science for that: Team development interventions in organizations. *Current Directions in Psychological Science, 20*(6), 365–372.

Shuffler, M. L., Diazgranados, D., Maynard, M. T., & Salas, E. (2018). Developing, sustaining, and maximizing team effectiveness: An integrative, dynamic perspective of team development interventions. *Academy of Management Annals, 12*(2), 688–724.

Spencer, L. M., & Spencer, P. S. M. (2008). *Competence at Work Models for Superior Performance*. New York, NY: John Wiley & Sons.

Tatikonda, M. V., & Rosenthal, S. R. (2000). Successful execution of product development projects: Balancing firmness and flexibility in the innovation process. *Journal of Operations Management, 18*(4), 401–425.

Wageman, R., Hackman, J. R., & Lehman, E. (2005). Team diagnostic survey: Development of an instrument. *The Journal of Applied Behavioral Science, 41*(4), 373–398.

Weick, K. E. (1995). *Sensemaking in Organizations*. Beverly Hills, CA: Sage.

Chapter 7

The Development of Collective Competence within an Inter-Organizational Group: A Proximity Perspective

Sihem Mammar El Hadj

Contents

7.1 Introduction

This chapter examines the development of collective competence within an inter-organizational group (IOG) in terms of proximity. Organizations enter into a variety of inter-organizational relations in order to cope with the changing environment in which they evolve and conduct their projects (Ring and Van de Ven, 1994). We define an inter-organizational relation as a formal or an informal (Ring and Van de Ven, 1994) connection (Tsasis, 2009) between organizations in order to achieve collective goals (Selden et al., 2006), but whereas some collaborations succeed remarkably, others fail to drive any collective action (Lawrence et al., 2002). Researchers and practitioners are therefore interested in means that might help inter-organizational groups to generate successful collective actions (Hardy et al., 2005).

Inter-organizational relations are reliant on the ability of their different members to pool their competences (Defélix and Picq, 2013); the major challenge is to develop a collective competence despite differences. We investigated this collective competence by selecting a level of analysis (inter-organizational groups) that is less widely studied and one concept: collective competence focusing on the collective work of individuals who are members of the inter-organizational group. It suggests that collective competence is developed as group members work together in the course of a joint action and create a set of inter-subjective meanings expressed in and through their artifacts (Ruuska and Teigland, 2009).

Such groups are particularly diverse, since an inter-organizational project group is composed of actors from different organizations. Inter-organization groups (IOGs) are defined as being "composed of members, representing parent organizations and community constituencies, who meet periodically to make decisions relevant to their common concerns, and whose behavior is regulated by a common set of expectations" (Schopler, 1987). That is, each person represents their home organization and its interests which may be divergent at times.

They often do not speak the same organizational language and sometimes do not have the same interpretation of the project objectives. However, they have to work together and build a collective competence in order to fulfill the inter-organizational objectives. This is why it may be difficult to develop a collective competence in inter-organizational relations over time: the group members need to overcome their differences, in order to pool their competence (Mammar el Hadj et al., 2015).

To understand the particularities of these groups better, we will use the concept of proximity. The literature on inter-organizational groups has mainly addressed the issue of the motivation behind the emergence of networks and placed emphasis on the notions of geographical distance or colocalization in a given territory. The notion of proximity seems to be an important point in an IOG, and it is for that reason that we are interested in the concept of proximity and the role it may have in IOGs and the development of a collective competence. We have therefore chosen to look into the concept of proximity in all its facets, over and above geographical proximity, for a better understanding of the dynamics at play within these IOGs. In addition to the motivations, we are seeking above all to understand the dynamics of the interpersonal relations in IOGs, which seem to us to be a largely underestimated factor in success or failure. Our research question is therefore: *How do the different forms of proximity influence the emergence of collective competence within inter-organizational groups?*

We conducted a longitudinal case study in the French cultural sector. This research has theoretical and practical aims. Theoretically, by highlighting the micro-processes in IOGs over time, it shows that the emergence of a collective competence requires interactions and proximity. It helps us understand how members of an inter-organizational group can develop a collective competence, leading to greater chances of success on the project.

First, we will introduce our theoretical background. Then we will introduce our field study and methodology. Finally, we will present our main results and discuss them.

7.2 Theoretical Background: Proximity's Impact on the Development of Collective Competence

7.2.1 Inter-Organizational Groups: Collective Competence Matters

Many studies of inter-organizational relations have focused on collaboration as a process of organizing relations in an inter-organizational context. Research has covered a wide range of collaborations and addressed different aspects that can favor inter-organizational collaborations, such as how to manage the collaboration or how to nurture collaborative relations (Vangen and Huxham, 2003), focused either on the individual or on the organizational level. Collaboration is also considered as an endpoint in most research (Bedwell et al., 2012) and is often described as an outcome at the organizational level.

While there are numerous studies of inter-organizational collaborations, few have analyzed the internal micro-processes of these collaborations within the group (Bedwell et al., 2012). We therefore propose to focus on the cornerstone of these collaborations that the IOGs face to achieve collective outcomes. To achieve a better understanding of how groups achieve success in projects, researchers make use of different concepts, such as collective competence (Ruuska and Teigland, 2009), team performance (Mathieu et al., 2008), and collective efficacy (Fernandez-Ballesteros et al., 2002). Collective competence has been defined as a collective ability of the inter-organizational project group to work together toward a common goal and its capacity to handle a situation that could not be managed by one member alone on account of its complexity (Defélix and Picq, 2013; Ruuska and Teigland, 2009).

Collective competence is a result of two concepts: the collective and work (Amherdt et al., 2000). The concept emerged in management science at the end of the 1990s, especially in the French-language literature, in answer to uncertainties raised by the development of dispersed, virtual, and asynchrone work groups and continuous change within organizations (Defélix et al., 2014). Collective competence is considered today as an organizational asset that is more than the sum of individual competences within the organization. Collective competence is drawn from individual resources and their interactions (Retour and Krohmer, 2006).

We refer to the work of Retour and Krohmer (2006) and consider that the attributes of collective competence are the following. *The common framework* emerges from the confrontation of representations and is built by pooling the competence of each member. It is the reference model that helps members agree on how to work in order to achieve the group's goals. *The common operative language* is a dialect that is specific to the team and helps it communicate, read between the lines, and save time by not having to explain or make comment. Then, there is *collective memory* that is composed of *collective, non-centralized, declarative memory*, based on acquisition of knowledge between members and the creation of new knowledge through interaction; *collective, non-centralized, procedural memory* is the result of the confrontation of knowledge and know-how between two or more individuals during joint work that is useful to accomplish the task. Finally, *collective judgment memory* is composed of knowledge emerging from the confrontation of individual judgment memories. Hence, when faced with a complex problem, the members confront their individual understandings of the situation through discussion, in order to come to a common understanding. The last component is *subjective commitment*. It is a cooperative process of problem resolution that helps the group make decisions, choices, or initiatives for which they are responsible.

In this chapter, we consider that the IOG is an entity that is constantly moving in regard to its purpose. This movement continuously requires a combination of resources and competences. We have adopted an interactionist approach to collective competence because we consider collective competence not to be a state, but a process that builds up and/or disaggregates over time. Many authors, such as Arnaud (2011), have insisted on the importance of interactions in the build up of collective competence. It is a concept that draws on interactions and linguistic activities. Our approach is based on a definition of competence which is by nature situated and evolving.

It is collective competence as a process that interests us at different stages of the evolution of the inter-organizational group: we study the inter-organizational group as it makes its way forward, establishing its norms and rules collectively and progressively. Hence we propose to study: *How the concept of proximity can shed light on the development process of collective competence, within an IOG?*

7.2.2 Proximity and the Development of Collective Competence within an IOG: Proximity at the Heart of Inter-Organizational Relations

IOG cooperation is a matter of proximity. The concept of proximity has been used in different fields in relation to other concepts: innovation, economic and regional development, and inter-organizational relations (Knoben and Oerlemans, 2006). It has been studied widely in the field of economic geography (Boschma, 2005). In this study, we will build on the five proximities operationalized by Boschma (2005): geographical proximity, institutional proximity (Kirat and Lung, 1999), organized proximity (Meisters and Werker, 2004), cognitive proximity (Nooteboon, 1999), and social proximity (Bradshaw, 2001).

Table 7.1 presents the operationalization of the proximity concept (Boschma, 2005) that we employ in this chapter, highlighting the key dimensions, definitions, and mechanisms at work.

In the proximity literature, it is recognized that *geographical proximity* favors the emergence of the other proximities, even if a number of studies suggest that this proximity has less effect when other proximities are present (Balland et al., 2015). Geographical proximity may produce or enforce the other proximities (Hausmann, 1996). It strengthens informal relations (through trust building), favors the emergence and development of norms and habits, and can replace *cognitive proximity* by reducing cognitive distance. Geographical proximity is essential for collaboration when cognitive proximity is low (Singh, 2005), but the combination of the two (geographical and cognitive proximities) favors learning (Boschma, 2005). However, the other proximities can replace geographical proximity. For example, geographical proximity can be supplanted by *organizational proximity* if there is a clear division of tasks and roles and a strong coordination (Boschma, 2005).

In addition to geographical proximity, in a collective action setting, we need some institutional proximity as it helps reduce uncertainties between members. *Institutional proximity* is important to the development of other proximities.

Table 7.1 The Five Proximities of Boschma (2005)

Proximity	Key dimension	Definition	Mechanisms
Geographical	Distance	Spatial and physical distance between economic actors, both absolute and relative	Brings people together Facilitates interaction and cooperation
Institutional	Trust (based on common institutions)	Socially embedded relations between agents at the macrolevel Common habits, routines, established practices, rules, and laws that regulate relations between individuals and groups	Glue for collective action Formal institutions: laws and rules Informal institutions: cultural norms and habits Common language, shared habits, and law system
Social	Trust (based on social relations)	Socially embedded relations between agents at a microlevel	Trust based on friendship, kinship, and experience Commitment
Cognitive	Knowledge gap	The similarities in the way actors perceive, interpret, understand, and evaluate the world	People sharing the same knowledge base and expertise may learn from each other Sharing the same perception of how to act Share goals and objectives, a common understanding
Organizational	Control	The extent to which relations are shared in an organizational arrangement, either within or between organizations. In regard to autonomy and control	A combination of interdepences between actors of different forms. Similarity: inter-organizational Membership: intra-organizational

However, *social proximity* can compensate to some extent for the absence of institutional proximity through trust. Geographical proximity favors social proximity by fostering social interactions and trust building. It can reduce cognitive distance between members in time. However, it can be supplanted by organizational proximity in certain conditions. Organizational and social proximities create strong ties between members, but rely on different mechanisms: the former on hierarchy and the latter on trust. Cognitive proximity favors interactions and communications between actors.

It is important to note that optimal proximity is a recurrent theme in proximity literature. Many studies have demonstrated that an excess of certain proximities can lock the group and hinder its development (Balland et al., 2015). In this chapter, we are not looking for the optimal distance, but for the combination of proximities that could help the group reach a collective competence at a given time.

Balland et al. (2015) shed new light on the dynamics of proximities within an inter-organizational context and put forward four types of proximities that are important to learning and innovation. They also consider that proximity can increase over time thanks to interactions between actors. They stress the dynamic nature of proximities that can change depending on the situation of the members of the IOG. This is why proximity must be studied as a dynamic process.

We will focus on understanding the development of collective competence in regard to this operationalization of proximity.

We introduced the concept of collective competence and the concept of proximity; in the following section, we propose to build on a case study within the French cultural sector in order to explore how these two concepts can combine. More specifically, we will investigate the way the four components of collective competence (common framework, common operative language, collective memory, and subjective commitment) may be influenced by the four types of proximity (geographical, institutional, social, cognitive, and organizational)

7.3 Methodology and Case Study Presentation

7.3.1 Methodology: Case Study

Our research is focused on micro-processes within inter-organizational groups, which is why we adopted intensive research (Tsoukas, 1989; Yin, 2015). We conducted an in-depth explanatory case study (Yin, 2015) and selected a successful case study in the region of Brittany, a collective of festivals between 27 festival organizers.

Our study is based on individual interviews, observations, and analysis of archives (Eisenhardt, 1989; Yin, 2015). We collected all the available data from the websites of the collective and government, and later the actors provided us with internal documents that helped us to understand the story better and complete the missing data. We summarized them and coded the transcriptions of some meetings and of our interviews (Miles et al., 2014).

We conducted the interviews in two phases. We carried out eight interviews from October 2014 to March 2015 with different members and four interviews with local authorities. The second phase took place between March and August 2016, with eight follow-up interviews with the same cultural actors and four interviews with local authorities. This represented about 18 hours of interviews and two non-participant observations. To analyze the data, we transcribed and coded our data using NVivo software, with a set of predefined codes derived from the literature. New codes also emerged during our data analysis (Miles et al., 2014). The data analysis method was based on the method of Miles et al., 2014, which consists in presenting the contents of the interviews, observations, and documents in a synthetic way.

Our interviewees were either volunteers or employees of the associations. They were all involved in this project, some since the beginning and others as new members.

7.3.2 Presentation of the Case Study: The "Collective for Sustainable Development"

The collective of festivals was created in 2005 and is now an association grouping together 27 festivals in the region of Brittany, all committed to sustainable development. The association committee is composed of five members from different festivals, a director, a communications officer, a coaching officer who helps the festivals, and an officer responsible for cultural events.

The 27 festivals were members at the time of the survey. Each had signed a charter and is thus committed to defining an action plan for sustainable development in relation to its own cultural project. This approach relies on joint work with an exchange of experience, knowledge, and information. The members discuss and debate common issues in order to find suitable solutions for each festival. The three main missions are to support the members in the implementation of the charter, investigation and experimentation with new actions, and the transmission of information and resources. We propose Table 7.2 to introduce the case study.

7.4 Proximity and Collective Competence Intertwined

7.4.1 Results Presentation

In this section, we analyzed simultaneously proximity and collective competence evolution through the different phases of the "Collective." We observed and

Table 7.2   Presentation of The Collective for Sustainable Development

Operating mode?	Different inter-organizational groups (IOGs) implemented in order to work on different subjects A group of employees coordinates the collective action of the different IOGs The collective was initiated by two important stakeholders in the sector	
Members	Festivals in the region of Brittany, 27 associations and a company	
Main mission	Respecting sustainable development rules during the organization of festivals in Brittany	
Key phases	Phase 1	2005: the beginning
	Phase 2	2007: signing of the "common values" charter
	Phase 3	2009: the establishment of the "collective for sustainable development" association between the festivals
	Phase 4	2014: signing of the fourth version of the charter
Existence	11 years	

analyzed the formation of different proximities and how they evolved during the lifetime of the group and its influence on the development of collective competence. Table 7.3 sums up the results.

First of all, we analyzed how proximity evolved and its impact on collective competence and then their interaction and the relationship with the results. For each phase, we analyzed the attributes of collective competence: common framework, common language, collective memory, and subjective commitment. We will present the process within each phase and then a global overview. We present a summary of the results in a table in order to show which proximity and attributes of collective competence were involved in each phase, and then we will explain each phase.

We divided the lifespan of the IOG into phases. During each phase, the group made an important step forward that then enabled the group to move on to the next phase. Then we will explain how the interactions between the proximities and the components of collective competence favored the attainment of the goal for each phase (see Table 7.3).

Table 7.3 Summary of the Results

Phase	Proximity	Collective competence	Example
Beginning	Geographical and institutional due to their belonging to the same sector (third sector economy) and the colocalization of actors Social proximity between the founding members	At the end of this phase, we observed the beginning of linguistic consistency	During this phase, the actors started working on a lexicon of common practices
Signing the charter	During this phase the actors benefited from social and cognitive proximities	During this phase, the actors formalized the common framework and collective memory	Members created a "common values" charter that united them
Founding of the association	During this phase, we observed a dynamic produced by social and organized proximities that became stronger	During this phase, we observed the affirmation of the role of declarative memory, during the interactions between members, favoring the collective decision process and the development of subjective commitment	The members created an association between them and decided on its main missions, procedures, and operating style
The new charter until today	On a daily basis, the social and cognitive proximities helped the members function collectively For new members, it is organized proximity that is at work	We observed a collective competence within each project	The members developed cultural and non-cultural projects collectively They established a platform for material loans

7.4.1.1 Getting Together

At this stage, geographical proximity was the cornerstone. The IOG is composed of actors located within the same region where there is a strong history of cooperation:

> It includes different festivals that are not alike. Brittany has a strong identity that brings us together and sustainable development too. We feel like a group. There are a variety of associations, but what brings us together is being Bretons, making music and our willingness to promote the image of Brittany.
>
> **(R4)***

Two main actors in the region launched this initiative as they believed they had similar issues with similar solutions:

> During a meeting in Brest in February, I met a director and during our discussion we noticed that in spite of our differences, there were a number of topics, issues that were similar.
>
> **(R9)**

Starting from there, the two directors of these two large regional associations decided to set up a network between them in order to address common issues centered on sustainable development. Both wanted to preserve the environment during their festivals. Later, they asked four other festivals to join them and started their collective work. In 2007, they produced and signed the first charter. In 2008, they decided to formalize the organization of their network and recruited an employee to coordinate the collective action. In 2009, they decided to start an association to manage the network and open up to new members. In 2012, the members signed the fourth version of their charter. Today there are 29 festivals, and they have expanded their missions. This network was initiated by its own members and not by the local authorities, as is sometimes the case.

In addition to social proximity, the respondents considered that geographical proximity favored interactions:

> We have a privileged relationship thanks to geographical proximity that helps us meet frequently.
>
> **(R4)**

We noticed that during this phase, geographical proximity gave rise to cooperation and that social proximity helped the actors understand and see their similarities

---

* In this chapter, we refer to our interviewees as "Rn."

and common issues. It was social proximity that connected the actors at an individual level:

> At the beginning there were 6 of them, it was a small group, but they knew each other. In Brittany, the technical teams know each other and meet often. The directors of festivals also knew each other because they meet at public events and conferences. They were different but they knew each other. There was a staff member that made the connection between a number of them, and they started debating about the management of the waste produced during festivals. They knew each other, there were connections and the teams knew each other. There was a technician that worked in one festival then in another. There was a close connection from the beginning.
>
> (R1)

It also helped them feel stronger in their contacts with the public authorities of the region:

> It's a help being together, we can make ourselves heard. When we have to write a letter to the authorities, I think it has more impact than each of us sending it alone.
>
> (R2)

It is also important to cooperate during these times when public funding is scarce:

> Being alone today in the cultural sector means death.
>
> (R4)

At the beginning of this phase, the institutional proximity derived from belonging to the social economy and being festivals provided a minimum linguistic base that facilitated the collective action:

> Being a festival helps us have a common reference.
>
> (R8)

We thus observed the standardization of the common language during this phase, thanks to the development of new forms of proximity.

7.4.1.2 Signing the Charter

This phase ended with the implementation of a common charter and took two years of collective work. We observed that the IOG developed cognitive proximity thanks to social and institutional proximities. As said before, the social proximity did not concern all the members, but existed between a few members that provided a connection between all the members. Each was linked to at least one other member by social proximity. In the end, it was cognitive proximity that favored efficient communication between the members.

This social proximity originated from friendships between actors within the same sector. It played an important role during this phase, as it favored exchanges and interactions between the members of the collective:

> We work a lot, but in the evening we go out together. They form a group, they are friends. I really think that's it.
>
> **(R6)**

This favored interactions between the actors and hence cognitive proximity.
During this process, a collective non-formalized procedural memory emerged.

> The collective helped us clarify what we were doing. We were already engaged in a sustainable development process, and the collective helped us do things in a better way and understand that even our organizational project was ecological in essence.
>
> **(R5)**

At the end of this phase, and thanks to the work on language and the common framework, the cognitive proximity emerged, as well as a mutual understanding and a common vision of the collective and its main missions:

> We did different things; we created a lexicon to agree on expressions, because sometimes the job name was different from one organization to another. We needed to understand the realities hidden behind these words. We conducted an overview of what was being done concerning social and cultural activities within the festivals; we've seen huge diversity during conferences, meetings and debates.
>
> **(R1)**

It was the debate around the common language and framework that strengthened cognitive proximity:

> In the collective, the idea was to have a structure and agree on a charter of committed festivals: what does committed mean? Committed to what? What is our goal.
>
> **(R10)**

These questions helped the members perceive the existence of a basis of common knowledge and create common knowledge and communicate efficiently.

At the end of this phase, we observed that the collective judgment memory enabled them to formalize their group and its operating method:

> We agreed quickly on the rule that is now the principle of the collective, that is: we work together, we experiment and we try to resolve our problems collectively. Knowing that, as I said, the solution can be different from one festival to another but the questioning is the same and the principle of working on them together, we are therefore all equal in the face of these problems. Each of us makes his own contribution.
>
> **(R8)**

All the debates resulted in work groups within the collective to foster exchanges and collective problem resolution. These work groups were organized by themes and the actors joined the group on the theme closest to their preoccupations. The members provided the work groups and created new ones in relation to their questions and issues:

> In the work group, it is the festivals that bring their realities; the collective is above all a collective of festivals.
>
> **(R9)**

The purpose of these groups was to initiate debates in small groups and give feedback to the other members, in order to facilitate debates and decision making. At the end of this phase, the common framework was produced.

7.4.1.3 Creating the Association

During this phase, the actors decided to create an association in order to formalize the group. At the beginning, cognitive and social proximities facilitated the enterprise. We noticed that later it was the collective as an entity that favored social proximity:

> The collective encourages the associations and favors the connection between them in order to collaborate. Thanks to the collective, we participated in joint purchasing that was useful to our festival.
>
> **(R4)**

The members started this phase sharing the observation that they all had something to offer to the collective:

> The festival landscape is rich, there are festivals of different shapes and sizes but the sector is in distress, so what can we do so that we can share our knowledge together and everyone can participate in all the dynamics. We are not competitors. We have things to discuss and debate. We do discuss.
>
> **(R9)**

The first members benefited from social proximity through friendships, but the new members initially had to build this proximity through affinity:

I built relationships with certain associations by affinity.

(R6)

Later on, it was shared experience that strengthened this tie.

Discussions and interactions became the operating mode of the group and favored the resolution of organizational problems in the members' festivals:

What I appreciate the most is having the support and the other members. Also, getting together and sharing issues that the other associations are facing. Meetings are friendly and I always leave them full of energy and motivation because I see the activities of the other festivals.

(R9)

Cognitive proximity between members increased over time and favored learning and creating new shared knowledge to facilitate the resolution of common problems:

discussions, mutual respect, collective emulation, that is the heart of this association. Shared values, listening, sharing, assistance … It can produce ideas for each one of us.

(R9)

It is a learning process that goes beyond the main mission of the collective:

the catering service is always complicated during a festival so we give each other a lot of ideas and advices.

(R2)

The members value this learning process, and it strengthens their commitment to the group.

It develops a collective judgment memory that favors making collective decisions, and it is a continuous learning process:

There were things we were already doing, and we confirmed them and we tried to see how to improve others.

(R8)

This process strengthens cognitive proximity and subjective commitment. The members are involved in the collective work and the decision making process, and their commitment is real.

Social proximity and acceptance favored expanding the group and attracting new members to the collective:

> The 6 members had to work hard to master the subject and then they welcomed new members. The other festivals showed interest in 2008 and started coming to meet us. In 2009, we created the association … we went from 6 to 14.

> **(R9)**

7.4.1.4 A Competent Inter-Organizational Group

Cognitive proximity strengthened by collective memory helped the group operate:

> We are all here to work, to accommodate our audience better. In addition to the fact that people in the collective are smart, and the festivals are awesome, people are working on themes of interest to everyone, and everyone had an interest in discussing and working well. There are good relationships, because it is simply a place where it is difficult to be worked up. If tomorrow you put other festivals together and tell them not to fight about programming, there will be tensions.

> **(R10)**

This helps the members organizing the work of the group to join together. As mentioned before, the social proximity is not at the level of the group as a whole, but between members at an individual level, and that does not change over time:

> We represent a festival but we are also a person with our own interests, competences and knowledge.

> **(R9)**

The group continues to update the common framework, building on collective memory and the commitment of the members to the collective process:

> This version of the charter is from 2012; we revised it and signed it in 12/12. It is the fourth version and a version that we wanted to be more technical in its values. We wanted to make the artistic project the central focus. Festival organizers are cultural stakeholders above all, and there was a value linked to it, that of placing the people at its center.

> **(R1)**

After the formalization of the group, the adhesion of new members followed a formal selection process. New members did not benefit from social proximity but from organized proximity, through the signature of the charter and the adhesion process that favored their commitment:

> Festivals that come to us know what they are looking for, and in return we ask them to really commit, to be present and to participate. The collective holds because there is an excellent team around X and its main job is to make the festivals feel at ease within the collective in order to participate fully.
>
> **(R1)**

During this phase, it was organized proximity based on shared values that favored the commitment of new members: "Participating in a collective with an ambitious object is of interest to us. I think that is part of shared values, sustainable development is a process and each festival has its own level of progress" (R4).

To conclude this section, we can say that the collective is working today, and the fact that the members can communicate efficiently boosts its development and the commitment of its members "We have realized that we are stronger, smarter, faster and more relevant together. The collective is a tool that we created to work better on our projects" (R8).

7.4.2 Analysis

7.4.2.1 At the Beginning There Was Geographical Proximity

When we share a territory, we share a history, an identity, and a common destiny. The members of the IOG are aware of belonging to the same territory with a strong identity, in addition to having local authorities that favor cooperation. At the beginning, it was geographical proximity and belonging to the same territory that fostered the link:

> Bretons like being talked about. This collective is unique in France. We do not fight each other, we do things together, we are proud of being capable of working together because we are all Bretons.
>
> **(R9)**

Moreover, facing the same difficulties created solidarity and social proximity:

> As we are together within the collective, what we see is our complementarities and the need to work together because outside is difficult, and it creates a solidarity because we are just festivals facing problems. Either we resolve them alone by competing and it will take a lot of energy for nothing, or we decide to cooperate and tell each other your experience

interests me and mine interests you so we can do more together. We chose to cooperate, it is smarter.

(R1)

Within this territory, public policy also favors cooperation:

When I see the number of networks created at national or local level, it is unbelievable. You know, for two years the public authorities have been asking for this kind of initiatives and supporting them. Before, they were in a more individual mindset.

(R4)

7.4.2.2 Social Proximity at the Center of the IOG

The particularity of this IOG is that it is composed of individuals bound by long-term ties of friendship. We observed from the beginning that the relations were at an individual level. Actually, the first members launched the collective process on the basis of friendship and trust and admitted new members later on the same basis:

For me, the collective is a network and persons that choose each other, that get together and decide to work together. It's true that there have always been collectives in Brittany, with different lifespans and histories, but this collective is more important to us, for me it is the collective of festivals.

(R1)

7.4.2.3 Cognitive Proximity and Collective Proximity Association

As demonstrated in this work, cognitive proximity favors the development of collective competence. Before achieving cognitive proximity, social proximity helped the members to meet, discuss, and debate. It was once cognitive proximity was achieved that we observed the development of collective competence, in an evolutionary approach.

Concerning the common language, it was cognitive proximity that allowed its construction:

It was about creating a common language in that field. We made one for another thing, it was a work group on artistic creation, I think. On social and cultural action, it was really to have a common language.

(R3)

This supported the group in starting the work on the common framework.

Collective memory with cognitive proximity helped the members' process of learning but also how to work collectively

> It is true that it is not the same when we are not isolated. We have a capacity of adaptation and open-mindedness that makes the debates livelier. When we are alone, we go round in circles and get tricked by habits.
>
> **(R1)**

The learning process enriches the organizational project and the collective project as well:

> What is interesting with the collective is that it helps us take a step back and debate, it is very important because sometimes we are over-whelmed and we can call another member to discuss the matter.
>
> **(R8)**

Finally, subjective commitment helps unite the members around common projects:

> The originality is in making festivals work together and having real discussions and debates, it favors a really rewarding collective dynamic.
>
> **(R10)**

This dynamic is valued by the members and favors commitment that is essential to the success of the group:

> We are lucky, the festivals participate, we can say it is a collective success: the participation of its members.
>
> **(R8)**

We notice that collective competence enforces cognitive and social proximity through its process:

> What is really interesting is that we are in a space where we can debate. We do not put on exactly the same festival, we all have our constraints, our contexts, but it enriches our viewpoints, helps us find new ideas and even go further.
>
> **(R8)**

Table 7.4 Synthesis of the Analysis

Collective competence ⇒ Proximity ⇓	Common framework	Operative common language	Collective memory	Subjective commitment
Geographical				Common territorial history
Institutional		Jargon of the business line and sustainable development vocabulary		
Social	Friendship and affinity ties favor interpersonal trust and interactions	Frequent debate and discussion on lexicon and common operational language	Mutual trust and common past experiences strengthen collective memory	Strong interpersonal relations favor collective decision making
Cognitive	A shared common vision and framework of the main purpose	Better understanding between members and efficient communication favored the creation of a common language	Collective learning and the creation of new common knowledge Better problem resolution capacities	Value to the common favors commitment
Organizational				Shared values favor commitment to the collective project

It is through the work on themes that common language is produced and in turn enforces cognitive proximity:

> For example, in our work on "social utility," it is clear that work was done in order to understand our own social utility and define and put words behind it and then commit to it together. It was an unknown notion for us all. The festivals that were in the work group did a good job and it was really a collective learning process.

(R1)

In Table 7.4, we present a synthesis of how the four components of collective competence (common framework, common operative language, collective memory, and subjective commitment) are influenced by the four types of proximities (geographical, institutional, social, cognitive, and organizational).

7.5 Conclusion

The main objective of this chapter is to understand the role of proximity in the development of collective competences within an IOG. Drawing on the work of Boschma (2005) on proximity and Retour and Krohmer (2006) on collective competence, we proposed an analysis grid that helped us observe interactions between the different proximities and attributes of collective competence.

We concluded that geographical proximity is essential to cooperation, but not sufficient. In fact, we observed that within inter-organizational groups, the different forms of proximity played a fundamental role at different moments in the group's life. Inter-organizational cooperation needs different proximities, and we observed that social proximity was the cornerstone of this kind of relations. Social proximity feeds on interpersonal relations that establish trust and foster collective action. Cognitive proximity is essential to communication between members coming from different organizations, as it helps to reach mutual comprehension and a shared vision. Proximities are also dynamic, and we observed that they changed over time to become stronger, in our case. The dynamic characteristic has an impact on the development of collective competence.

Some attributes of collective competence can also strengthen proximity. We observed that the collective framework and collective memory could enforce cognitive proximity and that subjective commitment could strengthen social proximity.

To conclude, we consider that within inter-organization groups, it is important to identify the type of proximity at play at a key moment of the group's life and manage it. In other words, managing proximity is more than just reducing the geographical distance, it is a matter of reducing other distances, such as social and cognitive ones.

References

Arnaud, N. (2011). L'ouverture du stock de connaissances de la compétence collective. Etude d'une conversation. *Finance Contrôle Stratégie, 14*(2), 101–135.

Amherdt, C. H., Dupuich-Rabsse, F., Emery, Y., Giauque, D. (2000). *Compétences collectives dans les organisations: émergence, gestion et développement*. Quebec City, Canada: Les Presses de l'Université Laval.

Bedwell, W. L., Wildman, J. L., DiazGranados, D., Salazar, M., Kramer, W. S., & Salas, E. (2012). Collaboration at work: An integrative multilevel conceptualization. *Human Resource Management Review, 22*(2), 128–145.

Balland, P. A., Boschma, R., & Frenken, K. (2015). Proximity and innovation: From statics to dynamics. *Regional Studies, 49*(6), 907–920.

Boschma, R. (2005). Proximity and innovation: A critical assessment. *Regional Studies, 39*(1), 61–74.

Bradshaw, M. (2001). Multiple proximities: Culture and geography in the transport logistics of newsprint manufactured in Australia. *Environment and Planning A, 33*(10), 1717–1739.

Défélix, C., Le Boulaire, M., Monties, V., & Picq, T. (2014). La compétence collective dans le contexte de la globalisation du management: retrouver le lien avec la performance. *@GRH, 11*(2), 31–50.

Défélix, C., & Picq, T. (2013). De l'entreprise étendue à la «gestion des compétences étendue»: enjeux et pratiques en pôles de compétitivité. *@GRH, 7*(2), 41–66.

Eisenhardt, K. (1989). Building theories from case study research. *Academy of Management Review, 14*(4), 532–550.

Fernández-Ballesteros, R., Díez-Nicolás, J., Caprara, G. V., Barbaranelli, C., & Bandura, A. (2002). Determinants and structural relation of personal efficacy to collective efficacy. *Applied Psychology, 51*(1), 107–125.

Hardy, C., Lawrence, T. B., & Grant, D. (2005). Discourse and collaboration: The role of conversations and collective identity. *Academy of Management Review, 30*(1), 58–77.

Hausmann, U. (1996). Neither industrial district nor innovation milieu: entrepreneurs and their contexts. In *An Actor-Oriented Framework and Case Studies From Greater London And Zurich*. Paper Prepared for the 36th Congress of the European Regional Science Association, Zurich, Switzerland (pp. 26–30).

Kirat, T., & Lung, Y. (1999). Innovation and proximity: Territories as loci of collective learning processes. *European Urban and Regional Studies, 6*(1), 27–38.

Knoben, J., & Oerlemans, L. A. (2006). Proximity and inter-organizational collaboration: A literature review. *International Journal of Management Reviews, 8*(2), 71–89.

Lawrence, T. B., Hardy, C., & Phillips, N. (2002). Institutional effects of interorganizational collaboration: The emergence of proto-institutions. *Academy of Management Journal, 45*(1), 281–290.

Mammar El Hadj, S., Chédotel, F., & Pujol, L. (2015). Construire un projet interorganisationnel dans l'économie sociale et solidaire-Quel lien entre l'identification et l'émergence d'une compétence interorganisationnelle? *Revue Française de Gestion, 41*(246), 159–173.

Mathieu, J., Maynard, M. T., Rapp, T., & Gilson, L. (2008). Team effectiveness 1997–2007: A review of recent advancements and a glimpse into the future. *Journal of Management, 34*(3), 410–476.

Meister, C., & Werker, C. (2004). Physical and organizational proximity in territorial innovation systems: Introduction to the special issue. *Journal of Economic Geography, 4*(1), 1–2.

Miles, M. B., Huberman, A. M., & Saldaña, J. (2014). *Qualitative Data Analysis: A Methods Sourcebook* (3rd Edition). Thousand Oaks, CA: SAGE.

Nooteboom, B. (1999). Innovation and inter-firm linkages: New implications for policy. *Research policy, 28*(8), 793–805.

Retour, D., & Krohmer, C. (2006). La compétence collective, maillon clé de la gestion des compétences. In Defélix, C., Klarrsfeld, A., & Oiry, E. *Nouveaux regards sur la gestion des compétences* (pp. 149–184). Paris, France: Vuibert.

Ring, P. S., & Van de Ven, A. H. (1994). Developmental processes of cooperative interorganizational relationships. *Academy of Management Review, 19*(1), 90–118.

Ruuska, I., and Teigland, R. (2009). Ensuring project success through collective competence and creative conflict in public–private partnerships–A case study of Bygga Villa, a Swedish triple helix e-government initiative. *International Journal of Project Management, 27*(4), 323–334.

Schopler, J. H. (1987). Interorganizational groups: Origins, structure, and outcomes. *Academy of Management Review, 12*(4), 702–718.

Selden, S. C., Sowa, J. E., & Sandfort, J. (2006). The impact of nonprofit collaboration in early child care and education on management and program outcomes. *Public Administration Review, 66*(3), 412–425.

Singh, J. (2005). Collaborative networks as determinants of knowledge diffusion patterns. *Management Science, 51*(5), 756–770.

Tsasis, P. (2009).The social processes of interorganizational collaboration and conflict in nonprofit organizations. *Nonprofit Management and Leadership, 20*(1), 5–21.

Tsoukas, H. (1989). The validity of idiographic research explanations. *Academy of Management Review, 14*(4), 551–561.

Vangen, S., & Huxham C. (2003). Nurturing collaborative relations: Building trust in interorganizational collaboration. *The Journal of Applied Behavioral Science, 39*(1), 5–31.

Yin, R. K. (2015). *Qualitative Research from Start to Finish*. New York, NY: Guilford Publications.

Chapter 8

How to Organize Territorial Competence Management?

Ingrid Mazzilli

Contents

8.1 Introduction

In the field of human resources management, competence was first conceptualized as an individual characteristic, before being extended to collective and organizational levels. More recently, the inter-organizational level and "territorial level" of competence have both been explored, mainly in Europe. Territory is defined as a form of collective action, embedded in a geographic space, where social and political compromises occur (Colletis and Pecqueur, 2018). European and in particular French literature on human resources management sciences has recently focused on studying HR management practices that can identify, organize, or even manage human capital on a territorial scale to better support a region's productive specialization or to revitalize regional economic activity. Previous research on "territorial competence management" underlines the necessary co-operation of actors over time, as well as whatever enables or hinders co-operation (Calamel et al., 2011; Michaux et al., 2011; Arnaud et al., 2013; Mazzilli and Pichault, 2015; Loubès et Bories-Azeau, 2016; Loufrani-Fedida and Saint-Germes, 2018). Instead, few works have contributed to explaining how to organize territorial competence management. This chapter discusses the "territorial" aspect of the concept of competence and illustrates more precisely the emergence and organization of territorial competence management. Drawing on empirical findings from the Provence-Alpes-Côte d'Azur region in France, this chapter sheds light on a specific means of organizing a territorial competence management project and its reliance on three main elements (collective governance, collective territorial knowledge, and specific local context). These findings contribute to regional development and competence literature in human resources development. The chapter is organized as follows: first, a panorama of what has been said about the concept of territory and territorial competence management, relying on economic geography, network organization cluster, and cross-sector partnership literature. Then, we shall introduce the field study, data, methods, findings, and results.

8.2 Territorial Competence Management Literature Review

8.2.1 Territorial Competence as a Result of Social Interactions

Territory is defined as a form of collective action, embedded in a geographic space where social and political compromises take place (Raulet-Croset, 2008). As a social construct, territory "reveals itself" when actors co-operate and partner across sectors (Colletis and Pecqueur, 2018). Regional development literature explains why some regions are more dynamic than others, indicating that they exploit natural resources while developing specific regional expertise and capacities (Boschma, 2004; Malmberg and Maskell, 2006). Territorial competitiveness is no longer based on exploitation of physical resources, but many studies show that immaterial resources, such as human capital and skilled workforce, play a significant role in developing territorial competitive advantage (Bathelt, 2001). Florida (2002) asserts that access to talented and creative people is to modern business what access to coal and iron was to steel, playing a decisive role in where companies locate and grow. In this context, territorial competence is considered the result of the "combination of geographically close resources allowing the territory to display a competitive specialisation" (Defélix and Mazzilli, 2009) and is an emerging property linked to social activity. Lawson (1999, p. 157) points out the relevance of actor interaction: "The relevant interaction will tend to take place between organisations and between different types of organisations. As such, the different means by which relationships emerge and are sustained between organisations becomes a central concern." The specific dynamics of social relations are viewed as the source of territorial competence. Defélix et al. (2009, p. 220) show how actor interactions contribute to territorial competence and use metaphor to illustrate dynamics: institutions and organizations (businesses, universities, technical centers, and local authorities) operating at the territory level are the "bricks" of a house; communities and exchange of practices, professional associations, inter-organizational projects, and informal ones are the cement; and the foundations are based on the territory's historical and cultural elements. In the field of regional development and in human resources management literature, many authors stress the importance of simultaneous interactions between numerous and various local actors to sustain regional innovation: firms, laboratories, public and financial institutions, customers, and users (Lawson, 1999; Vanhaverbeke, 2001; Husserl and Ronde, 2005; Mendez and Mercier, 2006; Defélix et al., 2009). It is then necessary to understand how these interactions, as units of analyses, could be organized or even managed.

8.2.2 Territorial Competence Management Actions and Projects

The field of regional development and spatial agglomeration (innovative milieu, regional innovation systems, learning hubs, and technology districts) has long since pointed to the relevance of human capital to sustained innovation and regional economic growth (Gössling and Rutten, 2007; Kasabov and Sundaram, 2016). Strategy researchers have increasingly investigated the influence of cluster network organizations in fostering innovation by focusing on the roles of knowledge transfer and human mobility (Hakanson, 2005; De Laurentis, 2006; Lambooy, 2010). More specifically, such research illustrates the emergent character of social dynamics, such as greater inter-firm employee mobility (Power and Lundmark, 2004; Eriksson and Lindgren, 2009), the emergence of "epistemic communities" (Hakanson, 2005), proximity and agglomeration effects, etc. Non-organized employee mobility contributes to the emergence of collective learning dynamics (Keeble and Wilkinson, 1999) and, *in fine*, to a skilled regional work-force (Saxenian, 1996; Dominicis et al., 2013). Few works mention the presence of labor market intermediaries (Benner, 2003) or acknowledge that public insti-tutions play a key role in sustaining regional development (De Laurentis, 2006; Casper, 2007). However, the literature review from Kasabov and Sundaram (2016) explains that the skills, competences, and capabilities of actors involved in devel-opment processes are rarely referenced, specifically in technology districts, and are mainly absent as a unit of analysis (Laasonen and Kolehmainen, 2017). Although there are mentions of skilled workers and links between territorial competitiveness and workforce competence, there is a paucity of research that directly addresses the issue of "space" in theorizing work and employment practices (Herod et al., 2007). However, Husserl and Ronde (2005) demonstrate that regional support and policies can benefit from innovative territorial initiatives, such as promoting educational programs and developing regional attractivity hubs. In Europe, specif-ically, certain clusters have launched practices to develop local workforce employ-ment, training, and skills (Hanssen-Bauer and Snow, 1996; Molina-Morales, 2001; Guidetti et al., 2009). Kasabov and Sundaram (2016) underline the interest of practitioners and policy-makers in externalities, proximity, and co-locationing and that cluster-planning tools have influenced local and national policies (Torre, 2008). Indeed, the increasing complexity of socio-economic development encour-ages greater involvement of local actors in inter-organizational collaborations (Geddes, 2008) and problem-solving they could not manage on their own (Selsky and Parker, 2005). These cross-partners and territorial competence projects repre-sent new opportunities for human resources teams (Beer et al., 2015; Colin and Mercier, 2017), who are therefore able to expand their actions with local partners under differentiated strategies (Uzan et al., 2017). At the same time, public orga-nizations are called to work more frequently in cross-sector partnerships (Bryson et al., 2015). Thite (2011) encourages a focus on cities and regions and examination of theory and practices in regional human resource development. In this context, European and particularly French literature has illuminated deliberate regional human resource management practices and, more specifically, how to organize territorial competence management (Calamel et al., 2011; Michaux et al., 2011; Arnaud et al., 2013; Mazzilli and Pichault, 2015; Loufrani-Fedida and Saint-Germes, 2018). Here, regional area is viewed as an area for mobility and mutual-ization (Loubès and Bories-Azeau, 2016). These projects can be led by public or private actors, seeking to develop local economic activities through the territorial competence management approach. Projects are generally sustained through pub-lic funding and bids for projects initiated by national or regional authorities. These HR actions are components of larger programs, or territorial competence man-agement projects initiated by public institutions, clusters, or business networks. Many managerial actions and HR practices launched in various contexts (such as mutualized training sessions, regionally developed recruitment platforms, and tal-ent recruitment campaigns) have been identified in previous works (Chabault and

Hulin, 2011; Loufrani-Fedida and Saint-Germes, 2015; Evon, 2018). However, implementing territorial competence management is problematic for several reasons; this chapter focuses on the following research question: How do we organize territorial competence management?

8.3 Research Context and Methodology

8.3.1 French Regulatory Context and the Case Site

In 2014, the Provence-Alpes-Côte d'Azur region launched a call for projects for employment centers to implement regional job and skill planning management programs to help companies assess current and future recruitment needs, while promoting employee inter-organizational mobility. The call specifically encouraged employment centers to collaborate with their stakeholders to achieve their missions. Employment centers are responsible for sustaining economic activities and employment by developing cross-sector partnerships in work, employment, and skills development. The West Provence Employment Centre (WPEC) participated in the 2015 project bid. The region's main economic activities are in petrochemicals and logistics and benefit many international firms located near the strategic Port of Marseille-Fos, France's leading port and the second largest Mediterranean port. Transport and logistics have consequently expanded in recent years, and many firms have located their warehouses in this strategic zone. In this context, the West Provence Employment Centre opted to build its own territorial competence management project to support transport and logistics in its territory. The West Provence Employment Centre operational team included a director and four project managers, responsible for project orientations and management.

8.3.2 Data Collection and Analysis

The research was performed as part of an agreement between the WPEC and the research team, to establish a research project on conditions for success in territorial competence management projects. The research position was limited to non-participating observation, concluding with a presentation of the research results at the end of the reporting period (April 2014 to April 2015). The corpus (see Table 8.1) was analyzed for thematic content, drawing up a starting list of three main themes based on the conceptual framework and research questions: emergence of a collaborative plan formulation; construction of shared meaning about territorial competence management project in transport and logistics; and difficulties in plan formulation. Then, by proceeding with an inductive codification (Miles and Huberman, 2003), we integrated common themes that had emerged from our analyses to present the history of this collaborative work.

Table 8.1   Empirical Data Collected

A total of 17 semi-directive interviews were conducted in the spring of 2015 with the WPEC team and collaborators: ■ Three interviews with the WPEC operational team;   ■ Fourteen interviews with partners (four logistics companies, a temporary work agency, three training organizations, three training center managers, a local mission, a chamber of commerce and industry, and one employers' group).   The interviews focused on each member's and partner's participation in the territorial competence management project, their expectations, roles, feedback, and future development paths. To complete the corpus, the authors participated in two plenary meetings and were added to the WPEC mailing list. At the end of the observation period, the research team organized meetings with the WPEC operational and board teams (September and November 2015).

8.4 The Territorial Competence Management Project Developed by the West Provence Employment Centre

8.4.1 Emergence of a Collaborative Plan Formulation

In 2014, the West Provence Employment Centre responded to a regional project bid, aimed at developing a tool for regional employment and competence planning. The WPEC first conducted a local analysis of socio-economic activities, as well as a survey, to better understand company skills and employers' needs. The results revealed transport and logistics to be among the most vibrant of industries, but they faced significant needs in recruitment and skilled labor, specifically in warehouse and handling jobs. Local firms stated that they were unable to recruit skilled workers quickly enough because many potential recruits held negative perceptions regarding the tasks involved (heavy loads, difficult schedules, poor job content, activity subject to hot or cold weather, etc.). Most importantly, transport and logistics are subject to seasonal activities, which create a high demand for temporal or seasonal jobs considered as insecure. Many logistics firms use a number of temporary employees, recruited and hired through temporary agencies. After the diagnostic and the survey were carried out, the WPEC summarized the information collected to reformulate the project's main objective and two sub-objectives: objective 1: support and strengthen territorial anchoring of transport and logistics activities; objective 2: "bring business and territory issues together" (WPEC's Action plan). The WPEC team then identified all local actors involved in work, training, employment, skills, and competence development in transport and logistics. All actors were considered as potential partners: companies and their warehouses, training centers, job centers, temporary agencies, technical schools and universities, management research centers, local and regional authorities, professional sector associations, trade unions, etc. The WPEC consulted all local transport and logistics stakeholders to construct a territorial competence management project adapted to their needs. The first challenge the WPEC faced would be to create a cross-sector partnership with voluntary participation from the stakeholders. The WPEC team invited all potential partners to a plenary session, where they asked each member to volunteer for a working-group. The three groups met twice over the following three months. They were first asked to articulate their needs and then considered how they could collectively support the WPEC territorial competence management project. Each working-group was led by a WPEC member and was represented by a referent who reported to a steering committee selected by the working-group. The first part of the project led the WPEC to prioritize ten actions to develop the "territorial competence management project."

8.4.2 Territorial Competence Management Action Plan

The ten actions (training, communication, mapping seasonality, identification of job mobility, etc.) were performed by the partners based on their own corporate mandate and specific expertise. The action plan consisted of three focus areas featuring the ten priority actions (see Table 8.2). "Job Security," the Nr.1 axis, included, among other actions, mapping the seasonality of logistics companies and identifying peak employment periods corresponding to off-peak periods to support professional mobility. It was also decided to experiment with "job-bridges," which allow employees to move easily from one job to another within partner organizations.

Table 8.2 WPEC Action Plan

AXIS 1: Securing Job and Promoting Professional Paths
ACTION 1.1: Securing temporary jobs
ACTION 1.2: Experiment with job mobility between partner companies
ACTION 1.3: Securing permanent jobs
AXIS 2: Improving Sectoral Attractiveness
ACTION 2.1: Work information and preparation
ACTION 2.2: Creating professional training sessions for logistics operators
ACTION 2.3: Workforce circulation within the three logistics platforms
ACTION 2.4: Creating a local, specific professional training sessions for managers in logistics
ACTION 2.5: Sustaining regional competitiveness and attractiveness
ACTION 2.6: Developing work for specific populations
AXIS 3: Promoting Local Firms and Public Stakeholder Partnerships
ACTION 3.1: Developing local socio-economical partnerships

The Nr.2 axis, "Improving sector attractiveness," has, for example, led to the development of operator training content (the logistics industry is lacking in operators and has difficulties recruiting), combining six training centers. Some collaborated in a common scheme called "Trans' Log," a tool to support skills development in logistics and to secure career paths (identifying skill gaps between the actual position and the "target" position). The Nr.3 axis, "Promoting local firms and public stakeholder partnership" organized discussions and information between economical, work, and training partners, aimed at developing economic monitoring to keep all actors fully informed about development projects at local companies and the requirements of HR firms. The objectives were formulated to meet the current needs of employees and partners as well as a "forward-looking" reflection. One of the actions focused on promoting transport and logistics professions among future employees. Actions were designed to create links with schools and higher education centers in the territory.

8.4.3 Construction of a Shared Meaning for the Territorial Competence Management Project

Analysis of the interviews revealed that participants also shared homogeneous understanding of the challenges in implementing the territorial competence management project: "It involves an approach at the territorial and professional sector level, to optimise resources, offers and applications, with a relatively long-term consideration, to do a foresight study" (training organization). According to them, the approach is based on their development in local employment, training, and skills in transport and logistics:

> The territorial competence project is a complex answer, allowing us to see that everything is linked, everything is complex; it's important to have institutional and political communication, etc. It is about mapping the skills, advantages and constraints of a territory to provide solutions and to work on continuous improvement. It deals with building a vibrant territorial and sectoral economy. You can see that no one can do anything alone! Everyone needs to be involved, there are key players: training organisations, employers.
>
> **(training organization)**

The WPEC played a "piloting" role by developing a participatory methodology to establish the territorial competence management project. It received strong support: network support for territorial actors developed through actions simultaneously implemented in previous projects; knowledge of the territorial logistics sector; and development of territorial competence management expertise through WPEC involvement in similar projects. The project was led by the local authority officer, who introduced the project objectives in person at the launch meeting. The WPEC drew on prior experience in the territory to develop a project where each player would participate and propose certain actions. The mobilization was received positively by most actors, according to our interviews:

> I found the project to be interesting, in part because there are a number of warehouses established in our region. This project allows us to take a step forward and to question ourselves

> **(temporary work agency)**

8.4.4 Territorial Competence Management Is Based on Collective Governance, Collective Territorial Knowledge, and a Local System Context

Constructing a territorial competence plan is a long-term process requiring long-term commitment from partners. This chapter illustrates how territorial competence management may be organized. It relies on the combination of three elements: first, a co-ordination team leading and managing "collaborative governance," based on "capacity for joint action"; second, partner collaboration to identify skills and actions in need of development for their industry based on "territorial knowledge"; and third, the existence of previous historical and social dynamics, contributing to cross-sector partnership projects over time.

The WPEC team did a tremendous job preparing the project, developing it as a collective program. They designed the project as participatory, fostering the gradual emergence of a "territorial group," which had not previously participated in a collaborative approach. They succeeded in establishing new relationships and collective learning through collaboration. They united regional key stakeholders on these issues, mobilizing them around co-construction and implementation of an action plan under their leadership to guarantee the project's sustainability. The ability to facilitate inter-organizational relationships was studied through a group of individuals. Emerson et al. (2012, p. 2) use the term "collaborative governance," defining it "as the processes and structures of public policy decision-making and management that engage people constructively across the boundaries of public agencies, levels of government, and/or the public, private and civic spheres in order to carry out a public purpose that could not otherwise be accomplished".

Collaborative governance is also conceptualized as the combination of three essential components: "principled engagement," "shared motivation," and "capacity for joint action." Drawing on Saint-Onge and Armonsting (2004, p. 19), the capacity of joint action is defined as "a collection of cross-functional elements that come together to create the potential for taking effective action" and serves "as the link between strategy and performance." The chapter illustrated that territorial competence management projects are based on the capacity of local partners to co-ordinate themselves, as identified by Défélix et al. (2009). This capacity for joint action is essential for developing a territorial competence management project.

The second observation illustrates that territorial competence management projects also rely on project stakeholders' capacity to identify actions to be developed for their industry on a specific territory. The WPEC's collaborative governance united project partners and facilitated the emergence of the action plan. But the proposed actions were based on the stakeholders' ability to identify actions, sustaining and promoting the territory's productive specialization, which in this case study was transport and logistics. The specific knowledge of the territory involves different actors, existing jobs, work techniques, working conditions, economic activity, job-hunting situations, recruitment context, and so on. Partners thus hold specific territorial knowledge and expertise, developing a relevant action plan based on this territorial and sectoral knowledge. The case shows that the WPEC made the territorial competence management project possible by articulating their collective territorial knowledge within the context of collaborative governance. Following Colletis and Pecqueur (2018), territorial resources have four characteristics: they are specific (they emerge in specific historical and socio-economical contexts); they can emerge or not, based on those specific conditions; they are not visible on their own unless activated; and they are sustainable. The collective territorial knowledge functions as a "territorial resource" (Colletis and Pecqueur, 2018) "activated" by the WPEC. This result also supports Sotarauta's (2010) and Laasonen and Kolehmainen's (2017) work: that regional development needs actors who are able to spot trends and their significance, who have a deeper understanding of their business sector, and who are able to use interactive processes.

Third, the authors observed that the territorial competence management project was developed by the WPEC, which had previously worked on projects of this type and were familiar with most of the partners. The WPEC is involved in professional and institutional networks on its territory. There were specific local conditions contributing to their project structure and reasons behind their major investment in the project. They also had an extensive history of co-operation with local authorities, which fostered mutual trust. Following Emerson et al. (2012), we assert that "collaborative governance unfolds within a system context that consists of a host of political, legal, socioeconomic, environmental, and other influences. This system context creates opportunities and constraints, and influences the dynamics and performance of collaboration at the outset and over time".

This study shows that territorial competence management projects are orchestrated within specific local contexts.

8.5 Conclusion

This chapter focuses on the following research question: How do we organize territorial competence management? The case study illustrates how the project framework established a cross-sector partnership and engaged voluntary public and private actors to identify local territorial needs in training, employment, and competence development. The findings show three founding elements of the territorial competence management project organization: (1) collaborative governance, which sustains (2) the emergence of a collective territorial knowledge, activated by (3) specific local systems. These findings contribute to regional development and to competence literature in human resource development. It targets the main aspects of the emergence of territorial competence management, bridging a gap in existing literature by linking regional development approaches to HR/competence management studies. First, this chapter contributes to the literature on HR/competence management and shows that territorial competence management projects offer a way of seeing urban growth and development from an HRM point of view. French HRM/competence research identified the emergence of territorial competence dynamics, but papers have focused on describing the collaborative implementation of territorial project processes or identifying different forms of territorial competence management (Calamel et al., 2011; Michaux et al., 2011; Arnaud et al., 2013; Mazzilli and Pichault, 2015; Loubès and Bories-Azeau, 2016; Loufrani-Fedida and Saint-Germes, 2018). Second, this chapter contributes to the literature on regional development and economic proximity. It has already been demonstrated that human capital and development of a skilled workforce are the driving forces behind regional competitiveness. Many authors stress the importance of simultaneous interactions between numerous and various local actors to sustain regional innovation competence (Vanhaverbeke, 2001; Husserl and Ronde, 2005). This work sheds light on social dynamics that effectively contribute to regional productive specialization and insists on a collective territorial resource held by local stakeholders. Although this case study is not developed within a cluster or network organization, it also contributes to this body of literature. Indeed, cluster literature recognizes the importance of human capital, but explicit references to skills and competences are rare in technology as a unit of analysis on their own (Kasabov and Sundaram, 2016). The regional development and competence approach adopted in this chapter allowed us to capture the complexity of territorial competence management organization and identify inherent key elements for its development. Given the relevance of territorial competence management in sustaining productive specialization and regional competitiveness, further field study on longitudinal research would be also be needed along with continued research in collaborative outcomes.

References

Arnaud, N., Fauvy, S., & Nekka, H. (2013). La difficile institutionnalisation d'une GRH territoriale: Une étude de cas exploratoire. *Revue Française de Gestion, 2*, 15–33.

Bathelt, H. (2001). Regional competence and economic recovery: Divergent growth paths in Boston's high technology economy. *Entrepreneurship & Regional Development, 13*, 287–314.

Beer, M., Boselie, P., & Brewster, C. (2015). Back to the future: Implications for the field of HRM of the multistakeholder perspective proposed 30 years ago. *Human Resource Management, 54*(3), 427–438.

Benner, C. (2003). Labour flexibility and regional development: The role of labour market intermediaries. *Regional Studies, 37*(6&7), 621–633.

Boschma, R. A. (2004). Competitiveness of regions from an evolutionary perspective. *Regional Studies, 38*(9), 1001–1014.

Bryson, J. M., Crosby, B. C., & Stone, M. M. (2015). Designing and implementing cross-sector collaborations: Needed and challenging. *Public Administration Review, 75*(5), 647–663.

Calamel, L., Defélix, C., Mazzilli, I., & Retour, D. (2011). Les pôles de compétitivité: un point de rupture pour la GRH traditionnelle? Une analyse des dispositifs RH au sein des douze pôles de la région Rhône-Alpes. *Management & Avenir, 1*(41), 175–193.

Casper, S. (2007). How do technology cluster emerge and become sustainable? Social network formation and inter-firm mobility within the San Diego biotechnology cluster. *Research Policy, 36*, 438–455.

Chabault, D., & Hulin, A. (2011). Embaucher et former le personnel au sein de grappes ou de pôles d'entreprises. *Gestion, 36*, 43–49.

Colin, T., & Mercier, E. (2017). Le territoire: de nouvelles opportunités pour la fonction RH ? *Management & Avenir, 5*(95), 107–127.

Colletis, G., & Pecqueur, B. (2018). Révélations des ressources spécifiques territoriales et inégalités de développement: le rôle de la proximité géographique. *Revue d'Economie Régionale et Urbaine, 5&6*, 993–1011.

Defélix, C., & Mazzilli, I. (2009). De l'individu au territoire : la longue marche de la gestion des compétences, In Retour, D., Picq, T., & Defélix, C. (Eds.), *Gestion des compétences: nouvelles dimensions, nouvelles relations* (pp. 97–209). Paris, France: Vuibert.

Defélix, C., Picq, T., & Retour, D. (2009). *Gestion des compétences: nouvelles relations, nouvelles dimensions.* Paris, France: Vuibert.

De Laurentis, C. (2006). Regional innovation systems and the labour market: A comparison of five regions. *European Planning Studies, 14*(8), 1059–1084.

Dominicis, L., Raymond , & De Groot, H. (2013). Regional clusters of innovative activity in Europe: Are social capital and geographical proximity key determinants? *Applied Economics, 45*(17), 2325–2335.

Emerson, K., Nabatchi, T., & Balogh, S. (2012). An integrative framework for collaborative governance. *Journal of Public Administration Research & Theory, 1*(22), 1–29.

Eriksson, R., & Lindgren, U. (2009). Localized mobility clusters: Impacts of labour market externalities on firm performance. *Journal of Economic Geography, 9*, 33–53.

Evon, J. (2018). *L'attractivité territoriale : de l'existence des ressources à leur valorisation en compétences* (Unpublished doctoral dissertation), Université de Tours, France.

Florida, R. (2002). The economic geography of talent. *Annals of the Association of American Geographers, 92*(4), 743–55.

Geddes, M. (2008). Inter-organizational relationships in local and regional development partnerships. In. Cropper, S., Ebers, M., Huxham, C. & Smith-Ring, P. (Eds.), *The Oxford Handbook of Inter-organizational Relations* (pp. 203–230). Oxford, UK: Oxford University Press.

Gössling, T., & Rutten, R. (2007). Innovation in regions. *European Planning Studies, 15*(2), 253–270.

Guidetti, G., Mancinelli, S., & Mazzanti, M. (2009). Complementarity in training practices: Methodological notes and empirical evidence for a local economic system. *Journal of Applied Economics, 8*(1), 39–56.

Hakanson, L. (2005). Epistemic communities and cluster dynamics: On the role of knowledge in industrial districts. *Industry & Innovation, 12*(4), 433–463.

Hanssen-Bauer, J. & Snow, C. C. (1996). Responding to hypercompetition: The structure and process of a regional learning network organization. *Organization Science, 7*(4), 413–427.

Herod, A., Rainnie, A., & Mc Grath-Champ, S. (2007). Working space: Why incorporating the geographical is central to theorizing work and employment practices. *Work, Employment & Society, 21*(2), 247–264.

Husserl, C., & Ronde, P. (2005). What kind of individual education for which type of regional innovative competence? An exploration of data on French industries. *Regional Studies, 39*(7), 873–889.

Kasabov, E., & Sundaram, U. (2016). Conceptualizing clusters as dynamic and path-dependent pools of skills. *Regional Studies, 50*(9), 1520–1536.

Keeble, D., & Wilkinson, F. (1999). Collective learning and knowledge development in the evolution of regional clusters of high technology SMEs in Europe. *Regional Studies, 33*(4), 295–303.

Laasonen, V., & Kolehmainen, J. (2017). Capabilities in knowledge-based regional development: Toward a dynamic framework. *European Planning Studies, 25*(10), 1673–1692.

Lambooy, J. G. (2010). Knowledge transfers, spillovers and actors: The role of context and social capital. *European Planning Studies, 18*(6), 873–891.

Lawson, C. (1999). Towards a competence theory of the region. *Cambridge Journal of Economics, 2*(23), 151–166.

Loubes, A. & Bories-Azeau, I. (2016). Les logiques de la GPEC élargie au territoire: une proposition de typologie. *Gestion 2000, 33*(2), 141–160.

Loufrani-Fedida, S., & Saint-Germes, È. (2015). Quand le territoire s'organise pour attirer à l'international et fidéliser en local les talents: le cas du cluster technologique de Sophia Antipolis. *@GRH, 15*(2), 99–125.

Loufrani-Fedida, S., & Saint-Germes, È. (2018). L'engagement durable des parties prenantes dans une démarche de GRH territoriale: le cas de la GTEC de Sophia Antipolis. *Revue de Gestion des Ressources Humaines, 110*(4), 18–40.

Malmberg, A., & Maskell, P. (2006). Localized learning revisited. *Growth and Change, 37*(1), 1–18.

Mazzilli, I., & Pichault, F. (2015). La construction des dispositifs de GRH territoriale: grille d'analyse et modalités du processus de traduction. *Management International, 19*(3), 31–46.

Mendez, A., & Mercier, D. (2006). Compétences-clés de territoires: le rôle des relations interorganisationnelles. *Revue Française de Gestion, 164*, 253–275.

Michaux, V., Defélix, C. & Raulet-Croset, N. (2011). Boosting territorial multi-stakeholder cooperation, coordination and collaboration: Strategic and managerial issues. *Management & Avenir, 50*(10), 122–136.

Miles M. B., & Huberman M. A. (2003). *Analyse des données qualitatives* (2nd edition). Bruxelles, Belgium: De Boeck.

Molina-Morales, F. X. (2001). Human capital in the industrial districts. *Human Management Systems, 20*, 319–331.

Power, D., & Lundmark, M. (2004). Working through knowledge pools: Labour market dynamics, the transference of knowledge and ideas, and industrial clusters. *Urban Studies, 14*(5/6), 1025–1044.

Raulet-Croset, N. (2008). La dimension territoriale des situations de gestion. *Revue Française de Gestion, 184*, 137–150.

Saint-Onge, H., & Armstrong, C. (2004). *The Conductive Organization Building Beyond Sustainability.* New York, NY: Elsevier.

Saxenian, A. (1996). Beyond Boundaries: Open labor markets and learning in Silicon Valley. In Arthur M. B. & Rousseau, D. M. (Eds.), *The Boundaryless Career: A New Principle for a New Organizational Era* (pp. 23–39). New York, NY: Oxford University Press.

Selsky, J., & Parker, B. (2005). Cross-sector partnerships to address social issues: Challenges to theory and practice. *Journal of Management, 31*(6), 849–873.

Sotarauta, M. (2010). Regional development and regional networks: The role of regional development officers in Finland. *European Urban and Regional Studies, 17*, 387–400.

Thite, M. (2011). Smart cities: Implications of urban planning for human resource development. *Human Resource Development International, 14*(5), 623–631.

Torre, A. (2008). On the role played by temporary geographical proximity in knowledge transmission. *Regional Studies, 42*(6), 869–889.

Uzan, O., Bonneveux, E., Bories-Azeau, I., Condomines, B., Delattre, M., Houessou, B., ... & Raulet-Croset, N. (2017). De la GRH instrumentale à la GRH partenariale : l'impact des stratégies territoriales. *Revue de Gestion des Ressources Humaines, 1*(103), 20–39.

Vanhaverbeke, W. (2001). Realizing new core competencies establishing a customer-oriented SME network. *Entrepreneurship & Regional Development, 13*, 97–116.

Chapter 9

Market for Competences: When Attractiveness Drives Competitiveness

Michel Ferrary

Contents

9.1 Introduction

Management strategy emphasizing competence is a critical resource for a firm to gain a competitive advantage over its competitors (Prahalad and Hamel, 1990). The resource-based view (RBV) (Barney, 1991; Wernerfelt, 1984) argues owning competences that are rare, valuable, imperfectly imitable, and non-substitutable contribute to firm competitiveness and is an entry barrier to an industry. In a dynamic perspective, entering into a new market supposes to acquire new competence. The more radical a strategic change is, the less the firm is endowed with the required competence and must acquire it outside its boundaries (Song et al., 2003).

A significant portion of competence that organizations need to acquire is embodied in individuals. Switching from the organizational level to the individual level highlights that competences are knowledge, skills, and abilities that belong to individuals. Tacit competences are even more embodied in individuals (Grant, 1996; Nonaka, 1994). Competence is difficult to separate from those who possess it, and employing individuals mastering strategic competences might give a competitive advantage. The resource-based view considers human capital as a potential strategic resource to deliver a superior customer value proposition (CVP) and obtain a competitive advantage (Delery and Roumpi, 2017).

However, RBV does not explore issues related to acquiring strategic competences embodied in individuals. Hiring individuals away from a rival firm is a way to acquire such competences (Singh and Agrawal, 2011). Song et al. (2003) highlighted that a firm recruits experts far from its core competence to develop new activities and to remove the firm from path dependency related to its core competence. Learning-by-hiring is a way for organizations to acquire new competence (Simon, 1991). Firms often find it less costly and faster to source externally available competences than to develop them internally (Tzabbar, 2009).

The current literature on competence is well-developed to analyze the strategic impact of competence on competitiveness and to define and manage them inside organizations. Strategic human resource management (HRM) makes the link between the organizational level and individual level and between strategic management and human resource management (Wright and McMahan, 2011), by focusing knowledge workers that provide strategic competence to the firm (Ferrary and Trepo, 1998).

Competition between firms on the labor market to acquire such strategic competence remains underexplored (Ferrary, 2010). Four theoretical issues related to the management of competence persist: How does attractiveness on the market for competences shape competitiveness on the product market? How to define competition on a labor market segmented by competence? How do HRM practices shape the firm's employee value proposition (EVP) and affect its attractiveness on the labor market? How to redesign EVP to make the firm more attractive?

In this chapter, it is argued that the firm's capability to attract competence by being more attractive than its competitors on the labor market affects its competitiveness on the product market. Attracting individuals is a critical way for firms to acquire new strategic competences through learning-by-hiring. The competence-based view of the firm needs to move one step further by analyzing the firm's attractiveness on the labor market. More precisely, that means identifying competitors on the labor market, the different factors that make them more or less attractive than the firm and, firm strengths and weaknesses on the labor market to attract talents.

A competence-based view switches strategic management issues from competitiveness on the "output" market to attractiveness on the "input" market. Any strategic intent to enter a new market requires previously owning related competences. The execution of a radical strategic move supposes to attract talented individuals on the labor market. Moreover, unattractiveness on the labor market might harm firm competitiveness and impede a strategic move. The competence-based view of the firm and knowledge management meeting to highlight how HRM practices contribute to competitiveness by making the firm attractive on the labor market (Ferrary, 2015).

This chapter investigates the managerial issues related to the acquisition of strategic competences on the labor market to be competitive on the product and services market. It is critical to note that competitors in the labor market may be the same as those on the product market. For example, luxury watch manufacturers such as Patek Philippe and Vacheron-Constantin compete on the product market (output) to obtain rich customers and also on the labor market (input) to attract watchmakers. However, competition on the two markets may be completely separate. For example, Google and Goldman Sachs do not compete on any product or services market, but they intensively compete on the labor market to attract IT engineers. Such a perspective requires that firms identify all their different competitors on the labor market for each segment of strategic competence, compare the relative attractiveness of their EVP, and improve their EVP or their employer brand to be more attractive.

This chapter contributes to the literature on competence by exploring why the human dimension of competence makes attractiveness on the labor market a critical issue to contribute to competitiveness on the product market. Competitiveness between firms on the market of products (output) is affected by the competition on the market for competences (input); the most attractive employer attracts the most talented individuals to deliver the best products and services. Such a proposition opens different perspectives on managerial practices. Firms should analyze and improve their attractiveness on the market for competences in the same way that they consider competition on their product market by analyzing competitors and designing competitive customer value proposition. That means segmenting the labor market by competence, identifying competitors in each segment, evaluating their relative attractiveness or unattractiveness compared with their competitors, exploring how their employee value proposition (EVP) matches or not with individuals' expectations, and whether it is more or less attractive than the EVP of its competitors. Such an analysis might lead the firm to improve the content of its EVP or improve its visibility through employer branding. In a competitive market for competences, HRM practices are considered in their contribution to the firm's attractiveness on the market. Employers need to consider competitive forces to design HR practices that make them more attractive on the market for competences. The sustainability of its attractive advantage depends on the reproducibility of its EVP by competitors.

9.2 Strategic Competence Embodied in Knowledge Workers

Recently, a Swiss bank in Geneva designed a new strategy to grow its business. The financial industry faces stricter regulation to tackle tax evasion and money laundering. Coping with such regulation induces huge investments in information systems. The bank perceived this situation as a market opportunity instead of a business constraint and decided to develop financial software to deal with the new regulation and to sell the software to small Swiss banks that do not have the financial resources to invest in such software development. The bank must combine competences in finance, tax, law, and computer science to implement this strategic intent. It owns the first three but lacks the last one. The bank must recruit IT engineers to implement its strategy. After a few months, the bank did not receive strong applications and discovered a tough reality: it was very attractive on the labor market for wealth managers but unattractive on the labor market for IT engineers. In Switzerland, IT engineers prefer to work for the European Center for Nuclear Research (CERN), Google, Swisscom, or Microsoft but not for a medium-level Swiss bank. Such unattractiveness prevents the implementation of the strategic intent by depriving the bank of required competences in computer science.

Competences such as knowledge, skills, and abilities are mainly embodied in individuals (Felin and Hesterly, 2007; Grant, 1996). Individuals are repositories for tacit knowledge and a great deal of explicit (codified) knowledge (Nonaka, 1994). Knowledge workers are a source of competitive advantage for the firm. By their competence, they help to differentiate the firm's offer in terms of quality and innovation. In a dynamic perspective, organizations learn competence through their workers and interactions of their employees. Simon (1991, p. 125) notes, "Organization learns in only two ways: by the learning of its members, or by ingesting new members who have knowledge that the organization did not previously have." This point links competence management and HR management. HR practices, such as recruitment, are key to access new competence through "learning-by-hiring" (Song et al., 2003). A dynamic perspective that considers how firms learn and acquire competence implicitly puts HR at the center, because competence flows in through hiring and training and flows out through individual departures.

The individual's embodiment of competence renders the employee essential to strategic management. Starbuck (1992) was among the first scholars to explicitly define knowledge workers. They are experts who master a specific field of knowledge and are characterized by their high levels of education. Individuals who trained at the best universities are assumed to have more and better competence and to have high intellectual potential to learn and accumulate tacit knowledge (Hitt et al., 2001). The industry tenure of executives is also a robust measure of expertise. Experience in industry equips the worker with contextual and tacit competence and increases his or her ability to acquire related competence (Rao and Drazin, 2002). Such reasoning may also apply to less qualified workers. For instance, truck drivers are skilled individuals that own strategic competences for a logistic company such as DHL or La Poste. Similarly, electricians and plumbers hold critical competences to develop a business in the building industry. More generally, any shortage on the labor market accentuates issues related to attractiveness.

9.3 Strategic Issues Related to Embodied Competence

A critical issue in the field of strategic management is how firms achieve a sustainable competitive advantage. Porter's (1985) seminal analysis of firm competitive advantage focuses strategic management on the competitiveness of the firm in its product market ("output" market). In this perspective, it is the firm's customer value proposition that gives it a competitive advantage.

Resource-based theory moves the focus of strategic management to the firm's resource combination. In this perspective, the firm's competitiveness is based on the specificity of this combination. Resources that create value and are rare, imperfectly imitable, and non-substitutable bring a competitive advantage and are needed to implement the firm's strategy (Barney, 1991; Wernerfelt, 1984). Competence is a strategic resource that introduces HR management into the field of strategic management (Becker and Huselid, 2006). In some cases, few highly skilled individuals can determine the competitiveness of the firm. However, as Grant (1996) noted, in contrast to arrangements over the ownership of physical and financial assets, employment contracts confer only partial and ill-defined ownership rights on employees' competence assets. The competence remains within the individual employee and cannot be readily transferred.

The use of competences implicitly raises the problem of acquiring competences. Most studies have focused on how competences are used. For example, knowledge-based theory (Grant, 1996) and dynamic capabilities theory (Teece et al., 1997) focus on how to coordinate knowledge and resources in organizations and do not explore the primary issue of bringing them into the organization. However, firms competing in output markets also compete for the same competence in the inputs market and their development depends on their capabilities to attract strategic individuals. From a theoretical perspective, there is a double dependency constraint. The competitive advantage of the firm on the output market depends on its resources combination, which depends, in turn, on the firm's attractiveness on the labor market (input). Any weakness in the second dependence undermines competitiveness on the first.

When individual competences are the main productive resources, owning it is crucial for entering a new market. Therefore, entry decisions must be based on the competences and capabilities of new entrants relative to the competition. Employing workers with the right knowledge is paramount to build a competitive resource combination and enter a new market. However, all competences required to launch a new product are not available within the firm, especially if the innovation is radically different from the firm's existing offer. It follows that issues such as skill acquisition, management of knowledge and know-how, and learning are fundamental strategic issues. For example, when Google decided to enter the mobile phone market, it bought Android, a start-up that developed an operating system for mobile devices and did its best to keep all the knowledge workers owning the competence. In high-tech industries, an acquisition strategy is a common practice to gain access to new competence but supposes the retention of individuals to be successful (Ferrary, 2011).

9.4 Recruiting Is a Critical Issue to Accessing Strategic Competence

Strategic human resource management emphasizes the importance of recruiting (Delery and Roumpi, 2017). Recruiting knowledge workers is often a precondition to enter a new market (Singh and Agrawal, 2011). Firms that are considering offering a new product but are lacking the requisite competence may proactively hire individuals with the necessary knowledge, skills, and abilities (Boeker, 1997). In the institutional perspective, the movement of personnel is an important precondition for learning from competitors and adopting their innovations (Song et al., 2003). In the resource-based literature, Barney (1991) noted that the recruitment of talent enables firms to acquire causally ambiguous and poorly codified competence.

Recruiting highly qualified employees is often a major obstacle, particularly because new ventures must compete for talents with existing employers. Therefore, the labor market can often serve as an important constraint to the development of a new activity. Cappelli (2000) described businesses realizing that, to create a new activity, it saves time by stealing new competences rather than developing them from scratch. Rao and Drazin's (2002) study of the US mutual fund industry showed that recruitment is a strategy to overcome competence constraints in an established professional services industry characterized by high interfirm mobility during a period of rapid growth. Boeker (1997) pointed out that executive migration between semiconductor companies in Silicon Valley, especially those with a functional background in research and development, product engineering, marketing, or sales, brings in knowledge workers with prior exposure to different products and strategies, which, in turn, is reflected in subsequent product market entry decisions by the executive's new firm. Kim (1997) described Samsung's deliberate strategy of hiring scientists and engineers from US firms to acquire critical competence to enter into the semi-conductors industry. Knowledge workers hired from large organizations give firms access to the competence of competitors. Individuals accumulate strategic competence through their professional activities and preventing their migration to competitors is a strategic tactic to protect the firm's competitive advantage. Because of the intensity of the competition to recruit talent, companies instinctively view retention and recruitment as competitive exercises (Cappelli, 2000).

9.5 Competition among Firms Is Primarily in the Labor Market for Knowledge Workers

While product market competition is clearly an important driver of the dynamics of organizations, there is also competition on the input side. Because organizations are aggregations of competences belonging to individuals, the extent to which firms compete for the same talented individuals drives the competitive dynamics in a specific industrial sector (Gardner, 2005). The nature of the competition among firms in the labor market has measurable consequences for the dynamics of competition among firms on the product market. The degree to which a core competence is distinctive depends on how well endowed the firm is relative to its competitors and how difficult it is for competitors to replicate its competences (Teece et al., 1997). Competences related to strategies and operations needed to succeed in an industry are often available to those already employed in the industry, especially when the competence of key success factors is not codified (Nelson and Winter, 1982). As a result, recruiting from competitors enables organizations without age-dependent routines to staff positions that have not previously been occupied and have no intra-organizational precedent.

Firms compete by poaching knowledge workers from each other. Firms regularly look outside the organization to find talented individuals to fill key positions. Once they identify attractive candidates, they do whatever is needed to lure them away from their current employers (Cappelli, 2000). A "raid" involves targeting a competitor's pool of employees as part of a systematic recruiting effort. If raiding is a necessity, the raiders may consider disguising their activities by: (a) having a delay between hirings; (b) approaching employees from the same company using different headhunting firms or divisions; (c) giving the poached employees different titles to disguise horizontal moves; and (d) coaching poached employees to disguise the nature of their new assignment during exit interviews (Gardner, 2002). Recruiting

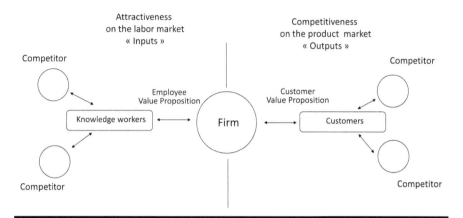

Figure 9.1 Interdependency between the competitiveness and the attractiveness of the firm.

knowledge workers from the competition has a double effect. First, it enhances the recruiting firm's competitiveness by increasing its strategic capabilities. Second, it weakens the competitors' competitiveness by depriving them of strategic knowledge workers.

Competitiveness in the product and services market (output market) depends on its attractiveness on the labor market (input market). In other words, the competitiveness of the firm's customer value proposition in the output market depends on the attractiveness of the firm's EVP on the labor market (Figure 9.1). The decline of a firm is usually due in part to its reduced attractiveness on the labor market. This decline may be accelerated if more attractive competitors are recruiting in the same segment of the HR market.

9.6 Drivers of Attractiveness and Competition on the Market for Competences

For each segment of a specific strategic population of knowledge workers, the firm must identify its competitors because the individual's choice depends primarily on his or her alternatives. As Barnard (1938) stated, a worker chooses whether he will enter into a specific organization based on: (1) purposes, desires, and impulses of the moment and (2) the external alternatives recognized by him (or her) as available.

9.6.1 The In-and-Out of Industry's Competition for Competences

The labor market is not a homogeneous one. It is segmented, and different competences represent different segments of the labor market. Competition differs in each segment, and each firm is more or less attractive in each segment. For example, in the segment of financial competence, a bank might compete with other banks but also compete with consulting firms. In the segment of IT competence, it competes with high-tech companies. The same bank may be very attractive in the first segment and unattractive in the second one.

Firms that compete for customers in the same industry or product market frequently have the same technologies, processes, resources, and skills. Therefore, for some competences, employers compete with firms in the same industry. The competitors in the product and services market (output) may be the same as those in the labor market (input). For example, the four major accounting firms PWC, EY, KPMG, and Deloitte compete over the same clients and potential employees. However, they might also compete with firms from other industrial sectors. The competition on the labor market does not strictly mirror the competition on the product market. For example, almost all firms and organizations compete for IT engineers. Therefore, a bank such as JPMorgan Chase that tries to recruit an IT engineer will face competition from all other firms and organizations interested in recruiting IT engineers. These may be other banks but also large companies (e.g., Nestlé, L'Oréal, General Electric), high-tech companies (e.g., IBM, Microsoft, Oracle), IT services firms (e.g., Accenture, Capgemini), public administrations (e.g., hospitals, universities), non-profit organizations (e.g., Amnesty International), or Internet start-ups.

For each segment of competence on the labor market, a firm should identify its competitors and diagnose its attractiveness by analyzing its strengths and weakness to recruit talents.

9.6.2 Geographical Dimension of Competition on the Labor Market

The attractiveness and competition faced by an employer on the labor market also depend on the geographical localization. An employer may be very attractive and well known in a country and less so in another. For example, the car maker Peugeot-Citroën is considered as an employer of choice by engineers in France but is not even considered as a potential employer in some other countries, such as the United States. Such a difference implies that the human capital constraint to develop an activity is weak in France and strong abroad. In other words, any strategic intent from Peugeot-Citroën to develop business in the United States would have to overcome its unattractiveness on the American labor market.

Moreover, the nature and intensity of competition differ depending on the localization. For example, the French bank Société Générale faces numerous competitors and intense competition on the labor market to develop its investment banking activities in London, where all the major investment banks worldwide are located. Conversely, competition for such competence is lower in Paris, where the company is headquartered. The geographical dimension of competition may lead employers to change their location to increase their attractiveness or reduce competition. For example, Zappos.com, an online shoe and clothing retailer originally based in San Francisco, moved to Las Vegas because of the huge competition from high-tech companies and start-ups in Silicon Valley. The same rationale explains why Uber settled its autonomous car entity in Pittsburgh and not in San Francisco, where the company is headquartered. In Pittsburgh, the expertise from Carnegie Mellon University in robotics and computer science is renowned worldwide. Uber is the main employer for autonomous car development in Pittsburgh and, hence, does not face the intense competition in Silicon Valley for such competence where Google (Waymo), Apple, Tesla Motors, and many other start-ups develop such activities.

9.6.3 Intensity of Competition in Different Segments of Competence in the Labor Market

Considering competition in the input market redefines the nature of competitors. Firms compete for competences in three different labor markets: expertise, industry, and geographic markets (Milkovich and Newman, 1993). The more overlap exists across these three dimensions, the more intense the competition will be (Figure 9.2). For example, the numerous Internet companies, large high-tech companies (e.g., Oracle, Intel, Apple, Google, and Facebook), and large firms (Ford, General Motors, Walmart, BMW, and Orange) developing Internet activities in Silicon Valley compete on all three dimensions. The location of these employers in the same region and transferability of employees' competences reduce the switching costs for knowledge workers migrating between companies and increase the competition among employers (Ferrary and Granovetter, 2009). In the 2000s, the failure of Yahoo!'s CEO's strategy to revamp the company was not related to the inadequacy of the strategic intent but to the inability to attract talented individuals to implement it.

To comprehend its attractiveness, a firm needs to analyze in which way its HRM practices that form its employee value proposition make it relatively more or less attractive than its competitors on each strategic segments of competence. Such understanding is required to design managerial innovation aiming to increase firm attractiveness.

	Industry	
	Same	Different
Close Geographical proximity	High competition	Moderate competition
Far	Moderate competition	Low competitition

Figure 9.2   Drivers of competition on the market for competence.

9.7 Firm Attractiveness Depends on Its Employee Value Proposition

Organizations facing competence scarcities will increase the competition for competences. However, how the attractiveness of the firm underpins the competitiveness of firms has yet to be explored. Firm attractiveness depends on its employee value proposition (EVP).

An EVP is not intrinsically attractive but its attractiveness is only relative to a competitor's EVP. This presupposes that the firm identifies its competitors in the labor market for each segment of competence and compares its EVP with those of its competitors to find ways to differentiate and create an attractive advantage. Depending on the industry and localization, each segment of competence values has different factors of attractiveness. An attractive EVP must be tailored for each specific type of individual the firm wants to attract. An attractive EVP also must be better than the other options that targeted individuals are considering. For example, to attract PhD graduates in finance for academic positions, business schools are competing with investment banks. Business schools' attraction in the competition with banks rests on the psychological (autonomy and work content) and sociological (prestige of an academic position) dimensions rather than on the financial dimension.

The firm's EVP is a strategic factor to attract knowledge workers. An EVP is "the holistic sum of everything people experience and receive while they are part of a company – everything from the intrinsic satisfaction of the work to the environment, leadership, colleagues, compensation, and more" (Michaels et al., 2001). The EVP is the set of associations and offerings provided by an organization in return for the knowledge, skills, and abilities the employee brings to the organization. An EVP comprises financial, sociological, and psychological rewards (Ferrary, 2012). These three types of rewards induce different types of motivation. Financial and sociological rewards equate with extrinsic motivation, and psychological rewards with intrinsic motivation. Connecting attractiveness and EVP in a competence-based view of the firm leads to considering HRM practices in another perspective of competence management. The strategic issue is to know whether the firm's HRM practices (e.g., compensation, benefits, training, and career path) make it more or less attractive than its competitors on the labor market.

The EVP contribution to firm attractiveness also depends on its visibility on the labor market. Employer branding increases attractiveness by communicating the EVP content to potential knowledge workers.

9.7.1 Financial Dimension of the EVP

Financial rewards can be short term or long term. They represent the worker's financial revenue. They include compensation (e.g., salary, bonus, and stock options), benefits (e.g., health insurance and retirement), and the career prospects (promotion opportunity, training, and employment security) offered by the firm. Financial rewards are an important aspect of a firm's attractiveness. A clear career path is also an incentive to attract and select knowledge workers. The "up-or-out" policy is widespread among knowledge firms such as law firms, consulting groups, investment banks, and IT services firms. Knowledge workers are recruited straight from elite universities and business and engineering schools and are set on a "partner track" and move up to the position of partner or leave the firm after approximately six years. The possibility of achieving partner status is a major source of motivation. The "out" policy is a guard against the lack of motivation and/or lack of competence.

In addition to the short-term compensation (salary and bonus), firms might consider ownership to attract and retain strategic knowledge workers (Ferrary, 2008). If most of the competence useful to the firm can only be applied by the individuals who possess it, the theoretical foundations of the shareholder value approach are challenged. Professional services firms, such as law firms, management consulting firms, auditing firms, and investment banks, are partnerships in which employees own the firm, and there are no or minority external shareholders. In this type of organization, those who learn the most and who are the most highly effective in using or applying their competence are eventually rewarded partner status and, thus, a stake in the firm. Partners have ownership stakes in their firms and usually share the profits earned. Thus, they have incentives to leverage their competence and social capital effectively (Hitt et al., 2001). Firms might use the bait of part ownership to lure knowledge workers and liquidity of stocks (possibility to sell them) to attract individuals.

The attractiveness of the ownership component of the EVP depends on the stage of development of the firm (start-up, growth, maturity, or decline). The stock price of a mature company has less potential to grow and, therefore, is less attractive to talent than rising start-ups. A start-up can be very attractive because of the potential gains linked to stock options. However, when the company becomes successful in its product market and goes public, the opportunity to make huge profits through stock options declines. Moreover, declining attractiveness might spark a vicious circle in which the company is finding it difficult to recruit critical competences to improve its products and innovate. The lack of innovation reduces competitiveness in the output market, further reducing its attractiveness on the labor market.

9.7.2 Sociological Dimension of the EVP

Sociological rewards are related to the social recognition induced by affiliation with the firm. This social recognition depends on the missions and values of the firm, its products, its CEO, its reputation, its ranking, its corporate social responsibility policy, and its work environment. Sociological rewards bring a sense of pride from working in the company. Firms differ in the sociological dimensions of their EVP.

Some are more prestigious than others and, therefore, are more attractive. The real issue for many companies is how to attract employees to work in less prestigious firms.

Corporate social responsibility affects attractiveness. Firms competing on this sociological dimension present themselves as "responsible" employers. They set up foundations to support non-profit organizations and contribute to the community. All publicize their support for human rights and environmental initiatives. Firms invest in corporate social responsibility not only to please customers but also to be more attractive on the labor market.

A firm may be more attractive on the labor market because of its reputation and the social status it provides. Non-governmental organizations such as Greenpeace or Amnesty International might be more attractive than law firms to attract legal experts because of the social recognition status and despite lower salaries. Conversely, some firms may be unattractive because they have a low social status. Tobacco companies are associated with a poor social status and face difficulties in recruiting talented individuals.

9.7.3 Psychological Dimension of the EVP

Psychological rewards are related to the content of jobs. The work content of a position can be defined by its various activities, the challenges it poses, the degree of autonomy, and its impact on the firm. The psychological dimension is related to intrinsic motivation. It refers to doing something because it is inherently interesting or enjoyable (distinct from extrinsic motivation, which refers to doing something because it leads to a separable outcome such as a financial or sociological reward). Intrinsic motivation means that the individual works for the fun of it or challenge. Intrinsically motivated behaviors, which are based on interest and satisfy the innate psychological need for competence and autonomy, are the prototypes for self-determined behavior (Deci and Ryan, 2000).

Knowledge workers are particularly sensitive to the psychological dimension of their work. Starbuck (1992) mentioned that most experts want autonomy and recognition of their individuality and that their firms should have egalitarian structures. For this reason, knowledge-intense firms downplay formal structure and achieve co-ordination through social norms and reward systems rather than hierarchical control. Many experts have a sense of their importance as individuals and a desire for autonomy, and too strict supervision would induce exit. Firm growth tends to lead to bureaucratization that reduces autonomy and psychological rewards and encourages employees to search for other jobs. However, individuals who are intrinsically motivated search for opportunities to create value but want their individual contributions recognized in their pay. Money is also related to psychological gratification. Compensation is critical to attract and maintain knowledge workers. Michaels et al. (2001) reported the findings from a survey that reward and recognition for high individual performance are seen as more important than the overall amount of cash or wealth they receive because many individuals see money as a scorecard for how well they have performed and how much the company values their talents.

9.7.4 Employer Branding

Employer brand is the organization's reputation on the labor market as an employer. Employer branding (Edwards, 2010) is the sum of the company's efforts to communicate to existing and prospective employees why it is a desirable place to work. The importance of company reputation increases the likelihood that potential applicants will apply for jobs in the organization. Employer branding programs tend to include external communication to increase recruits' awareness of the organization's EVP and its reputation. The employer brand can be evaluated. Rankings such as "The Great Place to Work for" and consulting groups such as Universum Global or Trendence measure the employer brand by workers and students, indicating the attractiveness of the firm.

The value of the employer brand can be reduced in various ways. Allegations about investment banks' responsibility for the 2008 financial crisis had an impact on their attractiveness. In 2008 and 2009, Goldman Sachs, one of the most prestigious investment banks in the world, was ranked 9th in "The Great Place to Work for" ranking published by Fortune, but fell to 24th in the 2010 ranking and 62nd in 2019.

9.8 Conclusion: HRM Innovation to Improve Firm Attractiveness

An EVP is a combination of three types of rewards: financial, sociological, and psychological. Highly attractive companies are attractive on the three dimensions. Prestigious firms that combine an "up-or-out" policy potentially to give access to partnership and offer interesting work content are attractive on the three dimensions of EVP. A consulting firm such as McKinsey scores high on all three dimensions. The firm is prestigious, regularly ranked as the best consulting group, and a favorite target of business school graduates. The firm applies an "up-or-out" policy that gives the best associates the opportunity to become partners and reap a share of the firm's profits. The work content is known to be very interesting, and young associates are quickly given responsibility. The combination of these features makes McKinsey very attractive for students from the best business schools and makes it difficult to out-compete on the labor market to attract the most talented workers.

Competence-based management should not focus only on highly qualified individuals but should be extended to any critical competence underlying a competitive advantage or required to implement a strategic intent. Recently, a famous French chef in the South of France has been forced to close his restaurant because of his inability to recruit skilled and motivated waiters and cooks. Even a well-designed strategy may require basic competence to be implemented. Considering firm attractiveness should be part of strategic thinking. The purpose is to design the right EVP to attract critical competences.

Strategic HR management focuses mainly on identifying HR practices creating value by managing competences inside the organization and underestimates the role played by interactions with direct competitors to attract required competences into the organization. Competence-based perspective should also assume that the firm identifies its competitors in the labor market and their EVP and finds ways to differentiate its EVP to make it more attractive. Identification of competitors is important because competing effectively on the labor market involves considering the impact on and reactions from competitors when the firm tries to make its EVP more attractive. Conversely, the firm needs to respond to the policy changes of competitors that may have an impact on its attractiveness. To attract strategic knowledge workers, it helps to gather systematic information on the activities of rivals competing for, especially, valuable pools of competences and apply counter-tactics to maintain a presence in the labor market (Gardner, 2002). A firm should identify the strengths and vulnerabilities of its EVP and decide which elements need to be improved to meet the needs of the targeted segment of competence in the labor market.

Firms use various tactics to gain an advantage over rivals on the labor market to attract talents such as initiating recruitment efforts and changing the pecuniary (e.g., wages, benefits, variable pay risk) and nonpecuniary (job design, autonomy) aspects of the employment relationship. Firms must design management innovations to improve their EVP and their attractiveness. Sherer and Lee (2002) showed that innovation in HRM practices in the head offices of large law firms is motivated by competitive pressure related to the scarcity of some competences.

A critical issue for an employer is to design management innovations to remain more attractive than its competitors on the labor market for strategic competences. However, innovations cannot be protected by intellectual property rights and information spreads quickly in the labor market, allowing rapid imitation by competitors. Some of the features of EVP that give an attractive advantage to a firm can be duplicated, forcing the firm to constantly innovate to maintain its attractive advantage in the labor market. The attractive advantage of the firm is related to the superiority of its EVP compared with that of its competitors. The sustainability of the attractive advantage of the firm depends on the reproducibility of its EVP by competitors in the labor market. Some parts of the EVP are reproducible (work environment and compensation), while others are less so (potential gains due to stock options or employer brand).

References

Barnard, C. (1938). *The Functions of the Executive*. Cambridge, MA: Harvard University Press.

Barney, J. B. (1991). Firm resources and sustained competitive advantage. *Journal of Management, 17*, 99–120.

Becker, B., & Huselid, M. (2006). Strategic human resources management: Where do we go from here? *Journal of Management, 32*(6), 898–925.

Boeker, W. (1997). Executive migration and strategic change: The effect of top manager movement on product-market entry. *Administrative Science Quarterly, 42*, 213–236.

Cappelli, P. (2000). A market-driven approach to retaining talent. *Harvard Business Review, 78*(1), 103–111.

Deci, E., & Ryan, R. (2000). Intrinsic and extrinsic motivations: Classic definitions and new directions. *Contemporary Educational Psychology, 25*, 54–67.

Delery, J. E., & Roumpi, D. (2017). Strategic human resource management, human capital and competitive advantage: Is the field going in circles? *Human Resource Management Journal, 27*(1), 1–21.

Edwards, M. (2010). An integrative review of employer branding and OB theory. *Personal Review, 39*(1), 5–23.

Felin, T., & Hesterly, W. (2007). The knowledge-based view, nested heterogeneity, and new value creation: Philosophical considerations on the locus of knowledge. *Academy of Management Review, 32*(1), 195–218.

Ferrary, M. (2008). Strategic Spin-off: A new incentive contract for managing R&D researchers. *Journal of Technology Transfer, 33*, 600–618.

Ferrary, M. (2010). Compétitivité de la firme et management stratégique des ressources humaines. *Revue d'Economie Industrielle, 15*(132), 1–28.

Ferrary, M. (2011). Specialized organizations and ambidextrous clusters in the open inno-vation paradigm. *European Management Journal, 29*, 181–192.

Ferrary, M. (2012). Attractiveness of the firm as a competitive advantage for knowledge-intense firms. In Dibiaggio, L. & Meschi, P.-X., *Management in the Knowledge Economy* (pp. 45–83). London, UK: Pearson, 323 p.

Ferrary, M. (2015). Investing in transferable strategic human capital through alliances in the luxury hotel industry. *Journal of Knowledge Management, 19*(5), 1007–1028.

Ferrary, M., & Trepo, G. (1998). La gestion par les compétences: Pour une opération-nalisation de la convergence entre la stratégie d'entreprise et la gestion des ressources humaines. *Revue Interactions, 2*(1), 54–83.

Ferrary, M., & Granovetter, M. (2009). The role of venture capital firms in Silicon Valley's complex Innovation Network. *Economy and Society, 38*(2), 326–259.

Gardner, T. (2002). In the trenches at the talent wars: Competitive interaction for scarce human resources. *Human Resource Management, 41*(2), 225–237 .

Gardner, T. (2005). Interfirm competition for human resources: Evidence from the soft-ware industry. *Academy of Management Journal, 48*(2), 237–256.

Grant, R. (1996). Toward a knowledge-based theory of the firm. *Strategic Management Journal, 17*, 109–122.

Hitt, M., Bierman, L., Shimizu, K., & Kochhar, R. (2001). Direct and moderating effects of human capital on strategy and performance in professional service firms: A resource-based perspective. *Academy of Management Journal, 44*(1), 13–28.

Kim, L. (1997). The dynamics of Samsung's technological learning in semiconductors. *California Management Review, 39*(3), 86–100.

Michaels, E., Handfield-Jones, H., & Axelrod, B. (2001). *The War for Talent* (200 p). Cambridge, MA: Harvard Business School Press.

Milkovich, G., & Newman, J. (1993). *Compensation*. Homewood, IL: Richard D. Irwin.

Nelson, R., & Winter, S. (1982). *An Evolutionary Theory of Economic Change.* Cambridge, MA and London: Belknap Harvard.

Nonaka, I. (1994). A dynamic theory of organizational knowledge creation. *Organization Science, 5*(1), 14–37.

Porter, M. (1985). *Competitive Advantage.* New York, NY: Free Press.

Prahalad, C. K., & Hamel, G. (1990). The core competence of the organization. *Harvard Business Review, 3,* 79–91.

Rao, H., & Drazin, R. (2002). Overcoming resource constraints on product innovation by recruiting talent from rivals: A study of the mutual fund industry, 1986–1994. *Academy of Management Journal, 45*(3), 491–507.

Sherer, P. D., & Lee, K. (2002). Institutional change in large law firms: A resource dependency and institutional perspective. *Academy of Management Journal, 45*(1), 102–119.

Simon, H. (1991). Bounded rationality and organizational learning. *Organization Science, 2*(1), 125–134.

Singh, J., & Agrawal, A. (2011). Recruiting for ideas: How firms exploit the prior inventions of new hires. *Management Science, 57*(1), 129–150.

Song, J., Almeida, P., & Wu, G. (2003). Learning-by-hiring: When is mobility more likely to facilitate interfirm knowledge transfer?. *Management Science, 49*(4), 351–365.

Starbuck, W. (1992). Learning by knowledge-intense firms. *Journal of Management Studies, 29*(6), 713–740.

Teece, D., Pisano G., & Shuen, A. (1997). Dynamic capabilities and strategic management. *Strategic Management Journal, 18*(7), 509–533.

Tzabbar, D. (2009). When does scientist recruitment affect technological repositioning? *Academy of Management Journal, 52*(5), 873–896.

Wernerfelt, B. (1984). A resource-based view of the firm. *Strategic Management Journal, 5,* 171–180.

Wright, P. M., & McMahan, G. C. (2011). Exploring human capital: Putting "human" back into strategic human resource management. *Human Resource Management Journal, 21*(2), 93–104.

Chapter 10

From the Transmission of Skills to the Concept of Competence: Lessons from a Case Study in the Aerospace Industry

Thierry Colin and Fabien Meier

Contents

10.1 Introduction

The transmission of knowledge and skills has become a prime issue in organizations. The success or failure of such actions may sometimes condition the performance and survival of a company. In management science, the transmission of competences is rarely seen as a separate issue, with most studies focusing on competences themselves (Defélix et al., 2006; Delamare-Le Deist and Winterton, 2005; Oiry, 2005; Singleton, 1978) or focusing on tools that enable the transfer of skills (Conjard et al., 2006; Kloetzer, 2015).

This chapter is based on the case study of a greenfield project of a factory in the aerospace industry that needs to deliver large quantities of parts, at rigorous quality standards, within short deadlines. To do this, the company scheduled a major recruitment drive, although the skills needed are not directly available in the labor market. Recognizing that this has been a major issue in the launching of the company, a strategy for transferring skills based mainly on peer tutoring has been implemented.

We had the opportunity to follow this approach for several years. In this longitudinal study, we investigated the mechanisms at work in the transmission of skills, and here we set out the lessons learned about the very concept of competence itself. Studying this skill transmission process based on peer tutoring helped us understand that employees were in fact building competences by performing their tasks. Competence here reveals itself as a combination of resources capable of evolution and reconstruction and of finding its place in the heart of any activity. Studying skills transmission offered us the possibility to explore this concept and also to have an alternative view on how competences are built.

We start by presenting the activity theory we have chosen to use. We focus in particular on the work of Engeström (1987, 2001) and the role of mediating artifacts. Our theoretical framework also draws on the contributions of professional didactics, and we explain several of its concepts here. Next, we present the case study and the methodology we used to conduct this longitudinal study. Then, we share the most significant results of this study, grouped by whether they are related to work situations, to actors in particular work situations, or to work organization.

Finally, we discuss these results in a way that draws out the lessons we have learned, both about the transmission of competences and about the concept of competence itself.

10.2 An Analysis of the Transmission of Competence Using Activity Theory

Our approach has been to observe work activity in order to understand the transmission of skills going on. We focus on activity to understand how production operators learn from each other. For this, we rely on activity theory, recently introduced into French-language studies in human resources management (HRM) (Colin and Grasser, 2014; Engeström, 2011; Gilbert and Raulet-Croset, 2012; Gilbert et al., 2013). This theory provides a detailed analysis of the link between employment and competence transmission. We propose complementing this approach by drawing on the contributions of professional training, (Pastré et al., 2006; Piaget, 1937), in order to highlight the mechanisms at work for individuals. While activity theory sheds light on how the transmission of skills operates from the viewpoint of collective organization, professional training theory allows us to focus on individuals. Using these insights provides a dynamic and original vision of the transmission of skills and the concept of competence.

10.2.1 Activity Systems

Activity theory (AT) was initiated by Lev Vygotsky (1978) and extended by Yrjö Engeström (2001). It has introduced the idea of mediation in the activity of individuals whereby a mediating artifact comes between a stimulus and its response. This conception of activity is often represented as a triangle (Figure 10.1). The subject is the person, the individual involved in the activity. The object is the raw material of the activity (using a tool, entering a doctor's surgery, reading a text out loud, etc.). In this representation, the subject is no longer involved in an immediate relationship with the object of her activity; but she enters a relationship mediated by an artifact. Vygotsky's seminal work has been extended by Engeström, who

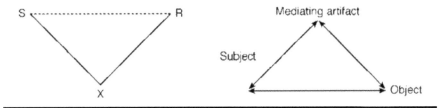

Figure 10.1   The basis of the activity system (Engeström, 2001).

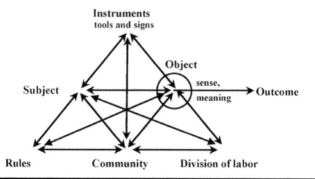

Figure 10.2   The structure of the activity system (Engeström, 1987).

connected the original triangle with "rules," "the community," and the division of labor" (Figure 10.2).

The components of an activity system are as follows:

- The subject refers to an individual or a subgroup whose point of view has been chosen as the perspective of the analysis (Engeström and Sannino, 2010). The subject accomplishes the object (or purpose) of the activity, as the subject is involved in an action that is directed toward an object.
- The object is the raw material of the activity system (Engeström and Sannino, 2010), so the activity is directed at it.
- The mediating artifact is one or more instruments (signs or tools) that transform the purpose of the activity and give it meaning.
- The rules are regulations, sets of laws, whether implicit or explicit, governing the action.
- The community is the entity in which the individual or subgroup is included, which pursues the same general object.
- The division of labor is the division of labor and tasks or the division of power found in companies.
- The result is the object stemming from the subject's action, which incorporates the meaning given by the collective activity and is relayed through the mediating artifact.

The whole point of activity theory is to situate work into a systemic framework which prevents analyzing an activity in isolation. Individual competences are employed and their transmissions are repositioned within a collective framework.

10.2.2 AT Allows the Interactions between Two Activity Systems to Be Analyzed

As noted by Gilbert et al. (2013, p. 71), "The specific contribution by Engeström also stems from his interest in the work that develops at the intersection of several

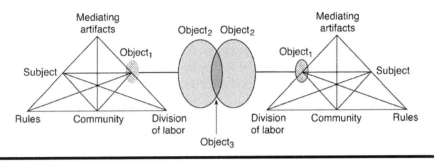

Figure 10.3   Two interacting activity systems (Engeström and Sannino, 2010).

activity systems". Engeström has put forward a model that positions individuals' actions within a community, in a way that shows how individual actions are transformed into shared and collective activities. This model is also relevant when analyzing the interactions at work when two people are engaged in a common activity. Activity theory makes it possible to understand better the exchanges between several interrelated activity systems.

Figure 10.3 shows two interacting activity systems. Engeström explains how *object 1* evolves from its original status as a raw material in the activity system to being *object 2*, which expresses the sense given to it by the activity system. Third generation activity theory even points to the possibility that the two interacting activity systems produce a shared *object 3*. The contradictions present within an activity system or between activity systems make it possible to understand how the system corrects itself and evolves.

10.2.3 The Contributions of Professional Didactics

Activity theory allows learning to be repositioned in the broader context of the system in which it takes place. However, it does not tell us much about individual cognitive mechanisms when acquiring a competence.

Professional didactics are a way of analyzing the activity of persons at work to understand better their development. Didactics builds on the work of Jean Piaget and Lev Vygotsky, who were mainly concerned by the development of children, by studying these changes in work-place situations. Professional didactics are based on both ergonomic psychology and the study of labor analysis in vocational training (Pastré, 2011, p. 11), introducing the notion of schemes.

Pastré et al. (2006, p. 149) draw on the work of Piaget and provide a definition: "the scheme is (…) the means of assimilating new objects and to accommodate oneself to the new properties they have, compared to the previously assimilated objects. At the same time, it has a twofold function, an action on reality, and an exploration of the properties of the real."

They add that the concept of the scheme concerns "the organization of the activity" and is the "cornerstone" of the analysis of the activity. To understand the mechanisms involved in the development of professional skills, Pastré et al. (2006) observed work situations and the representation individuals make of these situations. They point out that individuals may have very different representations of their work situation: "The meaning of a work situation or of training is both individual and shared: individual because the meaning given by any individual is specific and differs from one individual to another; shared precisely because the individuals of a community agree relatively well on the meaning in a given situation, for a given practice" (Pastré et al., 2006, p.149)

The transmission of competences takes place when an individual is able to share his representation of a professional activity as well as how he combines his resources. We refer to Piaget (Barrouillet, 2015; de Ribaupierre, 2015) to argue that the operator who is learning has an initial representation of a situation, which is then "destabilized" through observation or practice. She therefore has to create a new equilibrium by a process of accommodation and assimilation.

The learner operator will face problems (misunderstanding terms, misunderstanding requisite gestures, ignorance of tools, etc.) that will be highlighted when working with a qualified operator. She would have previously developed an understanding of the situation, albeit partial, and would have managed to reach a first point of equilibrium. This first equilibrium could well be quite incomplete or wrong but serves as a basic understanding of the situation and the way the operator needs to respond. The work then carried out in the tutoring situation with a skilled operator, by observation and by working with or under the supervision of the skilled operator, will cause representations to collide with one another.

The skilled operator has a direct impact on the patterns of the learner, via the information or corrections passed on. In this way, the learning operator changes the way she should combine her resources, i.e., by changing her understanding of the situation and the resources available. Professional didactics show that the transmission of skills goes beyond the transmission of knowledge which entails a simple transfer of resources, because the transmission of skills actually acquires learning a new combination of resources. It involves not only the transmission of information but the reconfiguration of operational schemes through the interaction (observation, discussion, and correction) with another employee.

10.3 Presentation of the Case

10.3.1 A New and Vital Technology for the Company

The AERO company was recently established in eastern France, and the transfer of competences is a major issue in the takeoff of the industrial project the company is pursuing, but also in the industrial sustainability of the site. AERO is a 100%

subsidiary of a large industrial group. The group, in collaboration with an American firm, produces a range of aircraft engines which have been a great commercial success. Among the features and technical advances of the new engine, certain parts are made of composite material (including the fan blades and engines' motor housing). Manufacturing parts out of composite material is not unprecedented for making aviation engines, but it is still uncommon. It yields significant gains in weight and engine noise without compromising strength. The group produces these composite material parts and has opted to set up several production plants in France but also in the United States and Mexico. AERO is the French factory responsible for the production of blades and housings made of composite materials. The company was founded in 2012 and has been located in eastern France since 2014. It is one of three companies in the world, with "sister" plants in the United States and Mexico which produce these parts too. The AERO plant is structured around two specialized production lines (blades and housings). Its supplier provides the company with a semifinished product. AERO is therefore essentially involved in tasks of finishing and quality control.

10.3.2 Issues Related to the Transmission of Skills

Starting with a core of trained operators in the US plant, the company had to increase its workforce to meet the expected increase in activity and had 200 employees in 2017. This increase in staff was considerable, and the human resources department had to face three major challenges.

First, it had to make sure that the company was able to continue production while respecting the high quality requirements of the aerospace industry, i.e., to ensure that persons recruited were able to mobilize all the competences required.

Second, it was important to ensure that the company could train employees for new jobs as well as for new parts, both within AERO and for the group to which it belongs.

Third, it was necessary to ensure the presence of sufficient staff at the right skill levels, while respecting a maximum two-year deadline. Thus, it is not only important to focus on the number of people and their level of qualification. Care also needs to be taken about setting up an organization that allows competence to be accumulated which is optimal in terms of quality and deadlines.

To face all these challenges, AERO adopted the solution of transmitting operator competences from trained operators to learning operators in tutorials.

10.4 Methodology: Observation, Interviews, and Video Recording

Our research is based on a case study (Yin, 1981, 2003). In this type of methodology, commonly used in HRM research, the choice of cases is based primarily on the potential ability to draw valuable lessons (Stake, 1994).

Data were collected as part of sponsored PhD research, so that one of the researchers held a position of responsibility in the company. He was therefore immersed in the organization being researched itself. We believe that knowledge – both practical and theoretical – is created in the working environment. To this end, we have been committed to following the methodological principles of intervention research (David and Hatchuel, 2007). The main objective of the research protocol implemented was to observe the actors in the transmission of competences when they were specifically trying to pass on their skills. To this end, we developed a three-step methodology.

Step 1: Understanding the practices and activities by observation

The first step of the research was focused on the observation of different production activities within AERO. It was indeed necessary to have precise knowledge of professional practices in the various trades.

Step 2: Investigating the transmission of competences using interviews

We next wanted to deepen our understanding, not of actors' activities themselves, but of how actors felt sharing their skills. Indeed, Step 1 of the practical observation showed that close relationships were formed between tutors and people needing to learn their craft: the operators/mentors on the one hand and the learners/mentees on the other hand. However, apart from the general framework set by the company, there have been no specific instructions on the methodology of imparting skills. Thus, the observation of practices revealed that the transmission of competences was fundamentally embedded in production activity. We therefore wanted to understand how tutors and newcomers operated a transmission of competences. To this end, we chose to question actors by drawing on a common guide for semi-directive interviews, used with all the actors working in production at AERO, as well as with employees in the US plant. We sought to identify a link between the activity of production and the transmission of skills. We also looked to see what the forces at work were and to understand if two activities are independent or not.

Step 3: Observing the transmission of competences through video recording

The interviews provided us information about the experience of the actors and gave us the subjective vision of "insiders" in the transmission of skills. They did not, however, make it possible to have an outside view of the activities examined. For this third step, we therefore opted for a research protocol that was as close as possible to actors' practices, while being the least intrusive, namely observation by automated video recording. This methodology has the advantage of capturing long video sequences that are then available for later study. To obtain sufficiently consistent data while keeping the volume of information to be analyzed to a "reasonable" level, we chose to limit the video recording to the gluing activities of operators and only film situations which brought together actors as competences were transmitted. We relied on the methodology of Gylfe et al. (2016) to draw out a scientific understanding of the accumulation of the raw video data. This helped to generate a multitude of data of scientific content, selecting important elements and seeking to establish groupings. We gathered more than 24 hours of video recording that enabled us to rely on robust material.

10.5 Results

The results of this longitudinal study were grouped into three categories. The first concerns the results focusing on the central role of artifacts in learning situations at work. The results addressing the negotiated aspects of the relationship between mentors and mentees constitute the second category, and the final one consists of results looking at learning outside peer tutoring relationship. At these three levels, we can see that the transfer of competences between skilled operators and learner operators is a process that goes beyond the transfer between two individuals. Instead, it involves a co-construction in which the environment, the organization, and the actors have a leading role. It allows us to go beyond the skill transfer analysis to observe how competences are constructed. We base our results on some of the (verbatim) transcripts and images of the videos.

10.5.1 The Central Role of Artifacts in Learning Situation at Work

Both the interviews and video observation stress the central role played by fan blades or motor housings as artifacts in situations of the transmission of competences. As shown in Verbatim 1, the presence of the artifact is fundamental to learning, as the tutor explains how it is essential to carrying out the transmission of skills. This result was confirmed with a number of (verbatim) interviews and video observations.

J: Right now it is not easy to tutor someone on the motor housing because **we are not working in a big business**. There are many of us in the team and we need everyone to practice. (…) **It is essential to have the part on which we work**.
Researcher: For you, the main tool is the part?
J: **It's the part**. The person has to see **what they will do**. I have tried to explain this to them, to make them read texts or show them photos. Seeing the part allows them immediately to be in a condition to work: "This is what you should expect." Only then is everything in place to give work instructions.

(Verbatim 1 J., Tutor – Gluing of Housing)

Figure 10.4   Focus of attention on the product.

In another example, shown in Figure 10.4, the attention of the tutor and the two learners who are watching is focused on the laying of a covering. To be meaningful, this activity cannot only be described. It must be observed and performed. It is only in actually performing the task that the learner can understand where exactly to place the coating, the pressure to be exerted, and the duration needed to maintain this pressure on the coating.

Our results also show that the availability of work instructions (WI) can have an impact on the dynamics of the transmission of skills. Even beyond the availability of work instructions, our study shows that the confidence of operators in these instructions is highly relative. It is moreover possible to observe a certain degree of skepticism and distance shown by employees about the knowledge made available to them by the company.

Researcher: The work instructions provided there, are they useful to you, a little? A lot?

M: We should use them more. Honestly. **They do not serve to explain the job or help work on a daily basis.** They are there. We show [learners] that they exist. But on a daily basis, we do not live with the work instructions.

(Verbatim 2 M., Learner – Fan Inspection)

During our observations, the use of the WI was not systematic: they were not used to guide the activity directly.

Researcher: In your training, were there tools at your disposal to learn well?

F: Not much. The WI are easy. To control … The WI are simplistic. They just say what to control, but not more than that. They don't go into the field of control; just to provide information as simply as possible.

(Verbatim 3 F., Mentee – Fan Blade Inspection)

However, we observed that as production picked up, employees gave greater importance to the work instructions. We noticed that they were sometimes used to adjudicate between certain nuances in employees' practices. We also observed that employees frequently pointed out differences between persons who actually carried out specific tasks and those who drafted the procedures.

The limits of the work instructions were indeed recognized by some engineers, even though AERO is operating in an industry where quality is paramount. The reply by a member of the methods team responsible in particular for drafting the WI is illuminating:

Researcher: Where does a good gluer create value added? What makes the gluer good?

H: If he [or she] glues well, properly. What is a good gluer? Someone who is conscientious, who will check the work done. All good practices are not in WI: some operators will add a tape end or cut the tape so that the glue does not flow. A good gluer is someone who thinks that quality is a top issue.

(Verbatim 4 H., Engineer – Gluing)

This engineer himself noted the difference between practices: "good practices" and those actually set out in the work instructions. He pointed out this difference as if the WI were a general framework, in which it was possible to formulate one's own more or less effective practices. It is clear that acquiring a competence in this framework cannot be equated with simply learning the work instructions. They are part of the resources to be mobilized, but are not enough to do the job well.

10.5.2 The Negotiated Side of the Relationship between Mentors and Mentees

The second family of results concerns relationships between employees taking part in the same situation of transmitting competences. We have seen through activity theory that the transmission of expertise is the result of a construction by two subjects. It therefore brings together at least two players, and our observations indicate that the relationships between these actors are marked by specific characteristics. In particular, our research has shown that the relationship between a tutor and a learner operator/mentee was systematically original, reconstructed by each pair or each group.

Researcher: Are you having problems? Are there some difficulties in teaching people the job?

M: I have made good progress, in terms of the way I was. I was a tutor in my previous job but I was really directive. Here I have learned to let people do things themselves, which means not waiting months and months before trusting them. Maybe it's the job that requires this; here the fan is already made. I try to let others practice. Then there are character problems. I don't explain to X like I do to others. The training changes according to people ... You have to adapt to the person across the street.

(Verbatim 34 M., Tutor – Fan Inspection)

The negotiation of this mentoring relationship takes place on several levels. It varies according to the time tutors spend with their mentees. Tutors spend different amounts of time with them, depending on tutors' work constraints, their perceptions of the skills level of their mentee(s), or depending on the number of people they have to supervise. The negotiation also changes the content which the tutor gives to the learner. Tutors will explain certain points, more or less, and agree to repeat themselves or not. Finally the negotiation takes place about how the work situation is organized, depending on whether the mentee is alone or not, in receiving explanations, if she has regular opportunities to compare her work with that of the tutor.

10.5.3 Learning Outside of the Peer Tutoring Relationship

Hierarchical relationships appear to be relatively absent. The tutors we consulted are aware of having had rare and crucial technical competences for when the business was launched. They also more frequently referred to a more clearly subordinate relationship with the methods department, which represents the technical expertise within the company, than with their direct supervisors. For their part, the learners/ mentees seem to consider their tutor as a supervisor, as their first point of reference, and they have no clear idea of what their actual superiors expect of them. Yet in our research and field study, we did not exactly observe the direct and exclusive transmission of knowledge between tutors and their mentees. We found that, although this relationship is especially important, learners had other relationships too and also learned from other actors in the company.

Researcher: Do you feel that you have learned from people other than your two tutors?
LZ: Oh that's clear. In gluing, by watching people work. Sometimes they call us to
highlight mistakes. We then also learn.

(Verbatim 5 L.Z., Learner – Blade Fan Inspection)

Video data show that learning is dispersed, that is to say, that mentees also learn from observation and discussions they have outside the mentoring relationship with other actors in the company. Video recordings show that some learner operators move around the production area and observe the working practices of others, in order to compare their own practices and those of their tutors'.

The requirement of tutors to do their production work and at the same time mentor learners was sometimes problematic. The interviews in particular revealed that tutors make trade-offs according to the urgency of production and their tutoring obligations.

10.6 Discussion

By basing our research on activity theory and professional didactics, we have tried to shed light on skill transmission while taking into account the full weight of work situations. By focusing on skills, our research helped us to understand the way competences are built within the context of mentoring in work situations. Similarly, our methodology has tried to be as close as possible to work situations, in order to understand how the transmission of skills operates. Here we try to discuss our main findings from the perspective of the conception of competences.

10.6.1 The Transmission of Work-Based Competences: An Activity Theory Approach

Connecting activity theory and skills transmission here seeks to understand and locate the transmission of competences within the work situation. We began in fact by considering skills, and we ended up dealing with the concept of competence. Let us now place these results within the framework of activity theory (Figure 10.5).

The transmission of competences takes place at the intersection of two activity systems. In situations where competences are transmitted during work, the two operators work together (object 2). As the results of the video recordings show, by working together, operators are required to exchange knowledge, correct each other, and give explanations through gestures or words. In other words, they

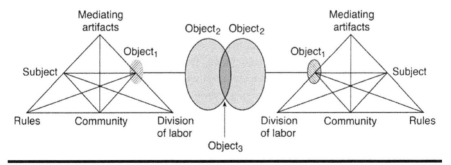

Figure 10.5 Representation of the activity systems of skilled operators and learners.

project the way they understand things and the way they arrange the resources at their disposal on the representation of their working situation (object 3). Therefore we understand that what we observed was not about skills but really about the competence transmission that takes place when skilled operators manage to share their representations, and especially, when they manage to project onto the work situation the way they assemble the combination of their own resources, while the learner operators manage to grasp them. In fact, it is through work that mentors and learners transmit skills together. Through observation, by mutual correction, and through supervising each other's work, the mentor and the mentee manage to reconstruct the combination of resources on which their competences are based. Accordingly, we understand that skill transmission leads to competence building in a dynamic way. This is not only about knowledge transfer or know-how learning: it is really about understanding resources and how to assemble them in the work situation.

10.6.2 *The Artifact: Keystone of Skill Transmission and Competence Building*

In activity theory, the role of the mediating artifact is of primary importance. It gives meaning to work. The fan blades and motor housings are the products on which production operators work at AERO. They are central to the professional activity of the company's employees. In our results, we have stressed their importance because the professional activity cannot be carried out without these products. And as the transmission of skills is at the heart of professional activity, no transmission of skills can take place without fan blades or motor housings. Without these products, professional activity is completely meaningless. Our results show that the transmission of skills is often hindered by the absence of a mediating artifact. This teaches us that the transfer of competences is at the heart of the activity and that it is a co-construction based on the activity itself, to such an extent that it is difficult to distinguish what belongs to professional activity and what concerns the transmission of skills. The mediating artifact allows a dialogue to take place between the tutor and the person being tutored about the professional activity. It is a tool, a support, and a tangible result of the construction of operational schemes at work, in the exercise of a professional activity. Thus the artifacts – here fan blades or motor housings – are not only the products on which operators ply their trade. They are also a means of expression, as much as being a means for operators to implement their schemes and so make them readable for other operators, with whom they work, opening up the possibility of improving their schemes. The importance of the artifacts in the process of the transmission of competences studied here emphasizes the situation in which the competence is contextualized. In a totally different context, our results are close to those of Dumouchel presented in Chapter 11 of this book.

10.7 Conclusion

In conclusion, it may be asked what the transmission of skills teaches us about the very concept of competence itself. This begins by confirming that competences exist within a work activity, that they are a process, a structure, underlying the activity. This study of the transmission of skills allows us to assert that competences are expressed by work, by a professional activity itself. When they are cut off from their working environment, they cannot express themselves or be transmitted from one individual to another.

These observations highlight the limitations of a decontextualized managerial approach to competence, what Sandberg (2000) calls "rationalistic approaches," and we advocate a contextualized approach to competence. In this perspective, professional didactics help us to understand that individual learning does not aim at the acquisition of competence, but much more fundamentally at the modification of actionable schemes. Such schemes are an individual's own mental organization that allows her to respond to the demands of the situation in which she is working.

The interviews we conducted, coupled with our video recordings, also confirm the idea that competence is a construct, a combination of heterogeneous resources. Our study shows that this combination is far from being static, but can evolve. It may be in equilibrium, yet such an equilibrium can be re-examined in the light of practices by third parties. The evolution of this combination of resources stems both from corrections contributed by a subject based on her personal experience and from the observations she may make about the activity of her peers, or of all the other interactions that can be found in collective work. The activity theory seems particularly interesting because it allows us to place the process of competence transmission within a collective context (the existence of rules, a community, a division of labor, etc.) and thus proposes a theoretical framework for an analysis of the interactions between the individual and the collective levels of competence. It may make it possible to take up the challenge proposed in the conclusion of this book for "a multilevel and contextualized perspective on competences."

References

Barrouillet, P. (2015). Theories of Cognitive Development: From Piaget to Today. *Developmental Review, 38*, 1–12.

Colin, T., & Grasser, B. (2014). Les instruments de gestion médiateurs de la compétence collective ? Le cas du Lean dans une entreprise de l'automobile. *@GRH, 3*(12), 75–102.

Conjard, P., Devin, B., & Olry, P. (2006). Acquérir et transmettre des compétences dans les organisations. In *XVIIème congrès de l'AGRH, IAE de Lille et Reims Management School* (pp. 16–17).

David, A., & Hatchuel, A. (2007). From actionable knowledge to universal theory in management research. In Shani, A. B., Albers Mohrman, S., Pasmore, W. A., Stymne,

B. & Adler, N. (Eds.), *Handbook of Collaborative Management Research* (pp. 33–47). New York NY: SAGE Publications.

de Ribaupierre, A. (2015). Piaget's theory of cognitive development. In Wright, J. D. (Ed.), *International Encyclopedia of the Social & Behavioral Sciences* (2nd edition, pp. 120–124). Oxford, UK: Elsevier.

Defélix, C., Klarsfeld, A., & Oiry, E. (2006). *Nouveaux regards sur la gestion des compétences.* Paris, France: Vuibert.

Delamare-Le Deist, F., & Winterton, J. (2005). What is competence? *Human Resource Development International, 8*(1), 27–46.

Engeström, Y. (1987). *Learning by Expanding: An Activity-Theoritical Approach to Developments Research.* Cambridge, UK: Cambridge University Press.

Engeström, Y. (2001). Expansive learning at work: Toward an activity theoretical reconceptualization. *Journal of Education and Work, 14*(1), 133–156.

Engeström, Y. (2011). Théorie de l'Activité et Management. *Management & Avenir, 2*(42), 170–182.

Engeström, Y., & Sannino, A. (2010). Studies of expansive learning: Foundations, findings and future challenges. *Educational Research Review, 5*(1), 1–24.

Gilbert, P., & Raulet-Croset, N. (2012). Lev Vytgotski: la théorie de l'activité. In Allouche, J. (Ed.), *Encyclopédie des Ressources Humaines* (pp. 1989–1995). Paris, France: Vuibert.

Gilbert, P., Raulet-Croset, N., Mourey, D., & Triomphe, C. (2013). Pour une contribution de la théorie de l'activité au changement organisationnel. *@GRH, 7*(2), 67–88. doi:10.3917/grh.132.0067

Gylfe, P., Franck, H., Lebaron, C., & Mantere, S. (2016). Video methods in strategy research: Focusing on embodied cognition. *Strategic Management Journal, 37*(1), 133–148.

Kloetzer, L. (2015). L'engagement conjoint dans la pratique comme clef du développement de l'activité des tuteurs. *Psychologie du Travail et des Organisations, 21*(3), 286–305.

Oiry, E. (2005). Qualification et compétence : deux soeurs jumelles ? *Revue Française de Gestion,* (158), 13–34.

Pastré, P. (2011). La didactique professionnelle. Un point de vue sur la formation et la professionnalisation. *Education Sciences & Society, 2*(1), 83–95.

Pastré, P., Mayen, P., & Vergnaud, G. (2006). La didactique professionnelle. *Revue française de pédagogie. Recherches en éducation 1*(154), 145–198.

Piaget, J. (1937). *The Construction of Reality in the Child.* Totton: Routledge.

Sandberg, J. (2000). Understanding human competence at work: An interpretative approach. *Academy of Management Journal, 43*(1), 9–25.

Singleton, W. T. (1978). *The Study of Real Skills.* Lancaster: University Park Press.

Stake, R. (1994). Case studies. In Denzin, N. K., & Lincoln, S. (Eds.), *Strategies of Qualitative Inquiry* (pp. 86–109). New York, NY: Sage Publications.

Vygotsky, L. (1978). Interaction between learning and development. *Readings on the Development of Children, 23*(3), 34–41.

Yin, R. K. (1981). The case study crisis: Some answers. *Administrative Science Quarterly, 26*, 58–65.

Yin, R. K. (2003). *Case Study Research: Design and Methods.* New York, NY: Sage Publications.

Chapter 11

Competences and Work Contexts: Learning from the French Ergonomic Approach

Nathalie Jeannerod-Dumouchel

Contents

11.1 Introduction: Organization, Work, and Competences

Any competences approach is interested in work (Ughetto, 2009). Job descriptions, competences frameworks, recruitment grids, training objectives, assessment procedures, or salary scales all try to grasp some aspects of work and formulate them in the appropriate language to feed the main human resource (HR) processes. In France, as a result of political and economic crises, the initial link between work, competences, and organizations gradually became loose as HR policies focused more on saving employment than on studying work organizations in response to the failure of Taylorian models (Oiry, 2009). In the past three decades, many French researches and HR practices about competences management concentrated on managing employment and some of its main aspects: recruitment, change management, employability, mobility, or layoffs. In doing so, they paid less attention to recognizing the difficulties workers face in their daily work situations and to their organizational causes (Loisil, 2009). In the meanwhile, competences have become a major strategic question, as core competences are the basis of sustained competitive advantage (Prahalad and Hamel, 1990; Chen and Chang, 2010). Organizations build their competitive advantage on valuable, rare, and difficult to imitate organizational competences (Prahalad and Hamel, 1990) through their specific culture, which creates a context in which individual competences are embedded and become unique (Chen and Chang, 2010). When facing deep transformations, organizations have to adapt both their core competences at the organizational level and job requirements at the individual level. This can be achieved through many different ways of managing the change, also depending on each national culture and its understanding and use of what is a competence (Delamare Le Deist and Winterton, 2005).

For Oiry (2009), new research in professional didactics, psychology, and sociology now helps rebuild the link between competences, work, and organization. This chapter is a contribution toward reactivating this link by drawing on the French roots of competences management in ergonomics. Through an empirical research in a large French company involved in a strategic transformation, we show that paying ergonomics-inspired attention to activity leads to a better understanding of the effects of work contexts on competences.

11.2 Competences Management: French Conceptual Roots in Ergonomics

Several authors have discussed the various definitions of the concept of "competence," questioning the theoretical perimeter, organizational level of use, or cultural assumptions implicitly conveyed through the different words to qualify it (Cheng and Dainty, 2003; Grzeda, 2005; Chen and Chang, 2010). There are clearly different usages of the concept in occidental countries as Delamare Le Deist and Winterton (2005) show by analyzing the behavioral approach in the United States, the functional approach in the UK, and the multi-dimensional approach in France, Germany, and Austria. Comparing the North American and French approaches on competences management, Bouteiller and Gilbert (2005) underline many differences. The authors show that the context of emergence of competences management, its conceptualization, instrumentation, targeted population, and even its main purpose are distinct on each side of the Atlantic Ocean. They also point out the difference in disciplinary roots: North American research was rooted in psychology while French research was clearly inspired by ergonomics and to a lesser degree by educational science. These roots lead to a specific way of considering competences at the individual job level, as we outline now.

Since the seminal works in ergonomic psychology (Ombredane, 1955), French ergonomics have paid much attention to the concept of "activity" with a distinction between *what* and *how* people work. More precisely, researchers analyzed the differences between task requirements and operational sequences to meet the requirements. While being inspired by the same fundamental works of Mayo (1933), Maslow (1943), and Herzberg (1959), French and Anglo-Saxon ergonomists soon diverged from one another (Lancry, 2016). Since the 1970s, Anglo-Saxons have focused on the *human factor* and its physiological and psychological dimensions in the human/machine interface while French ergonomists have concentrated on *activity* (Lancry, 2016). Largely inspired by Russian contributions of Vygotski (1992), Leontiev, and Bakhtine (quoted by Clot, 2008), French ergonomics have developed work situations analyses, in which technical and organizational contexts as well as production constraints are largely explored (Lancry, 2016).

From that period, the subjects of *health and work conditions* have become central in French management, for political and cultural reasons. journal May 1968 fostered an intense effort to improve work conditions in organizations and the French government created in 1973 a public institution dedicated to the subject* (Linhart, 2012). While Anglo-Saxon psychology studied work situations through detailed surveys (e.g., Hackman and Oldham, 1975), researchers from the "Société d'ergonomie de langue française"† were expanding outside laboratories to confront real workplace situations (Leplat, 1986, 1990; Teiger et al., 2014). This new approach was largely the result of a continuous cooperation with labor unions who wanted to understand the roots of workers' health problems. After many years of research, it led to the well-known difference between *prescribed work* and *real work*. Already emergent in earlier sociological studies, this duality is nowadays a reference for many disciplines (Daniellou, 2005, Teiger et al., 2014).

---

* ANACT: Agence Nationale pour l'Amélioration des Conditions de Travail (National Agency for Work Conditions Improvement).
† French-Language Ergonomic Society.

The difference between prescribed and real work is mainly based on the place given to *work context*. French ergonomists approaches, together with their colleagues in work psychodynamics, have long developed specific attention to the contextual dimensions of real work (Gaudard and Duarte, 2015). Real work is a succession of singular situations, always unique by their ever-changing context. Each work situation has its own set of relationships (customers, colleagues, and subcontractors), available material and procedures (tools, work position, and software) or specific objectives (production, quality, and deadline) (Flores, 1982). It is an unprecedented event in time and space for each worker. Moreover, there is always something unexpected in a work situation, which can come from any of the ingredients of the context (Dejours, 2003; Deranty, 2009). Real work is about what people add to prescribed work to take into account the contextual dimensions of each work situation (Dejours, 2003; Deranty, 2009). It can be called "intelligence of the situation" (Leplat and Montmollin, 2001). While prescribed work is a *decontextualized* vision of work applicable to any situation, real work is a succession of contextualized activities.

Following the evolutions of work over time, the focus of French ergonomics on work conditions and health turned from physiological to cognitive matters and their methodologies turned from diagnosis to prospective analyses to anticipate the effects of transformations (Daniellou et al., 2016; Delgoulet and Vidal-Gomel, 2014). The emergence of competences management is one of the evolutions of work. Considering the different designations of competences, ergonomists focused on *skills* for an activity (Leplat and Montmollin, 2001). A skill is always *for* an activity although the relationship between activity and skill is not always straightforward, as different skills may lead to perform in a single activity (Leplat, 1991). Montmollin (1984) defined competences as a set of knowledge, know how, conducts, standard procedures, and rationales that can be used without any new learning. They are plural as they derive from real activities. For him (Montmollin, 1993), and further colleagues, skills can only be studied from work situations as they cannot be isolated from the context in which they are mobilized.

From this short review, we can identify three interrelated concepts when studying competences management in a French ergonomics-inspired way at the individual job level: *activity* as a focus of ergonomics; *context*, understood with a "thick definition of work" (Deranty, 2009, p.69); and *competences*, for which we will use in this chapter the word *skills*, not as a replacement for competences, but as a possibility to enrich its understanding through an ergonomic prism. Using an empirical research, this chapter intends to show that focusing on *activity* is a way to grasp the work *context* and to study the potential interactions between these two and the required *skills*. Our research takes place in Enedis, a large French company, subsidiary of the French giant Electricité de France. It studies a major job transformation through the analysis of the contextual dimensions of work. Using some of the methodologies borrowed from ergonomics to analyze data and present our results, we show an example of what it means for French research on competences to be rooted in ergonomics.

11.3 A Large Transformation: Data Collection and Analysis

11.3.1 Our Field: A Large Transformation toward a New Versatile Job

In 2014, the French government made the final decision to modernize the electricity and gas distribution systems by wide-spreading the use of smart meters among all domestic consumers in France by 2022. These new meters are named *Linky* for electrical meters, run by Enedis, and *Gazpar* for gas meters, operated by GRDF (Gaz Réseau Distribution France). Both companies act under a public service contract for all French customers. This strategy is part of the French ecological transition plan as the new meters allow the development of smart grids, the monitoring of consumption in real time by customers, and remote operations to head toward a better use of electricity and gas distribution.

In both companies, many jobs are affected by this modernization. In Enedis (38000 employees), about 10000 technicians are concerned by the project, as it affects the two main technical jobs of the company: service technicians and network technicians. Table 11.1 describes the main activities of each job.

With the implementation of Linky, up to 70% of service technicians activities will be remotely and automatically operated instead of requiring an intervention at customers' homes. To deal with these deep evolutions, Enedis engaged in a large transformation of its two main technician jobs to create a new and unique job of *versatile technician*, skilled on both aspects of network and service. The aim is fairly simple: a versatile technician will be able to switch from one activity to the other several times a day, if necessary. It should lead to an optimization of activity planning, as the geographical area of interventions will be narrowed. The transformation is to be implemented over about three years, and it will affect the activity of most of the 10000 Enedis technicians.

The project has mobilized the collective energy of human resource departments, managerial line, and trade unions for years to prepare the change: new convergent information system; new organizational structure including centralized planning teams; new locations to gather technicians; new mixed managerial teams; and for specifically HR aspects, new job description, new competences framework, new training programs, and new ways of recognizing involvement in the transformation. The implementation started in 2016 in pilot sites, in urban or rural contexts. Our research mainly takes place in the urban pilot site in the city of Lyon, in two of

Table 11.1   Main Activities of Enedis Technicians

	Main activities
Service technicians	Take action on electric meters and circuit breakers at customers' homes, in response to customers' requests through Enedis call centers. Work alone, with an average of 10–12 interventions a day. ■ Carry out installation, commissioning, and termination of electrical equipment ■ Carry out contract amendments (increased capacity) ■ Repair electric equipment ■ Disconnect equipment when bills are unpaid
Network technicians	Take action on high voltage (HV) and low voltage (LV) networks and accessories, in distribution sub-stations, under pavements in cities, or on poles in the countryside. Work in pairs, with an average of 3–4 interventions a day. ■ Carry out building, maintenance, and repair on the cables ■ Carry out operations and protection needs in distribution sub-stations ■ Set up mobile generators ■ Make HV and LV connection accessories

the four operational bases chosen to gather technicians of both jobs. It is supported by Enedis Direction of Transformation to study the move toward versatility, trying to identify what is hindering and driving the process. This case is of particular interest as it allows us to study competences management at both strategic and individual levels.

11.3.2 Data Collection: A Qualitative Approach Centered on Activities

Data was collected between December 2016 and July 2017 through four sources allowing for comparison between prescribed and real activities: (1) 30 days on site observation mainly with technicians, (2) 23 interviews or non-participant observation of meetings with the main actors in charge of the transformation inside Enedis (transformation board, HR, and unions), and (3) collection of many documents related to the transformation (including confidential documents). At the end of the analysis, in December 2017, results were presented to three groups of actors inside the company, and their feedback (4) is included in the data. Table 11.2 details our sources.

Table 11.2   Four Sources of Data Collection

Sources	Data collection
1. 30 days on-field observations in two operational bases in the pilot site of Lyon	Non-participant observation of: ■ Morning briefs and evening debriefs ■ Network technicians on worksites and service technicians at customers' homes ■ Centralized planning team on their premises ■ Managers in their offices or in team meetings ■ Lunches with technicians
2. Main actors in charge of transformation	Interviews or non-participant observation of meetings or informal exchanges ■ Direction of transformation: eight occurrences ■ HR department: ten occurrences ■ Trade unions: three occurrences ■ Health and safety department: two occurrences
3. Internal documents	Secondary data collection, no restriction to access ■ All documents presenting the transformation (e.g., all documents discussed with unions and documents published on intranet site) ■ All HR tools related to transformation (e.g., job description and required practices)
4. Presentation of conclusions	Presentation of results by researcher: questions/validations/nuances ■ Board of directors of transformation ■ Board of managers at the pilot site ■ Local multidisciplinary board (HR, managers, unions, medical staff)

It is important to specify that at this period of data collection at the Lyon pilot site, each of the two observed new operational bases was setting up with around 40 people, half of whom coming from network activities and half from service activities. It was a cohabitation period, as very few technicians were starting to carry out versatile activities. Therefore we can consider that our observations collect data from the two previous jobs as they were *before* transformation toward versatility. It is also worth mentioning that this empirical work benefits from the researcher's deep knowledge of Enedis technicians' jobs and locally trusting relationships as it follows an ethnographic immersion of 17 months in these premises for a PhD work.

11.3.3 Data Analysis: Two Distinct Methodologies for Prescribed and Real Activities

Our data is made up of 352 pages of research notes, 8 transcribed interviews, and a large number of internal documents about the transformation. We used two different ways of analyzing data. The first one identifies what is prescriptive about the new versatile job, mainly in sources (2) and (3). In this chapter, we will focus on the list of required professional practices. The second one is directly inspired by the ergonomics models to analyze real activities, mainly for source (1). To pay specific attention to the contextual dimensions of work, we use Flores's (1982) suggestions to organize data in response to eight questions: Who (age, experience, and competences)? What for (purpose of the activities)? How (technologies, procedures, and work organization)? How much (objectives, deadlines, and quantity)? With whom (team, hierarchy, customers, and subcontractors)? When (schedule, duration, and time of the day)? With what (material, tools, and workstation)? Where (premises, worksites, and customers' homes)? In this chapter, we give some examples of the results of this analysis.

Following ergonomics logics, our aim is to focus on activity to understand how its contextual dimensions can have an effect on the required skills of versatile technicians.

11.4 Becoming a Versatile Technician

11.4.1 Prescribed Work: HR Tools to Show the Way

In this part, we present the way Enedis dealt with the strategic challenge of defining the activities and required practices of the new versatile job. To help the move toward versatility, the transformation department in charge of the project built two main references, drawing from previous HR documents and discussing them within workgroups with managers and trade unions: a job description and a list of required professional practices. Both documents offer precise descriptions of what is expected from the new versatile technician.

The job description (four pages) shows a single general mission ("to carry out network interventions on HV and LV equipment (repair, maintain, develop) and customers interventions on electrical columns and meters") and common purposes of "security, quality, customers satisfaction and uninterrupted electricity supply." However, the activities of the versatile technician are still separate between network activities (e.g., set up electric generators, supervise and maintain them) and service activities (e.g., carry out commissioning and termination). The context of the job is described as common to both previous activities and it covers the geographical zone; relationships (customers, subcontractors, and colleagues); available resources (vehicles, tools, and protection equipment); and security regulations and schedules.

The list of required professional practices (three pages) is called "Référentiel des pratiques professionnelles"* (RPP), underlining that it focuses on required work *practices* as a way of defining targeted skills. It seems to be very anchored in real work as it is also very precise, gathering 84 specific expectations around the new job, in a mix of technical acts to be carried out, skills to be acquired, and expected behaviors. It is presented as a table split into four sets of expectations, combined with four levels of appropriation: *begin, operate, optimize, and be a referent.* Table 11.3 gives some examples of the RPP content.

Analyzing the job description and RPP clearly shows the emphasis put on the common ground of practices between the two previous jobs. In the job description, they share the same general mission, the same purposes and the same context/environment. In the RPP, out of the 84 requirements described in the grid, only 26 show a distinction between network and service activities while 58 express the same expectations for both activities. From such a list, even if numbers do not say it all, it seems clear that the two previous jobs had a lot in common and that the move toward versatility mainly consists of adding technical acts to an already shared ground. This is highly consistent with the company's discourse on change management. These HR tools are the detailed result of many hours of elaboration including HR, managers, technicians, and unions. They were presented to personnel's representative bodies and accepted as such to guide future HR decisions in recruitment, training, assessment, career planning, mobility, promotions, or pay rises. They support the managerial line in the jobs' transformation toward versatility, emphasizing that the required move is an extension of technical acts set into a deep common ground of skills, practices, and behaviors. Logically, one of the main HR policies to help the move is to offer a large range of training sessions on technical aspects.

However, we can also identify that in the job description, apart from what surrounds the job either in very concrete elements (vehicles, tools, regulations, schedules, etc.) or in very abstract elements (purposes and mission), the required activities are very different. In addition, when focusing on the first set of skills (technical interventions) in the RPP, we can be surprised by the concentration of the differences between network and service skills on the average levels of appropriation, "operate," and "optimize": 22 out of 26 distinctive expectations. On the other hand, "beginners" and "referents" mainly share similar skills between the two activities. This somehow recognizes that there was a big difference between the two previous jobs, and that this difference will still be very visible for most versatile technicians, except when they start learning the job or when they will have come to master all the aspects of it.

Our field analysis inspired by ergonomics starts from there and digs into everyday work situations to pay attention to the context in real activities, in order to learn more about skills.

---

* Professional Practice Standards.

Table 11.3 Elements from the "Référentiel de pratiques professionnelles" (RPP) for a Versatile Technician

	Begin	Operate	Optimize	Be a referent
Network and services technical interventions	- 4 competences in common: "Identifies and takes care of tools and equipment" - 4 distinctive competences: (Network): "Identifies the nature and location of electric operating equipment on the geographical zone" (HV sub-stations, LV distribution stations); (Service): "Carries out routine interventions in conformity with the catalogue of services"	- 1 competence in common: "Knows and masters regulations and procedures of one's activity" - 10 distinctive competences: (Network): "Carries out notified operations on HV and LV networks and builds accessories according to his qualification and authorization"; (Service) : **"Carries out all routine interventions with effectiveness and autonomy"**	- 1 competence in common: "In case of a claim, provides factual elements to allow for elaboration of personalized mails" - 12 distinctive competences: (Network): "Carries out visits and controls on the electric operating equipment, on the public network and at its users locations; detects potential dysfunctions"; (Service): "Carries out any intervention with effectiveness and autonomy"	- 6 competences in common: "Proposes ideas to improve procedures and reinforce security for workers and other people" "Is able to adapt to any work situation" "Transmits one's knowledge in work situation"
Information systems	3 competences: "Learns and uses information systems tools associated with one's activity"	2 competences: "Masters information systems tools associated with one's activity"	2 competences: "Masters and uses in an effective manner all the tools associated with one's activity"	2 competences: "Proposes and implements relevant evolutions of the tools"

(Continued)

Table 11.3 (Continued) Elements from the "Référentiel de pratiques professionnelles" (RPP) for a Versatile Technician

	Begin	Operate	Optimize	Be a referent
Internal and external relationships	Internal: 3 competences "Has a positive attitude and makes oneself available" External: 4 competences "Tries to satisfy customers and adopts a positive behavior"	Internal: 3 competences "Actively participate in new projects or work groups" External: 4 competences **"Obtains customers satisfaction and checks it"**	Internal: 2 competences "Shows a critical mind, questions one's own positions and adapts oneself to job's evolutions" External: 2 competences "Proposes improvements to develop customers' satisfaction"	Internal: 2 competences "Positively capitalize on one's experiences and shares within the workgroup" External: 1 competence "Is recognized by hierarchy and colleagues for one's developed customers' orientation"
Quality, security, environment, and innovation	4 competences "Learns security instructions, prevention policies and prescriptions on general risks"	4 competences "Detects potentially dangerous situations, reports them to hierarchy and suggests solutions to handle them"	5 competences "Contributes to wellbeing at work inside the team"	3 competences "Is recognized for exemplary engagement in conducting prevention actions"

11.4.2 Prescribed Skills and the Effects of Work Contexts on Them

For that purpose, we choose to focus on two major elements of the RPP: "Carries out all routine interventions with effectiveness and autonomy" and "Obtains customers' satisfaction and checks it." In this part, we present results obtained through our field observations, using ergonomics-inspired data analysis (Flores, 1982), identifying some effects of work contexts on these two skills. New versatile technicians are supposed to carry out their interventions on one or the other of previous activities along the day, switching from one to another according to programmed activities in their area of intervention.

Where? In both jobs, most of the activities of technicians are carried out in autonomy outside the company's premises. However, there is a significant difference between both jobs regarding the workplace, and switching from one type of intervention to the other is not as simple as it seems on planning sheets or RPP. Service technicians mostly work inside houses or buildings, although the customer's meter may sometimes be in the street. Network technicians mostly work in the streets under the pavements or on poles, subject to all types of weather. On worksites, a technician quickly becomes dirty with mud if it is raining. Many technicians mention that it is not comfortable to rotate between activities : coming out from dirty settings, a network technician cannot go to a customer's home without washing himself and changing clothes. These very practical consequences of versatility are not mentioned in prescribed work: if the area of intervention will be the same, the workplace is not similar, and this represents a major change in work conditions. Carrying out routine interventions requires the appropriate outfit, and customer satisfaction is also related to this outfit.

With what? The job description specifies that versatile technicians are provided with a vehicle and necessary tools to cover their entire activities. Physical equipment is indeed a major aspect of this type of manual work. Particularly, the toolbox is a key equipment to work effectively and avoid wasting time going back to the van if some tool is missing. Each technician astonishingly personalizes his toolbox, in both jobs. Because it is heavy and has to be carried either to customers' homes or to worksites, the content of the toolbox needs to be optimized: it contains what may be needed to intervene (which is always partly unknown when leaving the van) and nothing else. The tools gathered in each box are a unique set, a result from years of practice. Obviously, the tools needed to work on circuit breakers or on network cables are partly different, and the toolbox cannot contain them all. When asking technicians to rotate between network and service interventions, they do not have the time to adjust their toolboxes, often miss a tool when working, waste time, and sometimes lose patience about their loss of effectiveness. In addition, customers may be less satisfied because of what may seem a lack of professionalism.

A similar problem arises with vehicles, which are an extension of toolboxes as the back seats are arranged to carry equipment. Network technicians drive little trucks because they often need additional large and heavy material, for example, to cut large cables. In a city like Lyon, it is always difficult to park with a truck. It often happens that after delivering the material on site, the technician takes some time to find a space to park. He can afford this because he is usually going to stay on the spot for a couple of hours. Service technicians drive small vans because they do not need additional equipment, and these smaller vehicles are a great help to park in the city. They often stay less than half an hour at customers' homes and need to be more flexible with their vehicles. When considering rotation between the two activities, technicians underline that their vehicles will be either too big for an easy parking or too small for larger tools. This affects the effectiveness of their work and customer satisfaction if they are late.

With whom? To support transformation toward versatility, the company's top management states that technicians from both previous jobs will learn a lot from one another. Service technicians will develop technical skills while network technicians will develop customer orientation. Our data confirms that technicians used to work at customers' homes pay a lot of attention to their satisfaction. However, because their production rate is fairly demanding (12 interventions a day on average), technicians often speed up the daily rhythm to prioritize the respect of appointment hours over patient explanations to customers.

Network technicians also deal with customers on worksites. However, their relationship is of a different nature. When customers wait for a service technician at home, they need his/her help to change the meter, get more power, or restore electricity. They know when and why the technician is coming and most of the time, (s)he is welcome. When customers talk to a network technician, it is rarely planned and is usually caused by an electricity power cut in their building, sometimes without warning when a problem arises. In such a situation, several curious people wander around the site to know how long it will last. At this specific time, however, the technician needs to concentrate in order to diagnose the problem and restore electricity as soon as possible. Clients are not welcome as they disturb him/her from this task. Working on dangerous settings, (s)he mainly tries to avoid having clients around the site. Therefore, if communication skills and customer orientation are part of the job demands included in the RPP, their use will diverge according to activities and will hardly require the same behaviors.

11.5 Practical and Theoretical Contributions

11.5.1 Prescribed Versatile Skills, Non-Versatile Contexts

Our analysis of job description and RPP pointed out that the move toward versatility required a large extension of skills to technically different acts, however seemingly set into a deep common ground of contexts, purposes, rules, practices, and behaviors. This analysis was in line with the strategic discourse supporting the transformation: with the appropriate training on technical acts, technicians should be able to perform versatile interventions during a working day.

Our on-field analysis using ergonomics-inspired methodologies reveals that it is more complex than it previously seemed: if technical skills can become versatile with the help of an appropriate training, *the contextual dimensions of the new activities are not versatile*: the toolbox, the vehicle, the workplace, and the relationships with customers all have effects on skills. Although not intended, rotation between activities brings its share of inefficiency that partly prevents technicians from "Carrying out routine interventions with effectiveness and autonomy." This loss of efficiency may affect the expected skill of "obtaining customers satisfaction" as this loss of efficiency is visible in missing tools in the toolbox, late arrivals due to parking problems, or unsuitable outfit following a dirtying activity.

These results were presented to three boards inside Enedis to get feedback on their validity. Even though sometimes uncomfortable with what seemed to question the overall project, most participants agreed that they had missed some important elements to manage the change. Many mentioned that putting words on the *non-versatile contexts* of the new job was a great help to understand what was previously qualified as a form of resistance to change. With that specific approach studying the contextual dimension of activities and their effect on skills, our purpose was to point out potential difficulties to help implement the transformation. Reactions differed according to the boards concerned. Managers at the pilot site felt relieved from a form of guilt, and that released new energies to deal with the problems raised by the transformation. Local multidisciplinary board (HR, unions, medical staff, and managers) adapted their management of the project on their geographic area by recognizing some of its limits. As for the board of directors in charge of the transformation, being very much involved in the prescribed work descriptions, it was more difficult to consider contextual elements as more than temporary obstacles. However, because of the strategic stakes of the transformation, and because of recurrent social tensions in technician teams, they have eventually adapted somewhat their way of managing the project.

11.5.2 Different Scales for Contexts

From this empirical research, we now present our contribution to restoring the link between organization, competences, and work. In the literature, competences are studied at different levels: national (e.g., Cheng and Dainty, 2003); organizational (e.g., Chen and Chang, 2010); or individual (e.g., Kim et al., 2009). In each of these levels, specific elements of the context need to be considered and used to reach a better understanding of the concept of competence. Mercier and Oiry (2010) consider that in social sciences, context is not a mere background scene but a key determinant of the studied processes, underlining the constant interactivity between context and processes. To help identify which elements of the context are relevant for a specific study, the authors suggest an analysis of context according to different scales (from micro to macro scales), arguing that each will bring its share to the overall intelligibility of the process. In this chapter, we follow this call and draw on ergonomics roots of French competences management to go a step further in the different scales of the contexts affecting competences: national, organizational, as an HR process, and at the activity level. At each of these scales, competences are reshaped in a constant move that can inform the other levels.

At the national level, because French approach to competences is multi-dimensional (Delamare Le Deist and Winterton, 2005), French organizations might be more willing to undertake this type of ergonomics-inspired research. We underline that it is a courageous stand from directors in charge of a very large project to allow researchers to dig into real work, and this probably benefits from a long understanding of the difference between prescribed and real work in France. Although the results of our analysis were somewhat uncomfortable to hear, their anchoring in French preoccupation about work conditions did help to integrate micro effects of the work context into the overall project. In nations culturally less familiar with these notions, it would be necessary to help the move with prior explanations.

At the organizational level, Chen and Chang (2010) underline the role of organizational culture, proposing that shared values, mutual trust, and mutual investment are cornerstones of competences, activating the link between core and individual competences. In our empirical research, the strategic vision of the transformation at the organizational level (ecologic transition, smart meters) is well understood and accepted by most of the technicians met during the research. They are ready to follow the move because they understand its stakes and feel part of it. However, this acceptance is not sufficient to align strategic ambition and individual skills toward versatility because the contexts of activities are not versatile. Although offering a detailed model of hidden and visible characteristics of competences at both individual and organizational levels, Chen and Chang (2010) do not highlight the activities contexts as ergonomics do, missing some key elements. It would therefore be necessary to enrich their model with that aspect.

Regarding the HR process of transformation, we underline the considerable work led by Enedis HR teams to manage the change and describe practices' expectations in a rather participative way. In the job description, context is mentioned (vehicles, tools, and workplace), but as a generic information that led us to believe it was common to both jobs. It is not. In the RPP, it seems that real work is captured in the 84 prescribed skills. It is not. It sets aside the contextual dimensions of activities, neglecting thereby, somehow unwillingly, their potential effects on skills. However, because competences have a social and managerial value and will be used as a management tool in most HR processes (recruitment, training, assessment, promotions, or wages), the RPP offers a simplified and narrower vision of competences. Consequently, the risk is high for human resource management (HRM) to stick to inadequate policies. We underline here that the contextual difficulties identified in our study (workplace, toolbox, vehicle, and customer relationship) are not temporary obstacles: they are the essence of work. Therefore, the classical managerial response of offering more training will not lift obstacles over time. The company has to recognize these elements and adapt to them.

Finally, at the activity level with an ergonomic lens, we showed that skills are deeply related to activities contexts, in a constant interaction. This understanding is a real opportunity to manage the change in a more efficient way. For Ughetto (2009), speaking of work in a prescribed form leads to denying real work. It produces requirements on what workers should do, but it does not aim at understanding the concrete obstacles they will meet on the way toward the target. Each action is set into a technical, spatial, and temporal context that needs an orthogonal perspective from the organizational point of view (Rogalski et al., 1995). From these elements, we can say, with Mazeau (1995), that analyzing competences would greatly benefit from a more detailed skills breakdown covering the contextual aspects of activities.

11.6 Conclusion

In this chapter, through an empirical research in Enedis, we show that French ergonomics help in focusing on activity as a way to grasp the work contexts and thus lead to a better understanding of skills at work. This allows for an enriched vision of competences, particularly of their interactions with contexts. We suggest that there are different scales through which it is relevant to analyze these interactions between competences and contexts, proposing theoretical and practical contributions.

While French ergonomics have developed a vast body of literature on the difference between prescribed and real work from the 1950s, they have not been very successful at translating their main results, as the world seemed to discover these concepts with the publication of *Resilience Engineering* by Hollnagel and Woods (2006) (Gaudard and Duarte, 2015). There would be more to say about the potential contributions of ergonomics, for example, in the analysis of differences between novices and experts to underline the role of time on competences (Gaudard and Weill-Fassina, 1999). For this chapter, we will conclude with Barbier and Durand (2003) and Daniellou (2005), who consider that the difference between prescribed and real activities has become a common ground to different disciplines in France such as psychology, sociology, professional didactics, management, or analytical philosophy. All of them draw on a conception of activities with common features: a comprehensive approach with no dissociation between action and cognition; an emphasis on situations and their contexts; an embodied vision of work and its physical dimensions; a socially negotiated activity; and a temporal continuity that does not separate past, present, and future. Accepting these principles in social sciences leads to consider human activity in its specific contexts and conditions, in its unprecedented situations.

References

Barbier, J.-M., & Durand, M. (2003). L'activité : un objet intégrateur pour les sciences sociales? *Recherche and Formation*, *42*, 99–117.

Bouteiller, D., & Gilbert, P. (2005). Réflexions croisées sur la gestion des compétences en France et en Amérique du Nord. *Relations Industrielles*, *60*(1), 3–28.

Chen, H. M., & Chang, W. Y. (2010). The essence of the competence concept: Adopting an organization's sustained competitive advantage viewpoint. *Journal of Management and Organization*, *16*(5), 677–699.

Cheng, M. I, & Dainty, A. R. J. (2003). The differing faces of managerial competency in Britain and America. *Journal of Management Development*, *22*(6), 527–537.

Clot, Y. (2008). *Travail et pouvoir d'agir*. Paris, France: Presses universitaires de France.

Daniellou, F., Dessors, D., & Teiger, C. (2016). Formation à l'analyse de l'activité et rapport au travail en ergonomie. *Travailler*, *35*(1), 95–103.

Daniellou, F. (2005). The French-speaking ergonomists' approach to work activity: Cross-influences of field intervention and conceptual models. *Theoretical Issues in Ergonomics Science*, *6*(5), 409–427.

Dejours, C. (2003). *L'évaluation du travail à l'épreuve du réel*. Paris, France: INRA Editions.

Delamare Le Deist, F., & Winterton, J. (2005). What Is Competence? *Human Resource Development International*, *8*(1), 27–46.

Delgoulet, C., & Vidal-Gomel, C. (2014). The development of skills: A condition for the construction of health and performance at work. In *Constructive Ergonomics* (pp. 3–16). Boca Raton, FL: CRC Press, Taylor & Francis Group.

Deranty, J.-P. (2009). What is work? Key insights from the psychodynamics of word. In *Thesis Eleven (98)* (pp. 69–87). New York, NY: SAGE Publication.

Flores, J.-L. (1982). *Approche ergonomique de la conception des autobus.* (Thèse de doctorat. Université Paris 8).

Gaudard, C., & Duarte, R. (2015). L'ergonomie, la psychodynamique du travail et les ergo-disciplines. Entretien avec François Daniellou. *Travailler*, *34*(2), 11–29.

Gaudard, C., & Weill-Fassina, A. (1999). L'évolution des compétences au cours de la vie professionnelle : une approche ergonomique. Extract from « Activités de travail et dynamique des compétences » . In *Les compétences en ergonomie* (pp. 135–146, 2001). Toulouse, France: Octarès Editions.

Grzeda, M. M. (2005). In competence we trust? Addressing conceptual ambiguity. *Journal of Management Development*, *24*(6), 530–545.

Hackman, R., & Oldham, G. R. (1975). Development of the job diagnostic survey. *Journal of Applied Psychology*, *60*(2), 159–170.

Herzberg, F. (1959). *The Motivation to Work*. Hoboken, NY: John Wiley and Sons, Inc.

Hollnagel, E., & Woods, D. (2006). *Resilience Engineering : Concepts and Precepts*. Boca Raton, FL: CRC Press.

Kim, T.-Y., Cable, D. M., Kim, S.-P., & Wang, J. (2009). Emotional competence and work performance: The mediating effect of proactivity and the moderating effect of job autonomy. *Journal of Organizational Behavior*, *30*(7), 983–1000.

Lancry, A. (2016). *L'ergonomie* (2nd edition). Paris, France: Presses Universitaires de France.

Leplat, J. (1986). L'analyse psychologique du travail », extrait de « Revue de psychologie appliquée ». In *L'analyse du travail en psychologie ergonomique* (pp. 23–39), 1992. Toulouse, France: Octarès Editions.

Leplat, J. (1990). Skills and tacit skills: A psychological perspective. *Applied Psychology: An International Review*, *39*(2), 143–154.

Leplat, J. (1991). Compétence et ergonomie. Extrait de « Modèles en analyse du travail ». In *Les compétences en ergonomie* (pp. 41–54), 2001. Toulouse, France: Octarès Editions.

Leplat, J., & Montmollin de, M. (2001). Préface. In *Les compétences en ergonomie* (pp. 7–10). Toulouse, France: Octarès Editions.

Linhart, D. (2012). Organisation du travail et participations des salariés. In *Encyclopédie des Ressources Humaines* (3rd edition, pp. 1044–1050). Paris, France: Vuibert Edition.

Loisil, F. (2009). Introduction. In *Du management des compétences au management du travail* (pp. 28–29). Paris, France: ANACT Edition.

Maslow, A. (1943). A theory of human motivation. *Psychological Review, 50*(4), 370–396.

Mayo, E. (1933). *The Human Problems of an Industrial Civilization*. New York, NY: The Macmillan Company.

Mazeau, M. (2001). Acquisition, maintien et développement des compétences. In *Les compétences en ergonomie* (pp. 89–94). Toulouse, France: Octarès Editions.

Mercier, D., & Oiry, E. (2010). Le contexte et ses ingrédients dans l'analyse de processus : Conceptualisation et méthode. In *Processus : Concepts et méthode pour l'analyse temporelle en sciences sociales* (pp. 29–41). Academia Bruylant.

Montmollin de, M. (1984). La compétence. Extrait de « L'intelligence de la tâche ». In *Les compétences en ergonomie* (pp. 11–26), 2001. Toulouse, France: Octarès Editions.

Montmollin de, M. (1993). L'ergonome, le pilote et la femme du directeur. Extrait de «Savoir et pouvoir : les compétences en question ». In *Les compétences en ergonomie* (pp. 55–60), 2001. Toulouse, France: Octarès Editions.

Oiry, E. (2009). La compétence, le travail et l'organisation : un lien en cours de (re)construction. In *Du management des compétences au management du travail* (pp. 30–45). Paris, France: ANACT Edition.

Ombredane, A. (1955). L'analyse Du Travail. Facteur d'économie Humaine et de Productivité. Extrait de « L'analyse Du Travail ». In *L'analyse Du Travail En Psychologie Ergonomique* (pp. 9–22), 1992. Toulouse, France: Octarès Editions.

Prahalad, C. K., & Hamel, G. (1990). The Core Competence of the Corporation. *Harvard Business Review, 68*(3), 79–91.

Rogalski, J., Rabardel, P., & Janin, R. (1995). L'identification des dimensions des changements de technologie, d'organisation du travail et d'évolution des compétences. Extrait de « Dossier : Compétences » . In *Les compétences en ergonomie* (pp. 95–100), 2001. Toulouse, France: Octarès Editions.

Teiger, C., Lacomblez, M., Gaudart, C., Théry, L., Chassaing, K., & Gâche, F. (2014). Dynamique de la compréhension et de la transformation du travail. Éléments pour une histoire de la coopération syndicats-recherche en ergonomie et psychologie du travail en France. *Nouvelle Revue de Psychologie, 18*(2), 195–210.

Terrsac de, G. (1995). Compétences et travail : compétences d'explicitation, d'intervention et d'évaluation. Extrait de «Savoirs théoriques et savoir d'action » . In *Les compétences en ergonomie* (pp. 113–120), 2001. Toulouse, France: Octarès Editions.

Ughetto, P. (2009). Une démarche compétence entre contrôle et accompagnement des salariés. In *Du management des compétences au management du travail* (pp. 46–67). Paris, France: ANACT Edition.

Vygotski, L. (1992). La méthode instrumentale en psychologie. In *Vygotski aujourd'hui* (p. 237). Lausanne, Switzerland: Delachaux et Niestlé.

Chapter 12

Situated Individual Competences, Practices, and Institutional Logics: Identification of Blended Practices among Front-Line Employees in a Railway Company

Nathalie Raulet-Croset and Régine Teulier

Contents

12.1 Introduction

In this chapter, we focus on competences of sales employees (referred to as "sales agents") in organizations, particularly the fact that organizations are subject to institutional pressures (Oliver, 1991). We analyze this environment from the perspective of the institutional complexity of the environment (Greenwood et al., 2011), and we consider the influence of institutional logics (Thornton and Occasio, 1999, 2008) on organizations and individuals. This theoretical framework is particularly appropriate in cases of organizational change where agents are subject to different and sometimes contradictory injunctions coming from their institutional environment. Thus, the agents face unexpected situations, particularly when they interact with other actors who convey the institutional logics, and they must adapt their practices and competences to those new situations. We adopt an interpretative approach of competence (Sandberg, 2000) and consider competences as developing at work and in situations, following the French academic tradition (Zarifian, 1995; Leplat and de Montmollin, 2001) and authors such as Loufrani-Fedida and Missonier (2015, p. 1221), who define competence as "the ability (…) to mobilize and combine resources (i.e., knowledge, skills, and attitudes) in order to implement an activity in situation." We thus consider competences as developing in situations where agents are directly confronted with an external environment and must cope with unexpected solicitations. In this interpretative and situated perspective, the evolution of an individual's competence refers to a new combination of resources, which results from the confrontation of the individual with a new situation. In particular, we propose to explore how the coexistence of two logics at a macro-level leads to individual practices that take into account both logics.

Our empirical context relates to the case of front-line sales employees in a large railway company in France. The company is subject to multiple institutional pressures, particularly to those of a public service logic that is rooted in its history and identity and, more recently, to those of a market logic due to the opening up to European competition and thus to a new customer orientation of the company.

We conducted ethnographic research in this company in 2007–2008, at the key moment of the arrival of the market logic. This field research lasted 18 months, and we spent 27 days observing the sales practices of the agents. This methodological approach is particularly adapted to detecting the detailed evolution of competences and practices in situ. Through this observation we propose an investigation of the evolution of competences of front-line employees in a sales situation. We show in this chapter that front-line employees have transformed their competences through the evolution of their practices by articulating both the new market logic and the historical public logic in their responses to customers. This influence of logics on practices was detected through elements of language, ways of being with the customer, and different uses of the sales dialog and of digital tools. We also observed a gap between the general discourse of the company and the fact that the agent must improvise in everyday situations. Some clients are still very attached to the public service dimension, others have more commercial expectations, and still others are sensitive to both dimensions. The pressure of logic also translates into hybrid expectations of consumers.

Our results are twofold. First, at the micro-level of individuals, we identify blended micro-practices, i.e., practices that combine the requirements of the two logics. Second, at the organizational level of the firm, we argue that the multiplicity of the individual employees' blended practices contributes to creating a global organizational response to institutional pressure. We therefore contribute to research on the organizational responses to institutional pressure (Oliver, 1991), and we highlight one particular response, the response based on the adaptation of individual practices and competences. In the case of institutional pressure that is exerted directly on operational agents through their close environment, we show that the organization relies indirectly on those employees in order to provide an appropriate answer to its novel, complex institutional environment.

12.2 Individual Competences, Practices, and Institutional Logics

12.2.1 Apprehending Competences through Practices: A Situated Approach

Some research on competences contrasts rational and interpretative approaches (Sandberg, 2000). Rational approaches consider competence as an individual's set of attributes, whereas interpretative approaches consider competence as developing in situations at work. Thus, the interpretative approach considers that lived experience in a situation comprises competence: competences are "ways of being"

(Sandberg and Pinnington, 2009). Sandberg (2000, p.11) also states "that attributes used in accomplishing work are not primarily context-free but are situational, or context-dependent."

Several research studies have already sought to establish links between competences and practices. Lindberg and Rantatalo (2014) propose to infer competences from practices. Practices, if considered as a set of shared action and know-how repertoires, are subject to changes related to environmental pressures. However, they are also the privileged place wherein to build a dynamic of individual competences. A practice-based approach allows us to go beyond the cognitive dimension and enlarge our comprehension of the evolution of competences. The analysis focuses on "practical understanding," defined by Jarzabkowski et al. (2013), relying on Schatzki et al. (2001), as "the know-how and embodied repertoires that compose a practice" (Schatzki et al., 2001, pp. 77–78) and that is grounded in actors and their actions, referring to a "feel for" how to perform a social order (Jarzabkowski et al., 2013).

12.2.2 How Do Competing Institutional Logics Influence Individual Practices?

We approach the issue of the evolution of competences and practices from an institutional perspective, particularly in cases of institutional complexity, when different logics coexist or conflict.

Various authors have analyzed organizations that endure the coexistence of explicit and visible logics in an organization that may endure them, as for example, in pluralistic organizations (Denis et al., 2007; Jarzabkowski et al., 2009; Kraatz and Block, 2008). These authors have identified different mechanisms that allow different logics to coexist and remain visible. They considered the response that an organization provides toward this complex environment in terms of adjustments among various groups of actors or organizational departments, each supported by a specific logic (Jarzabkowski et al., 2009; Pache and Santos, 2010; Reay and Hinings, 2009).

Some research has also been developed at the individual level. In the case of coexisting and contradictory institutional logics, most researchers have shown that actors are afforded a certain degree of freedom but must also exhibit coherent actions and practices and must give meaning to a situation that allows them, in spite of these contradictory logics, to remain true to themselves.

Pache and Santos (2013) identified different individual behaviors depending on the greater or lesser sensitivity of the individual to one logic. Other studies have deepened our understanding of the evolution of behaviors facing competing logics. Zilber (2002) concluded that different competing views provide greater possibilities for different interpretations by actors and emphasized that such interpretive acts are at the heart of their individual agency. In particular, she highlighted situations where actors attributed to a practice linked to one logic meaning that originated from the other logic. Using a similar perspective, Lê (2011) explained how actors draw on institutional logics as resources, which can lead to a reconfiguration of the relationship between competing logics. McPherson and Sauder (2013), studying a drug court, focused on the strategic individual choice of individuals facing a complex environment and showed that "although institutional logics are decidedly extra-individual, their construction, their transmission depend on people who themselves have interests, beliefs and preferences" (p. 168); they "portray actors as having a repertoire of logics – or tools that they can choose from when the need to influence, justify, or advocate arises" (p. 168). These authors also argue that actors have a pragmatic attitude and "creatively invoke available logics in order to manage everyday work" (p. 181). For their part, Svenningsen-Berthélem et al. (2018) examine individuals' propensity to either hybridize or compartmentalize multiple logics, depending on their structural position. However, studies on individual practices that confronted competing logics remain underdeveloped. We aim to contribute to this field of research, tackling the issue of the consequences of competing institutional logics on individual competences and practices.

In this chapter, we study the competences in a situation, what Sandberg (2000) calls "human competence at work," and their evolution caused by institutional pressure on the company. The importance given to the situation and the actors has led us to focus on the link between competences and practices (Lindberg and Rantatalo, 2014). We consider the notion of practice to be central because, contrary to competences, it is observable, and we answer to the following research questions: How can we characterize the evolution of situated competences resulting from the evolution of an institutional pressure? Does this evolution of individual competences allow a response at the organizational level from the firm to the institutional pressure?

12.3 Methodology and Empirical Context

12.3.1 Empirical Context

The case analyzed here focuses on change in a public organization confronted with a new market logic in the field of transportation. Despite the growing influence of market logic, the public service orientation is still present in most people's minds, practices, and organizational mechanisms. In addition, certain counterpowers, such as the trade unions, continue to actively nourish this orientation. This can be seen in the company's human resource management, modes of organization, management tools, and technical operations. This orientation dominates the technical departments where the majority of employees work. For example, in public service logic, the principles are: "All users have the same problem. More importantly, global service must be available to all of them," whereas in market logic, "Every customer is specific and every customer problem is specific."

Our research focuses on front-line employee competences (Harris and Ogbonna, 2000). These employees are in the front office and are directly in contact with customers; thus the new market logic has a strong influence, as it meets some clients' expectations and is supported by sales managers. However, it also confronts historical public logic, which is also at the heart of these agents' culture and practices. Thus, agents feel the pressure of both logics.

12.3.2 Methodology

The data were collected during an 18-month period. As a team of four, we interviewed 45 different front-office agents at different levels in the organization, including operational levels (agents and team managers) and managerial levels (middle and senior managers) (Collard et al., 2013). We spent 27 days observing salespeople and recorded 245 sales situations, varying in length from a few minutes to over 20 minutes. This methodological choice (observation) appears to be essential to access individual practices, in addition to interviews and discourse analysis (Rasche and Chia, 2009).

We then compiled a set of transcribed "situations." During long-term observations (half-days), we observed and recorded sales situations. During interruptions or during breaks, we also conducted short interviews, where we asked the sales employees for explanations of the situations observed. We then recorded the data as "situations" and, by comparing the situations among themselves, identified key practices that we then analyzed. At this stage, we observed various sets of behaviors emerging under different sales situations and identified individual sales practices that seemed to vary in accordance with the greater or lesser influence of either logic on a given agent.

Thus, having identified various situations in which blended practices were developed, we detected different micro-practices related to the selling process that seemed to have evolved because of the new institutional complexity. We decided to focus our analysis on two of them: (1) managing the customer relationship and (2) triggering the purchase. We observed how agents implemented these practices in situ and what skills they mobilized to do so.

12.4 Empirical Analysis

Here, we focus our analysis on sales situations, particularly on two practices (which we call micro-practices, as they occur at a microindividual level (Rouleau, 2005)) that appeared particularly representative and were more or less affected by the coexistence of the two logics. We observed that some agents manage to blend resources, values, knowledge, skills, etc., associated with these two logics in a very performative way.

The first micro-practice, called "managing the customer relationship," involves creating and maintaining a close, trusting relationship between the firm and the customer. Although we often observed this type of trusting relationship, we also observed that employees develop this relationship for different reasons: employees who are sensitive to the "public service logic" have a sense of participating, as a public transport service, in the history of their users. Other employees develop such a practice for market reasons, according to the market logic, in order to obtain a sale. We propose hereafter two contrasting examples of this micro-practice, one non-blended centered on the logic of public service (Section 12.4.1) and the other which blends the market logic and the logic of public service (Section 12.4.2).

The second micro-practice analyzed here focuses on triggering the purchasing act. It refers to the brief moment when the employee proposes and concludes the sale. This practice has become central for sales employees following the imposition of "market logic." In fact, triggering the purchase has become an implicit objective of the front-office employee–customer interaction, and it needs to take place very quickly during the interaction. This practice did not feature in the organization's pre-existing practices because triggering the purchase (of a ticket, a discount card, hotel, or rental car) was not an important objective for employees. However, we observed some people for whom this objective has now become important because of the arrival of the new logic. We propose two contrasting examples of this micro-practice, one non-blended centered on market logic (Section 12.4.3) and the other that blends market logic and public service logic (Section 12.4.4).

12.4.1 Public Service Logic in Managing the Customer Relationship – An Example of Non-Blended Practice

We contrast different situations where the practice of "managing the customer relationship" occurs differently. In the first case (detailed in Table 12.1), a customer explains that he would like train tickets for his children. In this situation, the approach pursued by the employee reveals the influence of the public service logic and is still not blended. This interaction lasts more than 13 minutes and does not ultimately result in a sale. In this case, the employee has not developed a blended practice nor a new competence. She has only kept the values proper to the public logic that we summarize by "listening to the customer and being part of his/her story."

12.4.2 Public Service Logic and Market Logic in Managing the Customer Relationship – An Example of Blended Practice

In this second case (detailed in Table 12.2), the employee combines familiarity with the customer, as in the logic of public service, with a close relationship from a market-oriented perspective, which seeks a better understanding of the customer in order to encourage a purchase. We interpret the employee's behavior as a blended

Table 12.1 Example 1: Public Service Logic in Managing the Customer Relationship – An Example of Non-Blended Practice

Example 1: Managing the customer relationship: listening to the customer and being part of his story	
Excerpt from interaction	*Analysis*
C (Customer): A (Agent): C: So I have a … I have a son that I … who [inaudible] to La Plagne there A: To La Plagne, yes. C: By the UCPA (a youth sports organization). A: By the UCPA. C: Yes. So they apparently have a quota of seats in the train … A: Okay. C: But it's full. But apparently we can … we can still find places apparently without going through them, whatever. A: Okay. Total duration of the interaction: 13.25 minutes	The customer explains that he would like train tickets for his children. The agent does not attempt to shorten the exchange. She is patient and empathizes with the client. She repeats the same sentences several times. The exchange lasts more than 13 minutes.

practice. She asks the customer to clarify the request and uses the personal data supplied by the customer to secure the ticket purchase. The employee listens to this personal information while continuing to search on the computer, thus not extending the interaction time. In this case, she has developed a competence of diagnosing the client situation while maintaining the competence of interaction that continues to give the customer a feeling of proximity with the company.

In fact, the practice of "managing the customer relationship" has evolved globally (see Figure 12.1). For some agents, it now combines "listening to customers" and "learning more about them in order to sell." The agent adapts to the new situation, forms new combinations of resources within the framework of the requests of both logics, and thus develops new competences. The agent proposes a response that draws on the history of the company and its values, as well as new market-oriented requirements, and so combines both logics.

12.4.3 Market Logic in "Triggering the Purchase" – An Example of Non-blended Practice

The excerpt in Table 12.3 shows a sales situation that refers mainly to the market logic: the sales agent tries to trigger the purchase without seeking any information about the client. The practice is not blended.

Table 12.2   Example 2: Public Service Logic and Market Logic in Managing the Customer Relationship – An Example of Blended Practice

Example 2: Managing the customer relationship: listening to the customer and learning more about her in order to sell	
Excerpt from interaction	*Analysis*
A: So the return will be … December 28th. The afternoon return? The afternoon? C: So, yes, from Albi (town), I usually travel around … one o'clock, I don't know. (3:34–4:04 on the recording) Searches on the computer (30 seconds of silence on the recording) A: Arrival 10:50 pm, is that late for you or not? At Montparnasse Station? No? C: Oh no, no, you know I … A: Uh, on the other hand, I have nothing but first class … In first class or second class, I'll see what I have. Otherwise, the thing is that there is a one hour wait at Toulouse. C: You know, the other time, I waited five hours … A: Really…? (slightly complicit laugh, but she does not go any deeper and continues to look on the computer) Uh … C: Then there was a delay … (C continues her explanation of the 5-hour delay) A: You'll have a departure at 3:50 pm otherwise from Albi changing in Toulouse, with a 55-minute wait, then arriving at 10:50 pm, and it will be a first [class] with 25%, not 50% … So wait, I'll look, you can maybe … (4:56–5:07, 11 seconds of silence on the recording) Searches on the computer. Oh … (a bit disappointed) the thing is that there is a change in Montauban (town) … No, do you prefer to change in Toulouse or Montauban? Or I have a train at 4:09 pm, with a change in Montauban, there is 20 minutes for the change there, and you arrive at the same time, at 10:50 pm. C: Really? A: It's better than waiting 55 minutes in Toulouse, isn't it? What do you think? The customer does not say anything. A: That one is better, where …? With the change at Montauban? C: Well … (several seconds) C: I prefer Toulouse… A: No? You prefer Toulouse? C: If something came up, someone could always take me to Toulouse by car A: Ah yes. (5:49–6:47 long silence, almost a minute) A: There, 10:50 pm, with a 55-minute wait … in Toulouse! (she starts the sentence in a tone that indicates she is focused on the computer)	The customer, an elderly person, expresses a personal habit. The agent takes the personal comment into account and asks whether the arrival time is too late. They laugh together (customer relationship) while the agent continues to search the timetables (efficiency). The agent combines a friendly relationship with efficiency. The agent proposes several possibilities. Then she takes into account the personal factors and proposes another route. However, for personal reasons, the customer prefers the first option. The agent ends the interaction and issues the ticket.

Public service logic

Market logic

Practice: Managing the customer relationship,
Listening to customers and being part of their stories

Practice: Managing the customer relationship,
Learning more about the customer in order to close the sale

Blended practice: Managing the customer relationship by listening to customers and learning more about them;
Building on the personal information provided by customers;
keeping the conversation brief while listening to customers

Figure 12.1 Blended practice: "Managing the customer relationship: listening to customers and learning more about them."

12.4.4 Market Logic and Public Service Logic in Triggering the Purchase – An Example of Blended Practice

In the example given in Table 12.4, the sales agent seeks to initiate a purchase that actually corresponds to a customer's need (he seeks information about the client) and that shows the customer that the purchase is worthwhile for him. The agent combines the need to quickly trigger the purchasing act via a search for information with the need to serve the consumer. Therefore, the practice synthesizes the two logics and resolves a tension. In this second situation, the agent has the ability to use proximity with the customer (which certainly comes from his history with the company and thus its closeness to the public logic) in order to rapidly trigger the purchase. This therefore creates an original way of responding to the customer, which is not the strict application of the commercial standardized script.

All in all, from these different situations, we observed that some agents succeed in mixing resources from the two logics and create a blended practice, whereas others do not. Figure 12.2 illustrates how the "triggering the purchase" practice derives originally from the market logic but is mixed with values and templates that derive from the public service logic to then become a blended practice. Agents who succeed in this blend of logics develop new competences and are better connected to the evolution of their internal and external environment, and hence to their clients' expectations.

We have observed that most agents integrate institutional pressures into their daily work practices and have often developed what we call "blended practices,"

Table 12.3 Example 3: Market Logic in "Triggering the Purchase" – An Example of Non-Blended Practice

Example 3: Triggering the purchase: a request for information that results in the purchase of a card	
Excerpt from interaction	*Analysis*

C: Hello Sir, I just want some information. I have to … I would like to get, tomorrow if possible, not today, I would like to get this replaced, can it be done immediately if I come to the counter?
 A: Well, yes … why not do it now?
 C: Well, because I wanted to decide this evening, it depends on my departure …
 A: It doesn't change anything; it can be dated for tomorrow.
 (…)
 A: You're leaving tomorrow?
 C: No, I'm leaving in a week.
 A: Well then, we'll put it for one week's time!
 C: Oh, how nice, yes, I don't leave until … one week's time … I'm going on the 11th.
 A: Why don't you get the ticket? Because the sooner you do it the better your chance of getting a reasonable price.
 C: Really?
 A: Yes (…)
  Where are you going?
  The agent begins the sales dialogue.
 .
 C: The card, I'll do it, but the ticket, I have to phone my friends tonight.
 A: Okay I'll let you think about it.
	The young agent is trained in the new sales strategy.
	 The agent attempts to trigger the sale of the card (market logic).
	 He shows the customer that the purchase will be quick and to his advantage.
	 The agent attempts to trigger the sale of the ticket (market logic). He also tries to obtain personal information and shows the customer that he will get a reasonable price based on his specific needs.
	 The agent does not use personal information and begins the sales dialogue.
	 However, the customer does not want to buy the ticket right away, as he wants to phone some friends first regarding the schedule.
	 Thus, the customer prefers to postpone the purchase.

i.e., practices that combine beliefs, values, and objectives that relate to both logics. Blended practices differ from one agent to another. By combining new commercial injunctions with the persistence of the public identity of the company, agents are tinkering, mobilizing new personal resources, and mixing beliefs relating to both logics. The framework of the coexistence of the two logics exists for each agent, but within this framework, we observed that the agents construct different responses.

Table 12.4 Example 4: Market Logic and Public Service Logic in Triggering the Purchase – An Example of Blended Practice

Example 4: Triggering the purchase: taking into account the customer's specific needs	
Excerpt from interaction	*Analysis*
A: But do you make at least four or five trips a year? It depends …? C: It depends … Because I often go to C every two to three months … or every month … A: Every month? It would be worth buying the XX card sir. It costs 49 euros, this card, right. For each round-trip on this journey, it saves you 14 euros 60 exactly. So if you do four round trips in a year, you're sure to save money. After that, the rest is clear profit. It works all over the country. (…) In my opinion it is a good package that would suit you, sir. C: And now, if I take it now? A: Well … Instead of paying 43 and a bit more euros, you will pay 29.20 euros. C: Yes … A: Okay, so I'll do that.	A young agent who is familiar with the sales requirements. The agent takes into account the customer's specific needs. He proposes to the customer a loyalty card that offers real savings. He adopts a protective attitude vis-à-vis the customer.

This set of different individual blended practices thus comprises an original response from the organization to the pressure of multiple institutional logics.

12.5 Discussion

Our first contribution is in proposing the concept of blended practices and in considering these practices as inventive responses to the requirement of two institutional logics in coexistence and confrontation. We refer to the interpretative approach of competences (Sandberg, 2000). We show that competences evolve in situations as a result of competing institutional logics that put pressure on agents, particularly on front-line employees in the context of situations of tension at work. Considering that competence emerges as the result of a recombination of resources, we show that institutional pressures bring knowledge and beliefs that are new resources available to agents. Agents feel compelled to mobilize beliefs and knowledge specific to the new logic. However, as the pre-existing logic is always present,

Public service logic

Market logic

Practice: developing a protective attitude towards the customer

Practice: triggering the purchase, and keeping the listening phase brief

Blended practice:
Triggering the purchase and considering the customers' needs
Shortening the listening phase while empathizing with the customer

Figure 12.2 Blended practice: "Triggering the purchase as quickly as possible and considering the customer's needs."

they hybridize the logics. This leads to blended practices. Lindberg and Rantatalo (2014) have developed the composite aspect of competences, which they defined as a "balance" between two skills. Here, we propose to consider "blended practices," which are not a mix of different skills but rather inventive responses that use the resources or requirements of two different, and sometimes contradictory, institutional logics and thus generate the emergence of new competences. The employees immersed in the action are at the origin of the inventiveness of the response.

As a second contribution, we highlight the link between the coexistence of logics and the blend of individual practices. Thus far, studies on competing logics have primarily focused on the consequences of the presence of different groups of actors, each carrying a different institutional logic within the same organization. This focus has led to the identification of the implications of the organizational structure and mechanisms that allow these groups to coexist (Reay and Hinings, 2009; Jarzabkowski et al., 2009) and cohere. In this chapter, we show that the two logics meet each other also at the individual level, in the mind and social practices of individual actors and thus in organizations. Our results complement Pache and Santos's (2013) and Svenningsen-Berthélem et al. (2018) work on the variety of individual responses to an embedded hybrid context. They also provide a contribution to research on how individuals capture the influences of institutional logic to build a response at their level (McPherson and Saunder, 2013). Our study also shows that this is a way for the firm to integrate agents with very diverse profiles (new or longer-term employees, employees with a commercial or technical background ...) and to meet the various expectations of customers.

As a third contribution, we argue that we identify a new form of organizational response to institutional pressure. We thus contribute to research on how organizations respond to new institutional pressures (Oliver, 1991). We have observed that agents improvise and provide different responses (Harris and Ogbonna, 2000), using different new individual competences, in order to respond to the requirements of the two logics. This set of varied individual responses comprises the organizational response of the company, enabling it to act in coherence with this double inspiration during a period of change and transition. Despite the variety of the blended practices, they appear to be part of a coherent set that allows and builds a collective response of the organization. Actually, our contribution explains the coexistence of contradictions and how the organization develops and composes a response to the customer that is both unique and multiple. This blending of practices makes for a response that is at once varied and unified.

12.6 Conclusion

We have outlined here the results of our study on the emergence of competences in situations characterized by the confrontation of two institutional logics. Our study is representative of the evolution of large companies facing new performance requirements and new forms of competition. We show that the response to these new pressures is also developed at the individual level and that agents respond by blending practices in order to be more efficient by responding in part to consumer demands. This leads to the identification of a new form of response to the pressure of the institutional environment: a set of individual blended practices that blends the logics in a varied way but that which also constitutes, at the same time, through this set of blended practices and the skills associated with them, a form of coherent organizational response that responds to the pressures of the two logics.

There are, of course, several limitations to our research that may form future lines of research. For example, we would have liked to deepen the collective dynamics or the interindividual interactions, which also occur under the pressure of the institutional logics. It would also be interesting to understand the individual reasons (personal history, personal strategy, etc.) that can lead to a more or less important blend within the practices.

References

Collard, D., Raulet-Croset, N., Teulier, R., & Suquet, J. B. (2013). Les managers de proximité face aux compétences: Une approche située. *Gérer et Comprendre, 113*, 62–72.
Denis, J. L., Langley, A., & Rouleau, A. (2007). Strategizing in Pluralistic Contexts: Rethinking Theoretical Frames. *Human Relations, 60*(1), 179–215.

Greenwood, R., Raynard, M., Kodeih, F., Micelotta, E. R., & Lounsbury, M. (2011). Institutional complexity and organizational responses. *The Academy of Management Annals*, 5(1), 317–371.

Harris, L. C., & Ogbonna, E. (2000). The responses of front-line employees to market-oriented culture change. *European Journal of Marketing*, 34(3–4), 318–340.

Jarzabkowski, P., Matthiesen, J., & Van de Ven, A. (2009). Doing which work? A practice approach to institutional pluralism. In Lawrence, T. B., Suddaby, R., & Leca, B. (Eds.), *Institutional Work. Actors and Agency in Institutional Studies of Organizations* (pp. 284–317). Cambridge, UK: Cambridge University Press.

Jarzabkowski, P., Smets, M., Bednarek, R., Burke, G., & Spee, P. (2013). Institutional ambidexterity: Leveraging institutional complexity in practice. In Lounsbury, M., & Boxenbaum, E. (Eds.), *Institutional logics in action, part B, Research in the sociology of organizations* (Vol. 39b, pp. 3–35). Emerald Publishing.

Kraatz, M. S., & Block, E. S. (2008). Organizational implications of institutional pluralism. In R. Greenwood, Oliver, C., Sahlin-Andersson, K., & Suddaby R. (Eds.), *The SAGE Handbook of Organizational Institutionalism*, (pp. 243–275). London, UK: Sage.

Lê, J. (2011). When contradictory logics coexist: How work practices and institutional accounts reconfigure institutional logics (Paper presented *AoM Submission* #13048).

Leplat, J., & De Montmollin, M. (Eds.). (2001). *Compétences en ergonomie*. Toulouse, France: Octares.

Lindberg, O., & Rantatalo, O. (2014). Competence in professional practice: A practice theory analysis of police and doctors. *Human Relations*, 68(4), 561–582.

Loufrani-Fedida, S., & Missonier, S. (2015). The project manager cannot be a hero anymore! Understanding critical competencies in project-based organizations from a multilevel approach. *International Journal of Project Management*, 33(6), 1220–1235.

McPherson, C. M., & Sauder, M. (2013). Logics in action: Managing institutional complexity in a drug court. *Administrative Science Quarterly*, 58(2), 165–196.

Oliver, C. (1991). Strategic responses to institutional processes. *Academy of Management Review*, 16(1), 145–179.

Pache, A., & Santos, F. (2010). When Worlds Collide: The Internal Dynamics of Organizational Responses to Conflicting Institutional Demands. *Academy of Management Review*, 35(3), 455–476.

Pache, A., & Santos, F. (2013). Embedded in hybrid contexts: How individuals in organizations respond to competing institutional logics. In Lounsbury, M., & Boxenbaum, E. (Eds.), *Institutional logics in action, part B, Research in the Sociology of Organizations* (Vol. 39b, pp. 3–35). Bingley, UK: Emerald Publishing.

Rasche, A., & Chia, R. (2009). Researching strategy practices: A genealogical social theory. *Organization Studies*, 30(7), 713–734.

Reay, T., & Hinings, C. R. (2009). Managing the rivalry of competing institutional logics. *Organization Studies*, 30(6), 629–652.

Rouleau, L. (2005). Micropractices of strategic sensemaking and sensegiving: How middle managers interpret and sell change every day. *Journal of Management Studies*, 42(7), 1413–1441.

Sandberg, J. (2000). Understanding human competence at work: An interpretative approach. *Academy of Management Journal*, 43(1), 9–25.

Sandberg, J., & Pinnington, A. H. (2009). Professional competence as ways of being: An existential ontological perspective. *Journal of Management Studies*, 46(7), 1138–1170.

Schatzki, T. R., Knorr-Cetina, K., & von Savigny, E. (Eds.). (2001). *The Practice Turn in Contemporary Theory*. London, UK: Routeledge.

Svenningsen-Berthélem, V., Boxenbaum, E., & Ravasi, D. (2018). Individual responses to multiple logics in hybrid organizing: The role of structural position. *M@n@gement*, *21*(4), 1306–1328.

Thornton, P. H., & Occasio, W. (1999). Institutional logics and the historical contingency of power in organizations: Executive succession in the higher education publishing industry, 1958–1990. *American Journal of Sociology*, *105*(3), 801–843.

Thornton, P. H., & Occasio, W. (2008). Institutional logics. In Greenwood, R., Oliver, C., Sahlin-Andersson K., & Suddaby R. (Eds.), *The SAGE Handbook of Organizational Institutionalism* (pp. 99–129). London, UK: Sage.

Zarifian, P. (1995). *Le travail et l'événement*. Paris, France: L'Harmattan

Zilber, T. B. (2002). Institutionalization as an interplay between actions, meanings, and actors: The case of a rape crisis center in Israel. *Academy of Management Journal*, *45*(1), 234–254.

Chapter 13

Social Innovation Processes and Collective Entrepreneurial Competence: The Case of the Jardins de Cocagne (Cocagne Gardens)

Brigitte Charles-Pauvers, Nathalie Schieb-Bienfait, and Caroline Urbain

Contents

13.1 Introduction

In recent years, research on innovation has highlighted new concerns with the aim of fostering a systemic approach to innovation, diversifying the sources and places of innovation (internal or external and open), and implementing organizational plans and managerial practices to develop the exploratory capabilities of teams and encourage collective creativity, the ultimate objective being to generate novelty and new ideas in processes, services, and business models (*via* fablabs, hackathons, crowdsourcing, etc.). The most recent research on innovation management has revealed opportunities for interaction, particularly within design phases, and the possibility of implementing organizational structures and incentive mechanisms that promote these innovation processes, such as mobilizing competences in situation (Defélix et al., 2006; Sandberg, 2000; Häland and Tjora, 2006; Sandberg and Pinnington, 2009; Lindberg and Rantatalo, 2015).

This approach, where competence becomes dynamic and transformative for actors and organizations, opens up interesting perspectives for the development of an organization's exploratory capabilities with regard to inventing new responses to needs (services, processes, partnerships, etc.). In this chapter, we address this issue within the somewhat less researched field of social innovation (SI) in the social action sector. Our aim is to study organizations that are interested in exploring new courses of action and draw on their collective entrepreneurial skills to stimulate social innovation and develop their learning capacities. Our approach is at the interface of different research areas, from research on skills and social innovation to research on design sciences. It helps us understand the competences at the heart of entrepreneurial dynamics in the field of social action.

For 30 years, the social action sector has been rich in entrepreneurial/intrapreneurial initiatives, which have all too frequently been grouped under the general term of social innovation. As pointed out by Bréchet and Schieb-Bienfait (2012), the ability to imagine, create, design, and carry out projects, as well as to take account of the values that action stands for and generates, is a major facet of the entrepreneurial action model. In our case, the entrepreneur as an individual interested us less than the competences mobilized by the actors and collectives of actors to carry out the activities launched by entrepreneurial initiatives in designing their social innovation projects. We chose a highly emblematic example of the social innovation approaches developed in France: the "Réseau de Cocagne" (Cocagne Network). Today the network is made up of 100 Cocagne gardens. Social innovation is the common driver behind its entrepreneurial dynamics (Klein et al., 2014).

It draws on the experience-based skills developed by the actors on various social projects. In this chapter, we investigate the mobilization of skills through different processes and collective dynamics and with one main question in mind: What skills are being created and developed in this "laboratory for experimenting with social innovation"?

We argue that the actors behind these collective action initiatives are entrepreneurs/collective intrapreneurs, who, given their intrapreneurial skills, have the capacity to envisage and imagine the future with stakeholder collectives from various backgrounds to carry out their experiments and launch new projects. These skills are a springboard for entrepreneurship and social innovation

13.2 Social Innovation and Collective Entrepreneurial Competences

Regardless of whether innovation is technological, organizational, or commercial, it is always connected to a set of invariably social practices and relationships that involve individual, collective, and organizational skills. Few studies look at social innovation from this competence perspective (Chédotel and Pujol, 2012).

13.2.1 Social Innovation: Addressing Social Problems

The various theoretical approaches to social innovation generally revolve around questions relating to its nature, novelty, and social purpose. There is also a general preference for meso- or macro-levels of analysis. However, recent conceptualizations of social innovation can but spark the interest of researchers in the field of competences: dealing with social innovation means looking at issues related to work, practices, knowledge, interaction, and learning (Cloutier, 2003). It also means looking at actors who seek to question their practices and reinvent their profession and missions every day in the face of new uncertainties within society, to bolster a social cohesion that has been somewhat undermined.

Social innovation focuses on addressing social problems defined in the following generally agreed manner: "any new approach, practice or intervention, or any new product, developed to improve a situation or to solve a social problem and which has been accepted by institutions, organizations and communities." In addition, social innovation generally seeks to contribute to the "well-being" of individuals and/or communities. It "consists of improving an approach, practice, process or service to contribute to the social development and well-being of the population" (CRISES, definition approved by the Quebec Ministry of Research, Science and Technology, 2001).

The conceptualization of social innovation is still a work in progress (Harrison, 2011; Richez-Battesti et al., 2012; Klein et al., 2016), with typological and conceptualization proposals made from different perspectives (Cajaiba-Santana, 2014). The close relationship between social entrepreneurship and social innovation constitutes a field of research with regard to the diverse range of activities, from care and dealing with neglected social needs to developing new solutions for a changing society. Social innovation should lead to collective action that is strongly anchored in the social economy (Bouchard, 1999; Lévesque, 2006; Mulgan, 2006; Murray et al., 2010; Besançon et al., 2013). Bouchard uses the term "social innovation laboratory."

Although social innovation is still in the process of being conceptualized and measured, its immaterial nature should not make it is less significant than the so-called "tangible" innovation. However, understanding social innovation is not easy as it addresses very different social problems and publics.

This last approach is characterized by a process of bottom-up and localized innovation driven by social aspirations or needs that are not a given, but result from co-construction between actors, the involvement of diverse and multiple actors and democratic governance, a market logic kept in check by two other economic principles – redistribution and reciprocity – and revealing a plural approach to the economy, and projects aiming to transform the framework and propose new directions.

The process-based approach invites us to look at how social innovation comes about. We decided to look at this in more detail to better understand the process/design work involved and the skills mobilized.

13.2.2 Social Innovation: Exploring and Designing

The concept of social innovation (SI) is now closely linked to the notion of "social change," or even the idea of "social transformation," through experiments and innovative projects that can actually transform the social system, or in other words, that can follow and keep in step with the long-term nature of organizations and institutions, with the objective of redefining society as more solidarity-based and fair, as well as more ethical, community-based, ecological, and civic.

The SI process is therefore based on the cooperation and participation of a whole range of stakeholders: "In most cases the success of the innovation will rest on the participation and involvement of a wide variety of interests – the users and beneficiaries of the innovation as well as the producers and suppliers" (Murray et al., 2010). SI "is about coordinating the relationships between the social actors involved in solving socio-economic problems to improve the performance and well-being of communities" (Harrisson and Vezina, 2006).

With all the major economic and financial transformations and the crisis of the welfare state, the inadequacy of social policies tends to be emphasized by the emergence of new social needs. Viewed on a continuum, social innovation seeks to satisfy or reveal diverse social needs or aspirations that need to be defined or reconsidered through concerted design and co-construction work with other stakeholders. These needs actually reflect diverse social realities that are considered as more or less unacceptable or insufficient (thus requiring a contextualized and temporal approach).

By focusing on SI through the prism of design work, we refer to the human, financial, social, and cultural capital; how it is mobilized to think about the social impact of SI; and how it can be used to benefit society – its symbolic status is earned through the appreciation and recognition it receives from the population. We also adopt a more detailed line of analysis, based on competences and organizational learning processes, by focusing on actors, their interaction processes, their organizational relationships, and the knowledge mobilized through action.

Since the 1960s, Herbert Simon (1969) and the artificial paradigm of design sciences have invited us to work on building a theory around the construction of entrepreneurial action, regardless of the level of thinking (Bréchet et al., 2006; Schieb-Bienfait and Urbain, 2004, 2006; Bréchet and Schieb-Bienfait, 2011). Why and how have the services offered by social stakeholders come to be at a time when the state and the market were failing? Why and how are alternative organic farming or fair-trade projects created and organized? Alongside SI, which refers to seizing a social opportunity (approach dominated by market logic with the aim of meeting social needs), we have opted to discuss the second conception of social innovation here, which is less about the market and its competitiveness and productivity goals. This second conception raises the issue of the skills mobilized in finding a solution to meet multidimensional social needs, or in other words, the skills at the heart of the processes and design activities undertaken by stakeholders in response to complex problems, which call for as much on-the-ground experience and knowledge as possible to be able to identify and analyze new situations.

13.2.3 From Individual to Collective Entrepreneurial Competence

The concept of competence is multidimensional (Kyndt and Baert, 2015). It is not about what the system or the support project does to individuals, but what they both do for individuals. It can thus be defined as "everything involved in an organized action and everything that makes it possible to report on how the action is organized" (De Terssac, 2011, p. 234). It is not a finite state but a continuous learning process (Le Boterf, 1994). When we use the notion of competence, we refer to the experience and learning actors acquire from supporting an activity and from the activity itself. It does not come from the resources themselves (knowledge, capacity, etc.) but from their mobilization. We can call it "knowing how to mobilize": "skills must be considered as a process and not as a starting point … The person who is qualified to become skilled in a field of knowledge will become competent."

Based on an observation conducted within a chemical company, Retour and Krohmer (2006) formalized the four "attributes" which characterize collective competence:

- a shared repository (operators have a common view of the work to be done);
- collective memory (including problems encountered and resolved together);

- common language (the team uses the same professional terms and jargon) and subjective engagement (there is a desire to work together);
- a learning process based on exchange and communication (Arnaud, 2016).

In her literature review, Chell (2013) groups the various entrepreneurial skills into six categories: cognitive (e.g., identification of opportunity, awareness of factors inductive to opportunity exploitation, etc.), personality related (ability to work out the means-end framework, innovative/creative ability to generate novel ideas, etc.), social and interpersonal (trust in one's own judgment, ability to manage other people, etc.), business specific (ability to garner necessary material resources, able to apply appropriate skills associated with different stages of business and drive its development forward, etc.), motivational (able to go the distance, energetic, motivation and effort expended, etc.), and learning (ability to learn the rules and make the right move at the right time). Luppi et al. (2019) identify five areas of entrepreneurial competences: team work and collaboration, critical and analytical thinking or problem solving, communication, creativity and innovation, and positive attitude and initiative.

All the researchers underline the difficulties that make them ambiguous: they involve dealing with material and social environment. These difficulties are often circumvented by the competence repository approach (Loué and Baronet, 2015; Brenet et al., 2017). They also concern collective entrepreneurial competence.

The concept of collective competence is essentially the one used in the French-speaking world (Chédotel and Krohmer, 2014; Defélix et al., 2006; Arnaud, 2016). Few studies from English-speaking countries address the notion of "collective competence," which could partly be explained by the individualized nature of practices, although individual competence is very much studied (Boreham, 2004). The collective dimension is most often associated with economic performance (Defélix et al., 2006). Le Bortef (1994) popularized this aspect, while ergonomists (Wittorski, 2007) or labor sociologists (Zarifian, 2009) studied it, and it became an essential part of the literature on human resources management in France and Quebec (Michaux, 2003).

Collective competence is context-based and thereby determined by the environment in which it evolves: the competence of an urban project will be determined by the relationships between stakeholders, the resources attributed to the project, the style of management, and how the work is organized to allow actors to exist within the project. According to Le Boterf (1994), "the competence of the teams cannot be reduced to the sum of the individual competences within them. It depends largely on the quality of the interactions that are established between the skills of individuals. It is forged through experience, being brought face-to-face with reality and collective momentum". The co-construction of this competence requires communication and exchange, which promotes the learning process (Arnaud, 2016).

13.2.4 Collective Entrepreneurial Competences and Exploration

While plenty of research has been carried out on entrepreneurial competence (Chell, 2013), collective entrepreneurial competence has been rather neglected by the academic community. Yet this collective dimension seems important to us, as the actors are more in favor of contexts where encounters and collective work take place (Charles-Pauvers and Schieb-Bienfait, 2009, 2010, 2012). Chédotel and Pujol (2012) confirm that collective entrepreneurship is a founding principle of social economy. Ben-Hafaïedh (2006) shows that entrepreneurship is collective but not well known and that team entrepreneurship should be discussed by the research community.

Design activity therefore involves skills for inventing alternative forms of action and intervention carried by collectives made up of multiple and diverse actors (Klein et al., 2014). So, which competences are used in this effort to create understanding and build when entrepreneurial action is led by a collective of actors?

Taking an interest in the skills required to carry out these exploration activities allows us to move away from a dominant paradigm in terms of entrepreneurial opportunity (Shane and Venkataraman, 2000) and toward an effective study of entrepreneurial work from a pragmatic perspective (according to the principles of the survey proposed by Dewey, 2006). This undertaking is nourished by inventive activities, research activities, and experiments, as well as meetings and interactions.

Creative activity enables innovation to be developed by experimenting with new environments or programs that may lead to new intervention strategies and new instruments of practice for managers and decision-makers. Gradually, this research helps to (re)establish a link with design activities, and, more specifically, with the issue of design work (Hatchuel and Weil, 2008), or in other words, with the idea of conceptualizing activities that reflect their own thinking, in our case, social work.

This point of entry through design activity, implementation, and learning in terms of human, organizational, social, cultural, and financial capacities enables us to study the competences behind the actual processes (design, organization, management, steering, etc.) within our empirical field. The relationships that these organizations have built with other actors and the objects involved in the situation in which action takes place are likely to transform this context from the point of view of relations between actors and in terms of the knowledge in play (current knowledge, new knowledge, and knowledge in construction). With this in mind, constructing the action in situation rests on a dynamic and transformative competence, because the action presupposes adapting the objectives within the action process and therefore within the experimentation and trial-and-error processes.

Moreover, constructing an action in this way means paying special attention to the situations in which social and professional support action takes place. These situations cannot be reduced to environments that are purely external to the supported organization and individual. The innovations envisaged must also take account of the public, of each individual case, and of the problems/difficulties faced.

Taking an interest in their exploratory activities leads us precisely to study which skills are developed and mobilized in undertaking these projects.

13.3 Jardins De Cocagne and Réseau Cocagne (Network Cocagne)

13.3.1 A Participation Observant Methodology

As members of the board of directors for ten years and having taken part in preparatory commissions and informal discussions with workers, we, the authors, played a role as observers and sometimes as participatory observers. It led us from theory to the field, with a "dual questioning of cases by theory and theory by cases" (Rasolofo-Distler and Zawadzki, 2011, p. 4). These experiments mobilized partners or other actors in the territory, pushing them to go beyond the scope of their intervention in situations of exclusion and poverty, thereby revealing different profiles and raising new issues. Through the work carried out with us, such as organizing days of reflection, and with the presence of researchers such as ourselves in their governance bodies, the actors sought to highlight their research activities, which are an integral part of their profession, but also to obtain help with taking a step back from their practices, the aim being to produce new knowledge about their activities and missions (Table 13.1).

This approach was therefore based on the "reflexive practitioner" concept, which consists of taking a step back and re-evaluating a fact or lived event in order to learn from it. Donald Shön (1983), an advocate of pragmatist sociology (Lorino, 2018), points out that practitioners can "work to implement the knowledge learned by continually adapting and refining it in response to changing and often unpredictable situations." It is a matter of putting practices hitherto used subconsciously or in an unplanned way into words.

Within the context of this on-the-ground approach (Bréchet et al., 2014), we observed effective practices of knowledge production and skills development within organizations working in the field of social inclusion. Through their work, these actors promote innovation strategies and are vectors of entrepreneurial/intrapreneurial dynamics. The organizations are rooted in the voluntary sector, with 70% of funding coming from public sources. The observation of their work revealed a commitment to research and experimentation, driven by a strong requirement: to explore new ways of taking action. The actors never cease to invent and design new ways of taking action, thanks to their in-depth knowledge of the needs of the supported public and the skills developed through providing this support: the types of public supported have often experienced difficult social situations and strong and

Table 13.1   History of the Cocagne Network (Réseau Cocagne)

Period	Activities & Innovations
1991	Creation of the first Jardin de Cocagne", after an experimental period of about 10 years
1993	Implementation of spin-off practices towards new gardens
1999	Creation of the Cocagne Network ("Réseau Cocagne")
2000	*50 gardens in activity*
2002	Launch of the quality approach
2010	Launch of the " 30 000 solidarity baskets" program for access to food
2011	*100 gardens with a diversification of activities to better accompany inclusion (activities involving green spaces, plants, processing, etc.)*
2012	Structuring of the R&D strategy
2013	"Maison de Cocagne" project with a change of scale
2014	Launch of Cocagne Investment & Cocagne Endowment Funds

diverse inequalities, exacerbated by new emerging issues, such as social division, deterioration of social ties, and increasing insecurity.

Where the "Jardins de Cocagne" (France) and the Cocagne Network are concerned, our investigations revolved around three questions: What are the characteristics of the approaches taken? What skills have been identified, particularly to define and address social problems and to build the solutions to provide support? Who are the actors mobilized?

13.3.2 From the Jardin de Cocagne to the Cocagne Network (Réseau Cocagne): Social Innovation Approaches

The idea of the Jardin de Cocagne was conceived and launched by the social worker Jean-Guy Henckel, while he was an educator in a shelter for people in difficulty (Table 13.2). Through the shelter and support initiatives, Jean-Guy discovered that these people were confronted with a combination of administrative, financial, family, and professional problems, often tightly intertwined and interrelated. Consequently, it was in the field of social work that the first experiments paving the way for inclusion through economic activity were undertaken in 1974–1975, with the creation of a carpentry workshop: "As soon as someone arrived, the shelter was able to give them a bed and a job immediately … we wanted those who worked to have an employee status, with pay slips, rights" (Henckel, 2009). This initiative brought huge changes for the actors and for practices. The experiment paved the way for the first Jardin de Cocagne, an extraordinary entrepreneurial project and a trailblazing vector of social innovation. This garden provided people in difficulty with work, from the joint development of local farming to the distribution of organic vegetables and the welcoming of consumer members. For more than 15 years, the Jardins de Cocagne has been promoting social inclusion through economic activity by creating gardens (organic market gardening inclusion workshops) to help people get back into active employment. A "Cocagne Network" was created to develop synergies and knowledge-sharing between social innovation initiatives and approaches.

Following its sustained ten-year dynamic of openness, the Jardins de Cocagne Network has become aware of certain vulnerabilities, particularly due to the reforms concerning inclusion through economic activity. Since 2012, the network has been following a research and development strategy to capitalize on the scattered initiatives undertaken in France and develop a more dynamic approach to spinning its initiatives off and searching for diversification projects.

Over the past three years, the network has begun structuring its approach around nine pillars to find financial support for actions and to engage the gardens in a more dynamic strategy in response to rising competition from organic vegetable offers based on short food supply chains (SFSCs).

The entrepreneurial initiatives carried out within the Cocagne Network belong to alternative food production systems; the gardens of the Cocagne Network bolster the primary activity of supporting social inclusion. Since their creation, the gardens have been a meeting place for several different professions and initiatives. This has led actors to constantly search for new ideas and question their practices, not only to propose alternative ways of thinking about inclusion but also to maintain a local organic vegetable production activity at a time when demand for organic products is increasing (in supermarkets and via SFSCs).

Over the past 20 years, the gardens have initiated new SFSC methods (from the sale of vegetable baskets to subscription systems), seeking to propose alternatives to the prevailing modes of regulation (both in terms of inclusion (main aim), but also in terms of the production and marketing of organic vegetables (secondary aim)). This alternative way of doing things is now much more common, and hence there is a need to search for new forms of action by diversifying activities (creation of an educational garden, processing activities – production of jam and plants – environmental maintenance activities, production of seeds, etc.) and also thinking more deeply about the future model of urban agriculture and experimenting with it.

At the same time, the social mission, and more particularly the social support mission, has become more complex because of the rise and combination of social problems experienced by the target public as well as the arrival of new types of public (young people, isolated women, illiterate foreigners, young migrants, political refugees, etc.) and new projects (related to supporting the long-term unemployed). People within these publics face some or all of the following problems: addiction, health problems, mental suffering, isolation, illiteracy, difficulty in accessing housing, debt overhang, legal issues, etc.

For the permanent staff at the gardens, their social and support mission is increasingly complex because of the extremely vulnerable publics involved and the deterioration of certain employment areas in recent years. These teams have become experts in developing innovative systems and services adapted to people's problems. They try to help them regain their dignity and get a job. However, this expertise needs to continue evolving, because, over the past few years, the garden teams have witnessed an increasing number of unemployed people requiring their support.

Finally, several changes have occurred in the support, regulatory, and financial contexts that have led to heavier and more time-consuming administrative and financial workloads. There is little research and development funding available where inclusion through economic activity and, more broadly, the social and solidarity economy are concerned. The gardens carry out their mission in an ecosystem that includes several social partners, who can have contradicting expectations (more often revolving around management issues – evoked in management discussions – than on innovation). They have in-depth knowledge of the gardens and their realities, which both need constant work.

In 2012, the network decided to create a research and development (R&D) activity, whose mission is to support the emergence and creation of innovative and socially motivated activities to reinforce both the social impact and the robustness of the Cocagne model. At the end of these first few years, the network would like to strengthen this activity and model its operations to make it more visible.

13.4 Identification of Entrepreneurial Competences

The analysis carried out on the Jardins de Cocagne made it possible to establish certain things and identify the problems met as well as the stakes related to identifying and recognizing the competences involved in this design activity. Although the organizations belonging to the Cocagne Network may have different activities going on, there are similarities in their role as pillars of entrepreneurial action and social innovation, which are collective activities undertaken by multiple yet highly interdependent stakeholders – associations, public authorities, institutions, volunteers – in the context of a social and solidarity economy.

13.4.1 Exploration Activities to Design and Develop New Services

The analysis of work activity makes it possible to measure the capacity of these actors to go beyond the idea or utopia stage to draw on internal competences and design projects based on several social innovations (services, organization, hybridization of resources, professional practices, etc.). This ability to generate new ideas and to conceive appears to be the driving force of social entrepreneurship in the field of social action. Paradoxically, this social entrepreneurship – an indispensable drive/lever for French public action – remains on the sidelines.

This R&D activity takes place within the sphere of competences, applied to a relational activity and a knowledge production activity involving users, partners, and institutions. These organizations experiment and develop new activities and new services as well as new partnerships, searching for creative hybrids that can be quite bold at times. Their objective is to design new services and to better support publics made up of varied profiles and to question prevailing rules. In the Cocagne Network, the permanent teams of each Cocagne garden regularly welcome new people (called the "gardeners"), who have problems whose nature is constantly changing and evolving. In recent years, work situations supervised by garden employees have become even more difficult to manage for various reasons. For example, some of the people welcomed do not know how to speak French, some are part of a nomadic community (e.g., Romani), and others are suffering from addictions (alcohol, drugs) or are even just out of prison (under surveillance with an electronic bracelet).

For the management teams, those explorations require initiatives, because each individual presents unique problems, which must be taken into account to reconsider and manage each work situation linked to market gardening activities (preparing crops, producing seeds, working on crops, preparing baskets of vegetables, etc.). Behavioral, psychosocial, and relational issues have to be taken into consideration, among others. To do this, the teams of employees carry out research on their own initiative to better understand the problems (research on drugs, on working positions for gardening, on the development of self-confidence, etc.). They take risks as they put into question their daily practices. They search to identify potential partners, so that they can design and test new proposals to adapt, modify, or even imagine work situations. With these experiments, they seek to overcome the problems which can hinder or even prevent them from accomplishing their social action and inclusion mission. They design a support and inclusion-through-work strategy that is both adapted to the individual and is part of the collective activities relating to market gardening. For example, they design and organize new workshops to learn French in parallel with discovering the gardening activity, they offer workshops to exchange and raise awareness about the effects of alcohol consumption, and they identify partners to conceive new approaches to support.

Their teams combine entrepreneurial skills and resources, which are often somewhat restricted, while developing strategies to access new resources (such as other actors, civil society, and foundations) within an action framework dominated by conflicting demands made by their supervisory bodies and/or by financial practices over which they have little or no control. These practices come in the shape of agreements, community budgets, labor, and employment management bodies, but also regulatory and administrative frameworks associated with public policy.

Their experiments concern the services offered, the modes of interaction with the different publics, their working frameworks and practices, and, albeit with more difficulty, their methods of evaluation with regard to the intangible/immaterial nature of the services offered. The social action – accompanying and integrating people (migrants/ Romani) – offers an illustration of skills mobilized to develop an ability to explore and conceive.

It started with the mobilization of the exploration skill, for identifying little or poorly met needs. This translated into the organization's ability to:

- make it easier for users to talk and observe its practices. This involved mobilizing "self-diagnosis" capacities (Internet access: What do they need? What do they want? Why?). Beyond revealing the instrumental aspect of carrying out administrative procedures, this also brought to light interdependent problems, such as a lack of vision, illiteracy, social and family isolation, loss of contact with pastimes and leisure activities, remoteness from current events, etc., and the organization's ability to be a "driving force behind proposals" (a place with free access, not necessarily dedicated to digital services – a café, a library, etc., practical training, such as "How to write an email? How to manage a mailbox? How to access websites? How to work on photos or videos? etc.," locating actors around where they live who can provide support, training, etc.);
- observe the practices of other actors in other fields or areas to take new ideas on board, find support, and adapt.

It then involved mobilizing the relational skill, for going out into in the field to find new or existing partners:

- identifying local actors and creating connections to build and sustain a network for mobilizing expert skills: trainers, health professionals, cultural institutions such as media libraries, the media, artists, lawyers, etc.;
- experimenting on the basis of priorities or opportunities.

Then there was a need for the solving skill, for creating and finding new resources by prospecting or convincing potential stakeholders:

- highlighting the social, economic, and societal utility of a systemic approach to the digital divide.

Then, formalizing experiments and learning and constructing the structure of services to encourage users to appropriate them were facilitated by mobilizing the skills of capitalization and production.

Finally, to develop intangible, formalized, and evolutive services enabling users to acquire knowledge and skills, it was necessary to design and model the system of resource hybridization.

Table 13.2 Summary of types of activities and characteristics of supported groups

Types of activity	Characteristics of the beneficiary
Psycho-social support	Degree of moral dependence
Professional support	Degree of physical dependence
Accompaniment for health problems, addiction	Degree of precariousness
Coaching/learning (French, maths, driving licence, etc.)	Urban/Rural Single/living as a couple/with child(ren)
Practical food education	Age
Accommodation	Level of education
Administrative procedures	Isolated/Presence of family
Leadership	French/foreign nationality
Going out to events, shows, etc.	Housing

Their supervisory bodies (city, conurbation, etc.) are neither aware nor very interested in these activities, which are not taken into account in annual reports, and even less so in the competences mobilized; these research and exploratory activities are little understood and rarely valued. This lack of interest is accentuated by the positions taken by the representatives of these supervisory bodies and by the inadequacy of the steering tools available. Nevertheless, non-profit organizations are increasingly questioning and studying the measurement of social utility or the use of economic models based on social activity.

Beyond social opportunity, the tricky issue of the skills mobilized in co-constructing responses to social needs arises: the analysis made underlines how central this co-construction process is to the research activity of actors and their daily support-based activity, as well as their relationship with their different publics. Table 13.2 shows the broad range needs and characteristics of their publics. It offers another insight into the tricky question of the processes involved in co-building needs and into the origin of the social initiatives and innovations designed by these organizations. It points out the diversity of dynamics and the skills combined to conduct this dual exploration and design activity.

13.4.2 Collective Entrepreneurial Competences

The organizations studied are complex entities. They lie at the intersection of different professions, fields of intervention, and statuses: their research activity is therefore complicated.

We identified the entrepreneurial competences that were involved in these design and innovative activities. The approaches taken are based on different avenues of exploration which revealed skills that are still largely ignored in the field of social action and social work (Table 13.3).

We identified several skills and various combinations that contribute to shaping a real capacity for design:

- the exploration skill, for identifying little or poorly met need(s);
- the relational skill, for going out into the field and building relationships with new or existing partners;
- the solving skill, for creating or finding new resources;
- the capitalizing skill, for making the most of the experiments carried out and knowledge gained;
- the production skill, for defining the structure of services;
- the design skill, for hybridizing resources to develop these immaterial and intangible services.

These different competences are mobilized in activities that are not systematically independent from the daily production activity of the support service. However, our presence as researchers can help actors better understand what can be explored and capitalized on. Researchers challenge, reassure, and legitimize the actors of these organizations (managers, employees) in their efforts. They question them about the processes they implement, and they also invite them to evaluate the experiments carried out.

Finally, we initiated and continue to initiate collective actions. These actions are never plain sailing, regardless of whether they are emerging after an initial

Table 13.3   Several types of business logic and associated skills

Types of conception activity logic	Skills put to use
Entrepreneurial/ intrapreneurial action logic	Ability to imagine and initiate new ways to design an offer that can satisfy needs that are presently unsatisfied or little or poorly satisfied
Logic of "societal" action	Ability to define other frameworks, new regulations to act on causes
Logic of territorial action	Ability to design new practices and structures for regional development (spin-off)
Logic of instrumental action	Ability to design mechanisms and tools to structure supply and activity
Logic of partnership action	Ability to design new partnership modalities

impulse and in fertile conditions, or already up and running with their activities being constantly updated and renewed. Although these actors have been regularly confronted with new problems of exclusion for the past 30 years, the related exploration work has rarely been taken into consideration. These activities carried out with and within the teams while searching for new ways and ideas to carry out their mission have remained a hidden, or even disregarded, part of their profession.

However, they apply R&D practices on an almost daily basis as their field of action is a quasi-permanent laboratory. In 2012, the Cocagne Network set up a research and development committee that meets four times a year to work specifically on new issues in urban agriculture, such as micro-farms with micro-greens and aboveground crops.

However, the lack of stable conditions for a proper R&D activity is a challenge for the gardens: time is an issue for employees, it is difficult to be objective, tensions are inherent to social work (Urbain et al., 2016), and support schemes are financed via calls for projects which prevents long-term structuring.

13.5 Conclusion

Our objective was to highlight the collective entrepreneurial skills of actors engaged in social innovation in all kinds of collectives of actors. It has been difficult to model the modes of operation and to describe the dynamics of collective and organizational competences accurately. The dynamics are driven by a variety of competences that evoke the do-it-yourself (DIY) and serendipity practices observed in research laboratories (Akrich et al., 2006), from "crazy" ideas formulated unexpectedly by employees and the presence of creative intrapreneurs to project design approaches, bringing together ad hoc skills to design new devices and trial-and-error approaches to experimenting with proposals. Our analysis underlines the importance not only of tacit knowledge and creating contexts that are favorable to the development of collective skills, interactions, and learning capacities, but also of the political dimension, in the semantic sense.

The analysis we carried out on the ground reveals that the skills required by the entrepreneurial process are not just those needed for the upstream design of an innovation. Competences are developed at stages when practices, behaviors, and needs of users and the supported public are taken into account. It is difficult to grasp the "lay" production process and its organization and management methods. It is above all a question of experience-based know-how, based on experiments, DIY, the ad hoc invention of new methods, and practices of innovation. The entrepreneurial process can only flourish in this context of social innovation if collaborative relationships are built on close ties, are synonymous with autonomy and well-being of all employees, and are rich in intense interactions in the field for all stakeholders (citizens, private companies, communities, etc.).

References

Akrich, M., Callon, M., & Latour, B. (Ed.) (2006). *Sociologie de la traduction: Textes fonda-teurs.* Paris, France: Mines Paris les Presses Sciences Sociales.

Arnaud, N. (2016). Pour une perspective communicationnelle et pratique de la compétence collective. *Communication Organisation,* (2), 215–244.

Ben-Hafaïedh, C. (2006). Entrepreneuriat en équipe: positionnement dans le champ de l'entrepreneuriat collectif. *Revue de l'Entrepreneuriat, 5*(2), 31–54.

Besançon, E., Chochoy, N., & Guyon, T. (2013). *L'innovation sociale: Principes et fonde-ments d'un concept.* Paris, France: Editions L'Harmattan.

Boreham, N. (2004). Collective competence and work process knowledge. In *European Conference on Educational Research,* Crete, Greece.

Bouchard, C. (1999). Recherche en sciences humaines et sociales et innovations sociales. Contribution à une politique de l'immatériel. *Conseil québécois de recherche sociale (CQRS), texte inédit.*

Bréchet, J.-P., & Schieb-Bienfait, N. (2012). *Entrepreneurship in search of its foundations.* EURAM, Rotterdam, Pays-Bas.

Brechet, J. P., & Schieb-Bienfait, N. (2011). Logique d'action et projet dans l'action col-lective: Réflexions théoriques comparées. *Finance Contrôle Stratégie, 14*(1), 101–129.

Bréchet, J. P., Émin, S., & Schieb-Bienfait, N. (2014). La recherche-accompagnement: une pratique légitime. *Finance Contrôle Stratégie, 17*(2), 17–27.

Brechet, J. P., Schieb-Bienfait, N., & Urbain, C. (2006). Les mains visibles du marché: Projets des acteurs et régulations dans les services à domicile aux personnes âgées. *Gérer et Comprendre. Annales des Mines, 83,* 67–77.

Brenet, P., Schieb-Bienfait, N. & Authier, J. (2017). Concevoir un référentiel de com-pétences pour les étudiants entrepreneurs: la démarche PEPITE. *Entreprendre & Innover, 33*(2), 29–43.

Cajaiba-Santana, G. (2014). Social innovation: Moving the field forward. A conceptual framework. *Technological Forecasting and Social Change, 82,* 42–51.

Charles-Pauvers, B., & Schieb-Bienfait, N. (2009). Compétences individuelles et collec-tives au cœur de la stratégie: une étude de cas longitudinale dans une SCOP du bâtiment. In Retour, D., Picq, T. & Defélix, C. (Ed.) (2009). *Gestion des compétences: nouvelles relations, nouvelles dimensions* (pp. 149-172). Paris, France: Vuibert.

Charles-Pauvers, B., & Schieb-Bienfait, N. (2010). La compétence entrepreneuriale: la ges-tion des ressources humaines au service des démarches d'accompagnement. Le cas des coopératives d'activité et d'emploi. *Gestion 2000, 3,* 107–122

Charles-Pauvers, B., & Schieb-Bienfait, N. (2012). Manager des collectifs, levier de la com-pétence organisationnelle? Étude de cas dans une société coopérative et participative. *Travail et Emploi, 130,* 57–75.

Chédotel, F., & Krohmer, C. (2014). Les règles, leviers de développement d'une compé-tence collective–deux études de cas. *@GRH, 3,* 15–38.

Chedotel, F., & Pujol, L. (2012). L'influence de l'identité sur la compétence collective lors de prises de décisions stratégiques: le cas de SCOP. *Finance Contrôle Stratégie, 15* (1/2), 35–47.

Chell, E. (2013). Review of skill and the entrepreneurial process. *International Journal of Entrepreneurial Behavior & Research, 19*(1), 6–31.

Cloutier, J. (2003). *Qu'est-ce que l'innovation sociale?* Online research book; Montréal: Crises, 1–46. CRISES research Center of Social Innovation (University of Quebec, Montréal), https://crises.uqam.ca/cahiers/et0314-quest-ce-que-linnovation-sociale

De Terssac, G. (2011). Savoirs, compétences et travail. In Barbier, J. M. (Ed.), *Savoirs théoriques et savoirs d'action*, (pp. 223–247). Paris, France: Presses Universitaires de France.

Defélix, C., Oiry, E., & Klarsfeld, A. (2006). *Nouveaux regards sur la gestion des compétences*. Paris, France: Vuibert.

Dewey, J. (2006). *Logique: la théorie de l'enquête*. Paris, France: PUF.

Håland, E., & Tjora, A. (2006). Between asset and process: Developing competence by implementing a learning management system. *Human Relations*, *59*(7), 993–1016.

Harrison D. (2011). Analyser les théories pour comprendre l'innovation sociale. 3ème colloque international du CRISES, *Pour une nouvelle mondialisation: le défi d'innover*, UQAM, Montréal.

Harrisson, D., & Vézina, M. (2006). L'innovation sociale: une introduction. *Annals of Public and Cooperative Economics*, *77*(2), 129–138.

Hatchuel, A., & Weil, B. (2008). Entre concepts et connaissances: éléments d'une théorie de la conception. In Hatchuel, A., & Weil, B. (Eds.), *Les nouveaux régimes de la conception. Langages, théories, métiers* (pp. 115–132). Paris, France: Vuibert.

Henckel, J. G. (2009). *Dans un pays de Cocagne: entretien avec Jean-Guy Henckel*. Conversations, Rue de l'échiquier.

Klein, J. L., Camus, A., Jetté, C., Champagne, C., & Roy, M. (2016). *La transformation sociale par l'innovation sociale*. Québec, Canada: PUQ.

Kyndt, E., & Baert, H. (2015). Entrepreneurial competencies: Assessment and predictive value for entrepreneurship. *Journal of Vocational Behavior*, *90*, 13–25.

Klein, J. L., Laville, J. L. & Moulaert, F. (2014). *L'innovation sociale*. Paris, France: Erès.

Krohmer, C. & Retour D. (2006). La compétence collective, maillon clé de la gestion des compétences. In Defélix, C., Klarsfeld, A., & Oiry, E. (Eds.), *Nouveaux regards sur la gestion des compétences* (pp. 139–173). Paris, France: Vuibert.

Le Boterf, G. (1994). *De la compétence, essai sur un attracteur étrange*. Paris, France: Éditions d'organisation.

Lévesque, B. (2006). Le potentiel d'innovation sociale de l'économie sociale: quelques éléments de problématique. *Économie et Solidarités*, *37*(1), 13–48.

Lindberg, O., & Rantatalo, O. (2015). Competence in professional practice: A practice theory analysis of police and doctors. *Human Relations*, *68*(4), 561–582.

Lorino, P. (2018). *Pragmatism and Organization Studies*. Oxford, UK: Oxford University Press.

Loué, C. & Baronet, J. (2015). Quelles compétences pour l'entrepreneur? Une étude de terrain pour élaborer un référentiel. *Entreprendre & Innover*, 27(4), 112–119.

Michaux, V. (2003). *Compétence collective et systèmes d'information: cinq cas de coordination dans les centres de contacts* (Doctoral dissertation, Nantes).

Mulgan, G. (2006). The process of social innovation. *Innovations: Technology, Governance, Globalization*, *1*(2), 145–162.

Murray, R., Caulier-Grice, J., & Mulgan, G. (2010). *The Open Book of Social Innovation* (p. 2). London, UK: National Endowment for Science, Technology and the Art.

Rasolofo-Distler, F., & Zawadzki, C. (2011). Proposition d'un cadre conceptuel pour les CIFRE: Illustration par deux thèses soutenues en contrôle de gestion. *Comptabilités, Economie et société*. May.

Richez-Battesti, N., Petrella, F., & Vallade, D. (2012). L'innovation sociale, une notion aux usages pluriels: Quels enjeux et défis pour l'analyse? *Innovations*, (2), 15–36.

Sandberg, J. (2000). Understanding human competence at work: An interpretative approach. *Academy of Management Journal, 43*(1), 9–25.

Sandberg, J., & Pinnington, A. H. (2009). Professional competence as ways of being: An existential ontological perspective. *Journal of Management Studies, 46*(7), 1138–1170.

Schieb-Bienfait, N., & Urbain, C. (2004). L'entrepreneuriat social, une autre façon d'entreprendre? Une étude exploratoire sur l'émergence organisationnelle dans l'univers des services à domicile aux personnes âgées. *Revue internationale de l'économie sociale: Recma, 293,* 68–92.

Schieb-Bienfait, N., & Urbain, C. (2006). L'entrepreneuriat social et solidaire: cas des associations de services à domicile aux personnes âgées. *Management et Sciences Sociales, 1,* 195–218.

Schieb-Bienfait, N., Charles-Pauvers, B., & Urbain, C. (2009). Émergence entrepreneuriale et innovation sociale dans l'économie sociale et solidaire: acteurs, projets et logiques d'action. *Innovations,* (2), 13–39.

Shane, S., & Venkataraman, S. (2000). The promise of entrepreneurship as a field of research. *Academy of Management Review, 25*(1), 217–226.

Shön, D. A. (1983). *The reflective practitioner: How professionals think in action/Donald A. Shon.* Basic Books, *374,* 55.

Simon, H. (1969). *Science des systèmes, sciences de l'artificiel.* Paris, France: Dunod.

Urbain C., Pailler D., Schieb-Bienfait N., & Lebot A. (2016). La construction d'une offre de services publics innovante par hybridation des ressources, des activités et des missions des acteurs: le cas d'un restaurant social municipal. In Klein, J. L., Camus, A., Jetté, C., Champagne, C., & Roy, M. (Eds.), *La transformation sociale par l'innovation sociale* (pp. 313–317). Québec, Canada: PUQ.

Wittorski, R. (2007). *Professionnalisation et développement professionnel.* Paris, France: Editions L'Harmattan.

Zarifian, P. (2009). *Le travail et la compétence: entre puissance et contrôle.* Paris, France: PUF.

Chapter 14

Contextualizing Intercultural Competences: Genesis, Concepts, and Research Agenda

Christoph Barmeyer and Ulrike Mayrhofer

Contents

14.1 Introduction

Intercultural competence – a person's ability to understand values, ways of thinking, and behaviors of other cultures, and to act in an appropriate and effective way – plays a role in various areas in multinational companies (MNCs) (Dias et al., 2017), which were then also recorded in research: initially, this included expatriation (Gertsen, 1990; Walther, 2014), but also leadership (Barmeyer and Mayrhofer, 2008), teams (Matveev, 2017), and knowledge transfer in multinational contexts (Mayrhofer, 2013), which are recently boundary spanning in MNCs (Barner-Rasmussen et al., 2014). Specific HR (human resource) strategies and personnel development measures such as intercultural training can help the actors to become interculturally more competent (Landis et al., 2004; Bennett, 2015).

Previous research on intercultural competence has been limited primarily to isolated individuals, who are also members of only one, mainly national, culture. Neither have interaction processes or diverse working contexts been sufficiently taken into account. The focus of this chapter is thus on the contextualization of intercultural competence. The authors provide a novel perspective of how to better capture the multiple dimensions of intercultural competence and their interactions in diverse cultural and historical contexts. The proposed research agenda should help future studies to contribute to a better understanding of the complexity of intercultural competence in multiple geographical and organizational settings.

This chapter is divided into five sections: after introducing the importance of the topic, we show that the historical genesis of intercultural competence has been influenced by the US context. Concepts and models of intercultural competence are then presented, followed by a section on the development and measurement of intercultural competence. The chapter ends with a context-related research agenda, which enables a differentiated research of intercultural competence.

14.2 Setting the Stage: Intercultural Learning and Intercultural Competence

People experience numerous development processes through intercultural influences and experiences – through their stays abroad, international working relationships, intercultural friendships, partnerships and families, or societal multiculturalism – which turn them into intercultural personalities (Vora et al., 2019). This process is called intercultural learning (Mayer, 2016). In intercultural learning, a change of perspective takes place through the adoption of new, different, cultural points of view (Hall, 1983). It should be emphasized that learning is a holistic process that is not limited to cognitive acquisition of knowledge, but also integrates emotions and behaviors (Barmeyer, 2004). In this respect, learning implies that behavioral patterns are modified and developed. This change of perspective also forms the basis for more understanding, tolerance, and empathy with regard to cultural differences and helps to question, relativize, and modify one's own attitudes and actions in intercultural situations (Deardorff, 2018). This change in attitudes means that new elements help to find new solutions for achieving goals – such as success or satisfaction – and to improve the quality of the relationship with other cultural interaction partners. Those can be integrated into the existing behavioral repertoire. Cultural otherness is perceived not only as irritation and disruption, but also as enrichment (Barmeyer and Franklin, 2016). Intercultural learning is thus not only an external process of goal achievement, adaptation, and integration, but also an internal process of personal development (Hoopes, 1979; Bennett, 2015). Central elements of intercultural learning are, on the one hand, the attitude of people to interculturality and, on the other hand, characteristics of intercultural competence as well as measures for its promotion and development (Bennett, 2015; Deardorff, 2018).

Originally developed within the framework of North American research in the field of intercultural communication and international assignments (Johnson et al., 2006), the concept of intercultural competence summarizes attitudes, personality traits, knowledge, and skills that facilitate a person's communication or interaction with individuals from other cultural backgrounds/environments. Intercultural competence can be understood as a person's ability to understand values, ways of thinking, communication rules, and behavioral patterns of another culture. In intercultural interaction situations, this enables the transparent communication of one's own points of view and thus to act in a culturally sensitive, constructive, and effective way. Intercultural competence thus leads to the achievement of personal or professional goals (Spencer-Oatey and Franklin, 2009).

14.3 Looking on the Origins: Genesis of Intercultural Competence Research

The research field of intercultural competence started with the development of intercultural communication research and intercultural training in the middle of the 20th century in the United States (Rogers and Hart, 2002; Matveev, 2017). The research developed out of practice. Some decades later, Croucher et al. (2015, p. 72) stated that: "Intercultural communication as a relatively new field of study is an answer to the communication complexities of a modern world with a wide range of cultural characteristics."

The origin of intercultural competence development in the United States can be situated around the time of the Second World War (Pusch, 2004). The Foreign Service Institute (FSI), founded in 1946, had the task of systematically and thoroughly preparing specialists and executives for foreign assignments in the fields of diplomacy, peace work, development cooperation, and the military: "After World War II, Americans began to reevaluate their knowledge and understanding of other countries, both in terms of their languages and in terms of their cultural assumptions. Along with general concern about the ability of Americans to interact with foreign nationals, the training and knowledge of American diplomats were issues, since deficiencies in those areas have substantial repercussions" (Leeds-Hurwitz, 1990, p. 264).

In the 1950s, the FSI commissioned renowned anthropologists and linguists to communicate cultural anthropological findings. One of these was Edward T. Hall (1956), who was among the first scholars to study intercultural situations using a micro-cultural analysis. The main focus was on how actors in intercultural situations dealt with unknown values and norms as well as foreign languages. Hall's research, published in books such as *The Silent Language* (1959) or *The Hidden Dimension* (1966), focuses primarily on spatial-temporal and nonverbal aspects of intercultural interaction. For him, culture represents a system of meanings and patterns of thought and action that can be understood like a foreign language. Gradually, preparations for international assignments developed the form of intercultural training. They enable actors in international contexts to become more capable of acting, i.e., interculturally competent, in foreign contexts. The development of various methods such as the critical incident method (Flanagan, 1954) and the culture assimilator (Fiedler et al., 1971), which are based on the micro-cultural analysis of interaction situations, should contribute to this empowerment.

The employees of the Peace Corps, an independent US authority founded by J.F. Kennedy in 1961 (Bird, 1989), played a particularly important role in the differentiation and professionalization of intercultural learning. The task of the Peace Corps was to promote mutual understanding between Americans and local residents, as well as trained specialists from other countries. Americans sent on technical and humanitarian aid missions should support the latter in their work. Volunteers worked abroad for about two years. In parallel with the human relations movement and the strengthening of personal responsibility and participation, a participant-centered learning approach was increasingly used, which placed experience-oriented interactions at the center of training (Rogers and Hart, 2002).

But intercultural competence did not only gain importance through international relations and stays abroad (Gertsen, 1990) or multinational companies (Bartel-Radic, 2013); it also gained importance through the development of US society into a multicultural society, i.e., through immigration, in which interethnic problems also led to discrimination and racism (Hoopes, 1979). Intercultural competence should help to better understand the different, parallel life worlds with their diverging values and practices and thus contribute to a more peaceful coexistence (Croucher et al., 2015). It becomes clear that both societal development and activities abroad (initially chiefly assignments in other cultural contexts), as well as the inner societal handling of interculturality in the form of diversity and multiculturalism, have also influenced two goals of intercultural competence development:

individual problem-solving and goal achievement as well as communal peaceful cooperation.

From the United States, the concept of intercultural competence spread to Europe and Japan (Rogers and Hart, 2002), and later also to China and Africa (Kulich, 2012). The development of intercultural competences was then promoted in the 1970s by associations such as SIETAR (Society for Intercultural Education Training and Research) and finally also by European organizations promoting youth exchange between European countries (Demorgon, 1989). Since 1990, the development of intercultural competence has become firmly established in multi-national companies within the framework of personnel and organizational development (Barmeyer and Franklin, 2016; Mayrhofer, 2013).

From this genesis, it becomes clear that the concept of intercultural competence originated in the United States and developed from the political environment, but also from human rights movements (Hoopes, 1979). It is thus strongly influenced by the temporal and spatial context of North America. Critical authors, such as Dahlén (1997), argue that intercultural research is based on political and military motives and that even respected ethnologists like Ruth Benedict have put their knowledge at the service of the US government. The intercultural development of competences has been increasingly discussed critically by postcolonial-oriented scholars, who reproduce the hierarchical and power structures that exist in Western-oriented contents and methods (Jack and Lorbiecki, 2003).

14.4 Defining Intercultural Competence: Concepts and Models

Many scholars and practitioners deal with intercultural competence. Central scientific disciplines, which illuminate the concept from their specific point of view, are among other communication studies, cross-cultural psychology, social psychology, linguistics, anthropology, and education. Anglo-Saxon research, in particular (Deardorff, 2009), has dealt with the concretization of intercultural competence on the basis of definitions, concepts, and models. The topic has also been researched in Germany and in France (Demorgon, 1989; Barmeyer, 2004; Mayrhofer, 2017). Even if definitions of intercultural competence are varied, there is a common understanding that intercultural competence is the ability to interact successfully and appropriately with individuals and groups from other cultures. In a more narrow sense, it means the ability to deal with people from different cultural orientations in a mutually satisfactory manner. Spitzberg and Changnon (2009, p. 7), for example, define intercultural competence as "the appropriate and effective management of interaction between people who, to some degree or another, represent different or divergent affective, cognitive, and behavioral orientations to the world."

14.4.1 Affective, Cognitive, and Conative Competences

A widespread structuring of characteristics (components) related to intercultural competence can be found, among others, in the so-called compositional models (see Table 14.1), originating from the US socio-psychological research (Rosenberg and Hovland, 1960), which investigated the research question of the extent to which personal attitudes determine behavior. The division into attitudes, knowledge, and behavior was transferred to characteristics of intercultural competence (Gertsen, 1990, p. 346), assuming an interaction of all three components:

> The *affective* component describes the social competence or emotional attitude of an individual toward cultural differences, which is expressed in personal attitudes such as empathy and openness toward other cultural worldviews.
>
> The *cognitive* component comprises both culture-specific and general cultural knowledge, which promotes the individual perception of similarities and differences between cultures as well as their values and ways of acting. Here, information is transformed into concrete knowledge.
>
> The *conative* component expresses the perceptible behavior required for appropriate interaction. The latter thus reflects the necessary implementation of emotional attitudes and cultural knowledge. This can manifest itself in the use of a foreign language or the general willingness and ability of an individual to communicate.

14.4.2 Models of Intercultural Competence

Researchers built on early work to further identify key variables in intercultural effectiveness or cross-cultural competence (Ruben, 1976; Hammer et al., 2003). A variety of models can be used to describe and record intercultural competence. These models have been discussed (Matveev, 2017) and systematized by Spitzberg and Changnon (2009), as shown in Table 14.1.

Frequently the question arises as to whether intercultural competence is a universal – etic – concept that can be transferred to any culture or is it rather a culture-specific – emic – concept that can be learned for each specific culture (Johnson et al., 2006). Moosmüller and Schönhut (2009) address the question of whether intercultural competence is not fundamentally context-bound – with the consequence that a specific intercultural competence exists for each specific context (e.g., school, partnership, small business, or multinational enterprise). Most models of intercultural competence, however, deal with different central characteristics, without making a contextualized allocation to specific cultures, occupational groups, etc. For example, the demands placed on engineers differ considerably from those placed on exchange students or politicians.

Table 14.1   Models of Intercultural Competence (Spitzberg and Changnon 2009)

Model	Concept	Criticism
Compositional Models	This type of model usually lists non-hierarchical human characteristics that are relevant in the context of intercultural competence and can be assigned to components, i.e., affective (e.g., impartiality, openness, and respect for other cultures), cognitive (e.g., cultural knowledge, tolerance of ambiguity, and role distance), and behavioral (conative) (e.g., friendliness, flexibility, communication skills, and problem-solving skills).	The central shortcomings of this type of model are its lack of coherence – what are the relationships between the individual components? – and decontextualization. While there is broad agreement that intercultural competence is at least partly context specific, component models list different characteristics without any allocation to specific cultures, occupational groups, etc.
Co-orientational Models	These models focus on the conceptualization of primarily interactive dimensions (e.g., change of perspective, empathy, and communicative commonalities). Their common frame of reference initially consists only of basic human needs and is always developed through interaction. Co-orientational models thus deal with the ability not only to accept other than one's own culture of origin, but also to adopt them, at least partially, into one's own orientation system and thus create something new.	Criticism of this type of model is that negative effects of interactions, such as misunderstandings, are not taken into account.

(Continued)

Table 14.1   (Continued) Models of Intercultural Competence (Spitzberg and Changnon 2009)

Model	Concept	Criticism
Developmental Models	These models emphasize the temporal dimension that has been neglected in previous models. Development models describe the development of intercultural competence as a learning process in the course of which several stages are passed through. Thus, more dynamic, systemic aspects are included. A first model, which states the development of intercultural competence through time and experience, comes from Hoopes (1979), with eight development phases such as ethnocentrism, awareness, understanding, acceptance and respect, appreciating and valuing, selective adoption, assimilation and adaptation, and biculturalism and multiculturalism. Building on this, Bennett (2001) developed the Developmental Model of Intercultural Sensitivity with six levels (denial, defense, minimization, acceptance, adaptation, and integration).	The linear sequence of the stages should be viewed critically, for example, because phases may be skipped or there may even be a relapse after negative experiences. Equally surprising is the freedom of culture and context with regard to the target society and situations of action: How do persons with different cultural backgrounds act? How do they relate to each other? For example, is a British person particularly sensitive and competent to certain target cultures, e.g., to a familiar European culture, which he or she does not feel toward an Asian culture?
Adaptational Models	These models are systemic in design: they identify different actors (interactants) involved in the process of intercultural communication and consider their constant mutual input. The interrelations between the actors and the process of mutual influence are emphasized. These models make it clear that an individual never develops in isolation and autonomously.	The criterion for competence is the adaptability of the actors. However, the ability to adapt alone and in itself is a dubious criterion for competence. A further problem is the processual character of adaptation: the individual stages of adaptation on both sides need to be further investigated and the term specifically defined.

(Continued)

Table 14.1   (Continued) Models of Intercultural Competence (Spitzberg and Changnon 2009)

Model	Concept	Criticism
Causal Process Models	These models examine specific relationships between components and represent path models in which individual components determine or influence the subsequent components. They describe linear systems, which makes them the easiest to translate into verifiable statements. An identifiable set of prerequisites (both individual and environmental) and capabilities leads to an identifiable set of results. Due to their logical structure, these models are often used in empirical research, for example, to measure the strength of influences using multivariate methods. The strength of Causal Process Models is the representation of cause and effect.	Their problem, however, is that too many paths lead in both directions, which makes it difficult to verify the individual directions and thus considerably weakens the validity of these types of models.

14.5 Developing and Measuring Intercultural Competence

Organizations that operate internationally or which are increasingly confronted with interculturality at home have a need for intercultural development (Bennett, 2015). They can support their employees in a professional, i.e., strategically and sustainably way. This is where intercultural competence development comes in. Interculturally oriented training and further education measures help to build, maintain, or restore qualifications and align them with requirement and competence profiles (Wagner et al., 2017). Multinational companies have been offering intercultural training for many decades, such as Airbus (Barmeyer and Mayrhofer, 2008) or Alleo (Barmeyer and Davoine, 2019), and public, non-profit, or social organizations are increasingly discovering the relevance of intercultural competence development (Wolff and Borzikowsky, 2018). The focus is on the development of intercultural competence through measures such as training, coaching, and consulting.

14.5.1 Intercultural Training, Coaching, and Consulting

Intercultural training is the most important measure of intercultural competence development, i.e., methodical, systematic educational measures that create awareness for cultural differences among the participants and at the same time promote skills for constructive adaptation and effective action under different cultural conditions. In terms of concept, content, and methodology, intercultural training combines findings from general training research and intercultural research (Landis et al., 2004; Bennett, 2015). The use of intercultural training methods for competence development should be contextual to take into account the specific characteristics of the participants. The success of intercultural training depends on the consideration of the participants' intercultural experiences and the development of their intercultural competence, but also on their learning styles (Barmeyer, 2004). Learning styles describe the preferred individual way to learn, i.e., to process information and feelings and translate them into knowledge and action (Simy and Kolb, 2009). The knowledge and consideration of diverging individual and cultural learning styles (Holtbrügge and Mohr, 2010) lead to better and successful learning.

Intercultural coaching and consulting are also possible measures for intercultural development and learning. Coaching and consulting are to be understood as process-oriented and individualized measures for intercultural competence development. They enable a stronger contextualization, in-depth response to situations, and concerns of organizations (Rosinski, 2003) than intercultural training

14.5.2 Measuring Intercultural Competence

Intercultural competence is a multidimensional construct and therefore difficult to measure. The concept covers affective (personal characteristics), cognitive (abilities and skills), and conative dimensions (actual behavior of actors). The models of intercultural competence presented by Spitzberg and Changnon (2009) emphasize the diversity of existing conceptualizations. Empirical studies often focus on personal characteristics such as personality traits and attitudes, assuming that they reflect the different components of intercultural competence. The study conducted by Bartel-Radic and Giannelloni (2017) shows that personality traits are not necessarily linked to other dimensions of intercultural competence, namely to cognitive abilities such as intercultural knowledge. Their contribution indicates that it is necessary to elaborate more adequate tools to measure the complexity of intercultural competence. Such tools should integrate affective and cognitive, but also conative dimensions. Their elaboration remains a promising research avenue for future studies.

To analyze and develop intercultural competence in the practice of organizations, various psychometric instruments are offered, mostly of the US origin (Koester and Lustig, 2015; Deardorff, 2009). The use of such self-assessment instruments can be useful, especially to obtain an initial assessment and then to initiate development steps (e.g., through coaching and training) (Spencer-Oatey and Franklin, 2009), to support a potential assessment and competence development for specialists and managers with regard to intercultural cooperation (Brinkmann and Weerdenburg, 2014).

A fundamental critique concerns the universalism of such instruments and also the "imperialism of Western management techniques" in the "cross-cultural training industry" (Jack and Lorbiecki, 2003, p. 213, 215). Characteristics and elements of intercultural competence development, such as content (stereotypes, intercultural misunderstandings, feedback, or the admission of one's own "deficits") and, above all, methods (interactive methods, such as simulations and other participatory processes, and self-reflections), are mostly Anglo-Saxon Western European. This can be explained by the genesis of practice and research on competence development: most of the interculturalists who contributed to the field of intercultural competence development came from the United States (Kulich, 2012) and from Western European countries (Hofstede, 1980). Moreover, they have developed a certain body of thought based on a special (self-determined, liberal, egalitarian, and participative) conception of people, communities, and organizations (Inglehart and Welzel, 2005). Only few ideas and publications can be found from other countries such as China, India, Russia, or the African or South American continent (Deardorff, 2009; Jackson, 2004). Research and practice of intercultural competence is therefore Western. Many basic assumptions are ethnocentric and can only be applied to a limited extent in other cultural contexts (Collier, 2015).

14.6 Proposing a Research Agenda: Contextualizing Intercultural Competence

Most studies on intercultural competence do not take into account any context of action and therefore regard it primarily as an individual and person-related phenomenon. This is probably due to the fact that research on intercultural competence has been driven and developed primarily by psychologists, who mostly use quantitative survey methods with standardized questionnaires. Other disciplines, such as pedagogy or (socio-)linguistics, have also dealt with intercultural competence, but the perspectives of sociology and anthropology, which understand competences not as an isolated individual but as a contextual and socially constructed phenomenon, are missing. Intercultural competence is usually described by individual personality traits and abilities. Intercultural competence goes far beyond the individual level because it can only become collectively effective and significant through (a) dynamic and reciprocal interaction with other (b) people, i.e., it is constituted, in certain (c) contexts.

Dynamic and reciprocal: Intercultural competence should not be viewed in isolation and individually. It rather constitutes itself within organizations from a complex combination of intercultural sensitivity and prior knowledge, regular intercultural interactions, and an organizational structure in which departmental and team leaders have been socialized in different countries.

Collective: This perspectival understanding of intercultural competence relates to collective interaction. It concerns the activation of diverse resources (e.g., knowledge and experience) and competences of other cultural employees through joint work (e.g., projects) in specific contexts (e.g., structures and departments) to achieve overarching goals.

Contexts: Since intercultural competences only become effective in social systems, i.e., in relation to organizations and management, different context factors can weaken or strengthen the meaning and value of intercultural competence. A contextual influencing factor is power: interculturality always takes place in spaces marked by power and interests. A central, but still too seldom, discussed topic is the question of mutual adaptation in intercultural interaction situations. Who has to adapt? How far do these adaptations reach and how often do they take place? This means that individuals who are in positions of power do not necessarily act in an interculturally competent way to enforce their goals, rules, and interests. On the other hand, people in subordinate positions are often forced to undertake intercultural adaptation processes. In the latter case, intercultural competence seems to have a higher value.

We can emphasize that only few academic studies have taken into account the specific context in which intercultural competence is developed (Bartel-Radic, 2013; Wang and Kulich, 2015). The study conducted by Bartel-Radic (2013) shows the importance of context and culture-specific intercultural competence in organizational learning in Brazilian MNCs. It illustrates on the basis of seven qualitative case studies that some specificities of Brazilian culture appears to be beneficial for the development of intercultural organizational competences: elements like flexibility, also illustrated through "jeitinho," as an informal problem-solving strategy in organizations (Duarte, 2006) or "estrangeirismo," as the Brazilian expression for ethnorelativism, help Brazilian managers to consider learning opportunities from other countries and cultures.

For the future of a contextualized research on intercultural competence, we propose the following research agenda, which will be carried out on three levels of analysis on the basis of the multicultural approach. This is also in accordance with the orientation of this research handbook and the recommendations provided by Collier (2015) and Martin (2015), who suggest that future research in the field of intercultural communication competence should elaborate more holistic frameworks considering multiple cultural identities and intercultural interactions. The authors consider that it is necessary to develop a new dialectical approach that allows for a historically and contextually situated conceptualization of intercultural communication competence. We build on their work by extending the research agenda to intercultural competence in general and by proposing concrete steps to achieve this goal.

14.6.1 Multiple Cultures Approach

Brannen (1998) points out that not only the context in which interculturality takes place must be taken into account, but also the cultural characteristics of the actors. The monolithic functionalist and national concept of culture is criticized as too deterministic (Fang, 2006). Actors in intercultural organizations are shaped by different cultural influences and thus have pluralistic cultural and identitary points of reference, which are far more diverse than just being shaped by national culture. This plurality is addressed by the multiple cultures approach of Sackmann and Phillips (2004). In accordance with this approach, intercultural competence is increasingly concerned with national culture, but also with other cultures such as industrial, organizational, departmental, and professional cultures (Sainsaulieu, 2014). Such cultural groupings or categories are known from diversity management (Özbilgin and Tatli, 2008), also referred to as stratification of subcultural characteristics (Zander and Romani, 2004) or as cultural mosaic (Chao and Moon, 2005). The perspective of multiple cultures thus enables a substantially differentiated picture of cultural realities and identities of actors in intercultural situations. Using this perspective, we argue that intercultural competence is not only linked to national culture but also to organizational culture, department, function and professional culture, position, experience, knowledge, and gender.

14.6.2 Three Level Analysis

Interculturality takes place in and between social systems that can be modeled as three interrelated, systemically influencing levels (Fink and Mayrhofer, 2009). In line with our understanding that intercultural competence is conceptual, we may ask the following questions. At the micro level, the focus is on actors and their international cooperation: Which persons are acting? Are they monocultural or bicultural? At the meso level, the focus is on organizational concerns, such as the development of an internationally oriented organizational culture: Which organizations (public or private, profit or non-profit, etc.)? At the macro level, the focus is on the influence of certain contexts in which organizations are embedded, such as institutions (e.g., state, laws, and education systems), but also media systems or the national language: Which countries, societies, and languages are concerned (centralistic or federal, modern or traditional, etc.). It helps to understand at which level of action (practice) or analysis (research) interculturality takes place. Fink and Mayrhofer (2009, p. 48) underline "the broad variety of possible levels and related units of analysis, many of them spanning across different kinds of boundaries. As usual, the concrete choice is determined by the various factors influencing the context of discovery. They include financial incentives by sponsoring agencies, economic or political relevance, personal interest of the researcher, assumed importance in the scientific discourse or contribution to a political, ideological or personal agenda".

Through societal evolution, each level will become increasingly pluralistic, intercultural, and multicultural, leading to the emergence and coexistence of multiple cultures that affect internal and interpersonal processes. At the micro level, there are more people with bicultural or intercultural backgrounds (Vora et al., 2019); at the meso level, teams and organizations become more multicultural and are characterized by cultural diversity (Dias et al., 2017). At the macro level, societies are confronted with cultural transfer and transformation processes such as migration (Guo and Al Ariss, 2015). An example for the three level analysis is provided in Box 1.

BOX 1: COMPETENCE DEVELOPMENT AT AIRBUS GROUP (BASED ON BARMEYER AND MAYRHOFER, 2008, 2014)

The European Airbus Group, formerly named EADS (European Aeronautic Defence and Space Company), which resulted from the merger of the French company Aérospatiale-Matra, the German company DASA ,and the Spanish company CASA in the year 2000, represents a particularly interesting case for illustrating the three level analysis of intercultural learning and competence development. The creation of a new organizational culture (meso level) enabled the company to overcome differences in terms of individual culture (micro level) and national culture (macro level). Confronted with individual, organizational, and national cultures that were diverging significantly, the Airbus Group put in place a human resources management policy that aimed to build a strong organizational culture. The different business units were involved in the harmonization and integration of human resources and the recruitment of new staff. The decision to organize intercultural training sessions and to adopt English as the official language of communication facilitated the process. The corporate culture of the company is based on teamwork, integrity, customer focus, reliability, respect, and creativity.

All levels are of interest for contextual and differentiated research on intercultural competence. It may be particularly relevant to examine bicultural and multicultural individuals (Fitzsimmons et al., 2013; Vora et al., 2019) who, due to their intercultural socialization, often possess pronounced/outstanding intercultural competences (Barmeyer and Franklin, 2016), which they may use in complex and demanding intercultural situations. Many bicultural individuals are, moreover, used to dealing with linguistic and intercultural challenges. Due to their insider and outsider intermediate position (they are not embedded in *one* cultural social systems but in different ones), as third culture perspective (Osula and Irvin, 2009), they can put themselves into different systems of meaning and action and better take on neutral metapositions than people who have grown up only in one socialization context (Thomas, 2008): metacognition enables individuals to evaluate which behavioral strategies are helpful and which are not. Additionally, metacognitive traits help individuals to recognize a sense behind foreign cultures and to cope with them. These multicultural specialists and managers can support the creation of synergies in interface functions within and between organizations. They can act as boundary spanners and interfaces and make – often unconsciously – valuable contributions to the understanding and functioning of multinational companies (Barner-Rasmussen et al., 2014).

In order to cope in a volatile, uncertain, complex, and ambivalent global environment – called VUCA world, actors need specific competences. If one considers the mentioned characteristics attributed to intercultural competence such as openness, diversity of perspectives, adaptability, tolerance of ambiguity, tolerance of frustration, and flexibility or knowledge of language and culture, it could be assumed that interculturally competent actors can find their way particularly well in the VUCA world.

14.7   Conclusion

This chapter has focused on the contextualization of intercultural competences. The authors have presented a historical genesis of intercultural competence research, defined major concepts and their measurements before proposing a research agenda for future studies. The proposed approach provides a novel perspective of how to better analyze the multiple dimensions of intercultural competence and their interactions in different contexts. The presented analysis should help future studies to contribute to a more accurate understanding of the complexity of intercultural competence in various national and organizational contexts.

References

Barmeyer, C. (2004). Learning styles and their impact on cross-cultural training. An international comparison in France, Germany and Quebec. *International Journal of Intercultural Relations*, 28(6), 577–594.

Barmeyer, C., & Davoine, E. (2019). Facilitating intercultural negotiated practices in joint ventures: The case of a French–German railway organization. *International Business Review, 28*(1), 1–11.

Barmeyer, C., & Franklin, P. (Eds.). (2016). *Intercultural Management: A Case-based Approach to Achieving Complementarity and Synergy.* London, UK: Palgrave.

Barmeyer, C., & Mayrhofer, U. (2008). The contribution of intercultural management to the success of international mergers and acquisitions: An analysis of the EADS group. *International Business Review, 17,* 28–38.

Barmeyer, C., & Mayrhofer, U. (2014). How has the French cultural and institutional context shaped the organization of the Airbus Group? *International Journal of Organizational Analysis, 22*(4), 426–448.

Barner-Rasmussen, W., Ehrnrooth, M., Koveshnikov, A., & Mäkelä, K. (2014). Cultural and language skills as resources for boundary spanning within the MNC. *Journal of International Business Studies, 45*(7), 886–905.

Bartel-Radic, A. (2013). "Estrangeirismo" and flexibility: Intercultural learning in Brazilian MNCs. *Management International, 17*(4), 239–253.

Bartel-Radic, A., & Giannelloni, J.-L. (2017). A renewed perspective on the measurement of cross-cultural competence: An approach through personality traits and crosscultural knowledge. *European Management Journal, 35*(5), 632–644.

Bennett, M. J. (2001). Developing intercultural competence for global leadership. In Reineke, R.-D., & Fussiger, C. (Eds.), *Interkulturelles Management: Konzeption, Beratung, Training* (pp. 206–225). Wiesbaden, Germany: Gabler.

Bennett, J. M. (Ed.). (2015). *The SAGE Encyclopedia of Intercultural Competence.* London, UK: Sage Publications.

Bird, A. (1989). The study of cross-cultural competence: Traditions and contemporary issues. *International Journal of Intercultural Relations, 13*(3), 229–240.

Brannen, M. Y. (1998). Negotiated culture in binational contexts: A model of culture change based on a Japanese/American organizational experience. *Anthropology of Work Review, 18*(2/3), 6–17.

Brinkmann, U., & Weerdenburg, v. O. (2014). *Intercultural Readiness. Four Competences for Working across Cultures.* Hampshire, UK: Palgrave Macmillan.

Chao, G. T., & Moon, H. (2005). The cultural mosaic: A metatheory for understanding the complexity of culture. *Journal of Applied Psychology, 90*(6), 1128–1140.

Collier, M. J. (2015). Intercultural communication competence: Continuing challenges and critical directions. *International Journal of Intercultural Relations, 48,* 9–11.

Croucher, S. M., Sommier, M., & Rahmani, D. (2015). Intercultural communication: Where we've been, where we're going, issues we face. *Communication Research and Practice, 1*(1), 71–87.

Dahlén, T. (1997). *Among the Interculturalists. An Emergent Profession and its Packaging of Knowledge.* Stockholm, Sweden: Almqvist & Wiksell.

Deardorff, D. K. (Ed.). (2009). *The SAGE Handbook of Intercultural Competence.* Thousand Oaks, CA: Sage.

Deardorff, D. K. (2018). Theories of cultural and educational exchange, intercultural competence, conflict resolution, and peace education. In Chou, C., & Spangler, J. (Eds.), *Cultural and Educational Exchanges between Rival Societies* (pp. 23–38). Singapore: Springer.

Demorgon, J. (1989). *L'exploration interculturelle. Pour une pédagogie internationale.* Paris, France: Armand Colin.

Dias, D., Zhu, C. J., & Samaratunge, R. (2017). Examining the role of cultural exposure in improving intercultural competence: Implications for HRM practices in multicultural organizations. *The International Journal of Human Resource Management*, *31*(11), 1359–1378.

Fang, T. (2006). From "onion" to "ocean": Paradox and change in national cultures. *International Studies of Management and Organization*, *35*(4), 71–90.

Fiedler, F. E., Mitchell, T., & Triandis, H. C. (1971). The culture assimilator: An approach to cross-cultural training. *Journal of Applied Psychology*, *55*(2), 95–102.

Fink, G., & Mayerhofer, W. (2009). Cross-cultural competence and management – setting the stage. *European Journal of Cross-Cultural Competence and Management*, *1*(1), 42–65.

Fitzsimmons, S. R., Lee, Y.-T., & Brannen, M. Y. (2013). Demystifying the myth about marginals: Implications for global leadership. *European Journal of International Management*, *7*(5), 587–603.

Flanagan, J. C. (1954). The critical incident technique. *Psychological Bulletin*, *51*(4), 327–358.

Gertsen, M. C. (1990). Intercultural competence and expatriates. *The International Journal of Human Resource Management*, *1*(3), 341–362.

Guo, C., & Al Ariss, A. (2015). Human resource management of international migrants: Current theories and future research. *The International Journal of Human Resource Management*, *26*(10), 1287–1297.

Hall, E. T. (1956). Orientation and training in government for work overseas. *Human Organization*, *15*(1), 4–10.

Hall, E. T. (1959). *The Silent Language*. New York, NY: Anchor Books.

Hall, E. T. (1966). *The Hidden Dimension*. Garden City, NY: Anchor Books.

Hall, E. T. (1983). *The Dance of Life. The Other Dimension of Time*. New York, NY: Anchor Books.

Hammer, M. R., Bennett, M. J., & Wiseman, R. L. (2003). Measuring intercultural sensitivity: The intercultural development inventory. *International Journal of Intercultural Relations*, *27*, 421–443.

Hofstede, G. H. (1980). *Culture's Consequences. International Differences in Work-Related Values*. London, UK: Sage.

Holtbrügge, D., & Mohr, A. (2010). Cultural determinants of learning style preferences. *Academy of Management Learning & Education*, *9*(4), 622–637.

Hoopes, D. S. (1979). Intercultural communication concepts and the psychology of intercultural experience. In Pusch, M. D. (Ed.), *Multicultural Education. A Cross-cultural Training Approach* (pp. 9–38). Chicago, IL: Intercultural Press.

Inglehart, R., & Welzel, C. (2005). *Modernization, Cultural Change and Democracy*. New Jersey: Princeton University Press.

Jack, G., & Lorbiecki, A. (2003). Asserting possibilities of resistance in the cross-cultural teaching machine: Re-viewing videos of others. In Prasad, A. (Ed.), *Postcolonial Theory and Organizational Analysis* (pp. 213–231). New York, NY: Palgrave Macmillan.

Jackson, T. (2004). *Management and Change in Africa: A Cross-Cultural Perspective*. London, UK: Routledge.

Johnson, J. P., Lenartowicz, T., & Apud, S. (2006). Cross-cultural competence in international business: Toward a definition and a model. *Journal of International Business Studies*, *37*(4), 525–543.

Koester, J., & Lustig, M. W. (2015). Intercultural communication competence: Theory, measurement, and application. *International Journal of Intercultural Relations*, *48*, 20–21.

Kulich, S. J. (2012). Reconstructing the histories and influences of 1970 intercultural leaders: Prelude to biographies. *International Journal of Intercultural Relations, 36*(6), 744–759.

Landis, D., Bennett, J., & Bennett, M. (Eds.). (2004). *Handbook of Intercultural Training*. London, UK: Sage.

Leeds-Hurwitz, W. L. (1990). Notes in the history of intercultural communication: The Foreign Service Institute and the Mandate for Intercultural Training. *Quarterly Journal of Speech, 76*, 262–281.

Martin, J. N. (2015). Revisiting intercultural communication competence: Where to go from here. *International Journal of Intercultural Relations, 48*, 6–8.

Matveev, A. (2017). *Intercultural Competence in Organizations: A Guide for Leaders, Educators and Team Players*. Cham: Springer.

Mayer, C.-H. (2016). *Mori-Joe: Exploring Magical Path. A Reading Companion to Intercultural Learning and Personality Development*. Münster, Germany: Waxmann.

Mayrhofer, U. (2013). (Ed.). *Management of Multinational Companies: A French Perspective*. Basingstoke, UK: Palgrave Macmillan.

Mayrhofer, U. (2017). *Management interculturel. Comprendre et gérer la diversité culturelle*. Paris, France: Vuibert.

Moosmüller, A., & Schönhut, M. (2009). Intercultural competence in German discourse. In Deardorff, D. K. (Ed.). *The SAGE Handbook of Intercultural Competence* (pp. 209–232). Thousand Oaks, CA: Sage.

Osula, B., & Irvin, S. M. (2009). Awareness in intercultural mentoring: A model for enhancing mentoring relationships. *International Journal of Leadership Studies, 5*(1), 37–50.

Özbilgin, M., & Tatli, A. (2008). *Global diversity management. An evidence based approach*. New York, NY: Palgrave Macmillan.

Pusch, M. (2004). Intercultural Training in historical perspective. In Landis, D., Bennett, J., & Bennett, M. (Eds.), *Handbook of Intercultural Training* (pp. 13–36). London, UK: Sage.

Rogers, E. M., & Hart, W. B. (2002). The histories of intercultural, international, and development communication. In Gudykunst, W. B., & Mody, B. (Eds.), *Handbook of International and Intercultural Communication* (2nd edition, pp. 1–18). Thousand Oaks, CA: Sage.

Rosenberg, M. J., & Hovland, C. I. (1960). Cognitive, affective and behavioral components of attitudes. In Rosenberg, M. J. and Hovland, C. I. (Eds.), *Attitude Organization and Change: An Analysis of Consistency among Attitude Components*. New Haven, CT: Yale University Press.

Rosinski, P. (2003). *Coaching Across Cultures. New Tools for Leveraging National, Corporate & Professional Differences*. London, UK: Nicholas Brealey.

Ruben, B. D. (1976). Assessing communication competency for intercultural adaptation. *Group and Organization Studies, 1*, 334–354.

Sackmann, S. A., & Phillips, M. E. (2004). Contextual influences on culture research: Shifting assumptions for new workplace realities. *International Journal of Cross Cultural Management, 4*(3), 370–390.

Sainsaulieu, R. (2014). *L'identité au travail: Les effets culturels de l'organisation*. Paris, France: Presses de Sciences Po.

Simy, J., & Kolb, D. (2009). Are there cultural differences in learning style? *International Journal of Intercultural Relations, 33*(1), 69–85.

Spencer-Oatey, H., & Franklin, P. (2009). *Intercultural Interaction. A Multidisciplinary Approach to Intercultural Communication*. London, UK: Palgrave Macmillan.

Spitzberg, B., & Changnon, G. (2009). Conceptualizing intercultural competence. In Deardorff, D. K. (Ed.), *The SAGE Handbook of Intercultural Competence* (pp. 2–52). Thousand Oaks, CA: Sage.

Thomas, D. C. (2008). *Cross-Cultural Management. Essential Concepts*. Los Angeles, CA: Sage.

Vora, D., Martin, L., Fitzsimmons, S. R., Pekerti, A. A., Lakshman, C., & Raheem, S. (2019). Multiculturalism within individuals: A review, critique, and agenda for future research. *Journal of International Business Studies, 50*(4), 499–524.

Wagner, M., Perugini, D. C., & Byram, M. (Eds.). (2017). *Teaching Intercultural Competence Across the Age Range: From Theory to Practice*. Multilingual Matters.

Walther, M. (2014). *Repatriation to France and Germany: A Comparative Study Based on Bourdieu's Theory of Practice*. Wiesbaden, Germany: Springer.

Wang, Y., & Kulich, S. J. (2015). Does context count? Developing and assessing intercultural competence through an interview- and model-based domestic course design in China. *International Journal of Intercultural Relations, 48*, 38–57.

Wolff, F., & Borzikowsky, C. (2018). Intercultural competence by international experiences? An investigation of the impact of educational stays abroad on intercultural competence and its facets. *Journal of Cross-Cultural Psychology, 49*(3), 488–514.

Zander, L., & Romani, L. (2004). When nationality matters. A study of departmental, hierarchical, professional, gender and age-based employee groupings' leadership preference across 15 countries. *International Journal of Cross Cultural Management, 4*(3), 291–315.

Conclusion to the Handbook: Toward a Multilevel and Contextualized Approach of Managing Competences

Benoît Grasser, Sabrina Loufrani-Fedida, and Ewan Oiry

In the conclusion of this Handbook, we acknowledge that research on competence management, particularly in France and more broadly in Europe, offers two complementary perspectives that enrich the American literature: a multilevel approach and the contextualization of competence management. The second perspective proposed by this book responds to the call from the French scientific community for more contextualized research. We consider, indeed, that competence management is contextualized and does not fit into supposedly universal "best practices." On the contrary, competence management relies on, is shaped by, and contributes to transforming the internal and external environment in which it develops. Let's consider the example of frameworks of required competences necessary for a job to be carried out, regardless of the line of business or organizational context. Required competences are often based on rather general definitions of competences. They can refer to competences within a professional domain (e.g., managers in general) or even to a professional field, covering all possible professions and domains by considering competence as something that goes beyond specific professions and domains. Required competences are often found in reference lists, job descriptions, or competence frameworks. Accordingly, required competences usually offer a deterministic, universal, or even ideal view of competences required from individuals for them to perform: we here seek to identify "good" competences (Boyatsis, 1982; Spencer and Spencer, 2008). Chen and Chang (2010) hereby refer to "person-job fit," where the required competence enables quantitative measurement and captures more visible characteristics, such as knowledge, skills, and abilities (KSAs). Thus, competence becomes a "human asset" with generic attributes transferable to many organizations. Employees with superior performance may seek promotion in their own firm or switch to other firms for increased individual employability (Van Der Heijde and Van Der Heijden, 2006). Nevertheless, in today's highly turbulent business environment, the effect of organizational context on employee competence is increasingly receiving attention from strategic human resource management (SHRM) scholars (e.g., Capaldo et al., 2006; Håland and Tjora, 2006; Sandberg, 2000). Recognized competences are strongly linked to the work the person actually carries out (Capaldo et al., 2006). An interactive "process" between a person and an organization generates competence (Hayton and Kelley, 2006). This context-dependent competence seems more important in a dynamic situation, leading to "firm-specific" employee competence (Cardy and Selvarajan, 2006). This perspective in which competence is embedded in an interactive "process" between a person and an organization has been more widely valued (Håland and Tjora, 2006; Hayton and Kelley, 2006; Lindberg and Rantatalo, 2015). Appreciating whether an individual possesses a competence is quite difficult. It can only be done in specific work situations. Competence is an unstable and flexible construct, interacting between the individual and its context (Sandberg, 2000; Sandberg and Pinnington, 2009). The concept of competence has thus moved from an employment-related context (context of independence) to an organizational context (context of dependence). In this book, different contexts have been studied: a Canadian business school (Chapter 4), an airline company (Chapter 5), hospital and humanitarian emergencies (Chapter 6), a collective of cultural festivals (Chapter 7), a territorial employment center (Chapter 8), a company in the aerospace industry (Chapter 10), a large transformation of the electricity and gas distribution systems (Chapter 11), a railway company (Chapter 12), the specific context of the social and solidarity economy (Chapter 13), and intercultural contexts (Chapter 14). The results presented in this book therefore call for a global rethinking of competence management toward a renewed vision that is both holistic and pluralist, adapted to the diverse contexts and situations of work. It goes beyond the classical vision of competence management, both deterministic and universal, which was inherited from the Taylorian philosophy of scientific management. The response to this call also has methodological consequences. Taking into account the context in which the competences are implemented calls for qualitative methods (case studies, ethnography, and research action) that allow for the longitudinal, process-based, and dynamic analysis of complex phenomena in their specific contexts.

The first perspective is the adoption of a multilevel approach to thinking about competence management in contemporary organizations. A multilevel approach refers to the simultaneous and integrated study of at least two levels of analysis (Kozlowski and Klein, 2000): for example, the individual and the group, the organization and the network, the functional department, the company, and the line of business. This book demonstrates that the essence of the concept of competence is multilevel in management sciences. The concept of competence has "naturally" carved its place within the company by first positioning itself on three levels of analysis: the individual (with individual competences), the team (with collective competences) and the organization (with organizational competences, some of which are considered strategic). Since the opening of organizational boundaries and outsourcing strategies, a fourth level has emerged: the inter-organizational level (with inter-organizational competences, some of which are territorial). This book favors research conducted at multiple levels of competence: the individual (Chapters 2, 3, 4, and 5) but also the collective, intra-organizational (Chapter 6) and inter-organizational (Chapter 7), the territory (Chapter 8), or the labor market (Chapter 9). However, according to Hitt et al. (2007), researchers mobilizing a multilevel approach of managing competences must not only specify the different levels of analysis, but also consider the possible articulations of the levels between them. It is therefore essential today to recognize and understand the nature of the interactions between the different levels of competence management. What are the factors that facilitate or hinder the interrelationships between the different levels of competence management? What can be the constituent bases of a distributed competence? How can a greater or lesser degree of alignment be achieved between the different levels of competence management, the HRM system, and the other key elements of company management?

Moreover, the two perspectives – multilevel and contextualized of managing competence – put forth in this book are complementary. Appositely, taking into account the context leads to the integration of the multilevel in the competence analysis. For example, contextualizing a competence by simultaneously analyzing the employee exercising his/her activity (individual level) and his/her work situation leads to taking into account the organizational level, since this work situation is very largely prescribed by the organization. This analysis conceptualizes the competence of the individual as a relationship between two levels of analysis, and not as an individual attribute that could exist identically outside of this singular relationship, these singular levels, and this specific context. The multilevel approach feeds the question of contextualization in three ways. Firstly, it forces us to systematically consider at least two levels, making it impossible to consider the different components of competence as disjointed entities that are external to each other. Secondly, it then requires us to specify the levels chosen, which means that we must not be satisfied with general definitions of the different levels of analysis (from the micro level to the macro level) but must instead describe precisely and concretely the levels to which we are referring. Thirdly, it requires proposing a "theory" of how the different selected levels combine. This requires the explanation of the hypotheses relating to the way in which each level acts on, influences, and transforms the other. In this way, rather than considering the context as a simple environment, the multilevel approach proposes a conceptual and methodological approach that places the dynamic interactions between the different levels at the heart of the analysis. It then becomes possible to understand why and how the different levels of competence determine and transform each other, to form, overall, a set of resources specific to each organization, inserted into its social dynamics, and contributing to its performance.

In conclusion, multilevel and contextualized approaches provide a global framework for thinking about contemporary competence management issues and allow a renewal of research on the subject. They are clearly fertile breeding grounds for management to conduct more research in order to enrich and revise our knowledge in a world where the complexity of human resources and organizational phenomena no longer requires us to grasp the organization as an entity but to articulate the different levels of organizations and territories. Thus, we strongly invite researchers to adopt more multilevel and contextualized approaches to better understand competence management as a multilevel and multi-context reality and hope that this book can serve as a basis for defining relevant research orientations.

References

Boyatsis, R. E. (1982). *The Competent Manager: A Model for Effective Performance*. New York, NY: Wiley.

Capaldo, G., Iandoli, L., & Zollo, G. (2006). A situationalist perspective: To competency management. *Human Resource Management, 45*(3), 429–448.

Cardy, R. L., & Selvarajan, T. T. (2006). Competencies: Alternative frameworks for competitive advantage. *Business Horizons, 49*(3), 235–245.

Chen, H. M., & Chang, W. Y. (2010). The essence of the competence concept: Adopting an organization's sustained competitive advantage viewpoint. *Journal of Management & Organization, 16*(05), 677–699.

Håland, E., & Tjora, A. (2006). Between asset and process: Developing competence by implementing a learning management system. *Human Relations, 59*(7), 993–1016.

Hayton, J. C., & Kelley, D. J. (2006). A competency-based framework for promoting corporate entrepreneurship. *Human Resource Management, 45*(3), 407–427.

Hitt, M. A., Beamish, P. W., Jackson, S. E., & Mathieu, J. E. (2007). Building theoretical and empirical bridges across levels: Multilevel research in management. *Academy of Management Journal, 50*(6), 1385–1399.

Kozlowski, S. W., & Klein, K. J. (2000). A multilevel approach to theory and research in organizations: Contextual, temporal, and emergent processes. In Klein, K. J., Kozlowski, S. W. J. (Eds.), *Multilevel Theory, Research, and Methods in Organizations: Foundations, Extensions, and New Directions* (pp.3–90). San Francisco, CA: Jossey-Bass.

Lindberg, O., & Rantatalo, O. (2015). Competence in professional practice: A practice theory analysis of police and doctors. *Human Relations, 68*(4), 561–582.

Sandberg, J. (2000). Understanding human competence at work: An interpretative approach. *Academy of Management Journal, 43*(1), 9–25.

Sandberg, J., & Pinnington, A. H. (2009). Professional competence as ways of being: An existential ontological perspective. *Journal of Management Studies, 46*(7), 1138–1170.

Spencer, L. M. Jr., & Spencer, S. M. (2008). *Competence at Work, Models for Superior Performance*. New-York, NY: John Wiley and Sons.

Van Der Heijde, C., & Van Der Heijden, B. (2006). A competence-based and multi-dimensional operationalization and measurement of employability. *Human Resource Management, 45*(3), 449–476.

Index

Note: Page numbers in *italics* denote tables and figures.

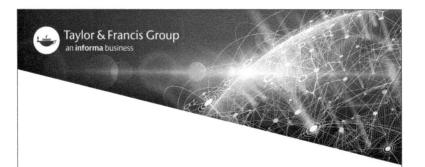

For Product Safety Concerns and Information please contact our EU
representative GPSR@taylorandfrancis.com
Taylor & Francis Verlag GmbH, Kaufingerstraße 24, 80331 München, Germany

www.ingramcontent.com/pod-product-compliance
Ingram Content Group UK Ltd.
Pitfield, Milton Keynes, MK11 3LW, UK
UKHW021831240425
457818UK00006B/163